Software Architecture with Spring 5.0

Design and architect highly scalable, robust,
and high-performance Java applications

René Enríquez
Alberto Salazar

BIRMINGHAM - MUMBAI

Software Architecture with Spring 5.0

Commissioning Editor: Richa Tripathi
Acquisition Editor: Sandeep Mishra
Content Development Editor: Anugraha Arunagiri
Technical Editor: Subhalaxmi Nadar
Copy Editor: Safis Editing
Project Coordinator: Ulhas Kambali
Proofreader: Safis Editing
Indexer: Aishwarya Gangawane
Graphics: Tom Scaria
Production Coordinator: Shraddha Falebhai

First published: August 2018

Production reference: 1310818

Published by Packt Publishing Ltd.
Livery Place
35 Livery Street
Birmingham
B3 2PB, UK.

ISBN 978-1-78899-299-2

www.packtpub.com

`mapt.io`

Mapt is an online digital library that gives you full access to over 5,000 books and videos, as well as industry leading tools to help you plan your personal development and advance your career. For more information, please visit our website.

Why subscribe?

- Spend less time learning and more time coding with practical eBooks and Videos from over 4,000 industry professionals

- Improve your learning with Skill Plans built especially for you

- Get a free eBook or video every month

- Mapt is fully searchable

- Copy and paste, print, and bookmark content

PacktPub.com

Did you know that Packt offers eBook versions of every book published, with PDF and ePub files available? You can upgrade to the eBook version at `www.PacktPub.com` and as a print book customer, you are entitled to a discount on the eBook copy. Get in touch with us at `service@packtpub.com` for more details.

At `www.PacktPub.com`, you can also read a collection of free technical articles, sign up for a range of free newsletters, and receive exclusive discounts and offers on Packt books and eBooks.

Contributors

About the authors

René Enríquez works as technical leader in a multinational company headquartered in Silicon Valley. He worked on different projects using Java Enterprise Edition and Spring Framework. He currently works with different Spring projects to maintain legacy code and write microservices applying best practices to deliver products using Agile techniques with a strong focus on testing at different levels. During the last years, he worked as a software consultant for private and government companies and as an instructor of courses to develop enterprise and mobile applications. He was also a speaker at the ScrumDay and JavaDay conferences in Quito-Ecuador.

Alberto Salazar is an entrepeneur, passionate Java consultant, JUG leader, Auth0 ambassador and founder of the Java User Group of Ecuador, an associate member of the Java community process and a Java evangelist/trainer. He founded a consulting company in Latin America 10 years ago, where he creates and offers technical solutions based on Java. He has been working for 2 decades creating higly scalable and transactional systems. He is a regular speaker at multiple Java conferences and meetings. He recently organized a Java Conference in Ecuador with Java Champions and co-organized a Java Hackdays event in Spanish that brought together 11 different cities from around the world and 9 Spanish-speaking countries.

About the reviewer

Yogendra Sharma is a developer with experience in the architecture, design, and development of scalable and distributed applications. He was awarded a bachelor's degree from Rajasthan Technical University in computer science with a core interest in microservices and Spring. He also has hands-on experience in technologies such as AWS Cloud, Python, J2EE, NodeJS, Angular, MongoDB, and Docker. He is currently working as an IoT and cloud architect at Intelizign Engineering Services. He constantly explores technical novelties, and is open-minded and eager to learn about new technologies and frameworks. He has also technically reviewed books and video courses for Packt.

Roland Alden has been the founder as well as co-founder of three technology startups and has decades of experience managing software engineering teams distributed around the world (Armenia, China, India, Micronesia, Nigeria, Pakistan, UAE, Ukraine, and Zambia). His background includes large companies (Data General and AT&T) and venture capital backed startups (Forethought, Go, and Eo). Currently, he works at ioet Inc., a software outsourcing firm based in Silicon Valley and Ecuador. He is a co-author of the *Working with Computers* and *Working with Microsoft Office* series of textbooks published by Houghton Mifflin.

Packt is searching for authors like you

If you're interested in becoming an author for Packt, please visit `authors.packtpub.com` and apply today. We have worked with thousands of developers and tech professionals, just like you, to help them share their insight with the global tech community. You can make a general application, apply for a specific hot topic that we are recruiting an author for, or submit your own idea.

Table of Contents

Preface   1

Chapter 1: Software Architecture Today   7
  Defining software architecture   8
    I know my land   9
    I want to stay ahead   9
    Predicting the future   10
  Architecture and architects   11
  Software architecture principles   13
    Components   13
    Low coupling   14
    High cohesion   17
  SOLID principles   18
    The single responsibility principle (SRP)   18
    The Open–Closed Principle (OCP)   19
    The Liskov substitution principle   20
    The interface segregation principle (ISP)   21
    The dependency inversion (DI) principle   23
  Conway's law   23
  Choosing the right technology for you   25
  New trends   27
  Summary   28

Chapter 2: Software Architecture Dimensions   29
  Dimensions   30
    The business dimension   30
      Managing user requirements   31
      Identifying and tracking business metrics   32
    The data dimension   32
    The technical dimension   35
    The operations dimension   37
      How to deploy an application   37
      How interaction occurs among your components   37
      Dealing with infrastructure   37
        Understanding the infrastructure   38
        Versioning   38
        Testing   39
      Cloud versus on-premise   39
      Deploying your application   40
  The C4 model   41
    Context diagram   42

Container diagram	42
Components diagram	43
Class diagram	43
Summary	44
Chapter 3: Spring Projects	45
Why Spring appeared	46
Spring projects	46
Spring Initializr	47
Spring Boot in a Nutshell	48
Servlet container integration	48
Autoconfiguration	48
Dependency management	48
mvnw and mvnw.cmd	49
pom.xml	49
DemoApplication.java	50
The application.properties file	51
DemoApplicationTests.java	51
Avoiding redeployment with developer tools	51
Spring Data	52
Supporting EIPs with Spring Integration	53
Spring Batch	55
The read step	55
The process step	56
The write step	56
Securing applications with Spring Security	56
Embracing (Spring) HATEOAS	58
Spring Cloud and the microservices world	59
Configuration server	59
Service registry	60
Edge services	60
Microproxy	61
API gateway	61
Circuit breaker	61
Reactive and Spring	62
Publisher	62
Subscriber	62
Subscription	63
Processor	63
Project reactor	63
Mono	64
Flux	65
Back pressure	66
Reactive Spring Data	67
Reactive REST services	68
Summary	69
Chapter 4: Client-Server Architectures	71
Understanding client-server architectures	72

Server   72
   Scaling   73
Request   75
Client   75
Network   76
Where to apply client-server architectures   76
Implementing client-server architectures with Spring   78
The server   78
   SOAP web services   79
   RESTful web services   79
   CORBA   80
   Sockets   80
   AMQP   80
Implementing the server   83
   Banking-domain   83
   Banking-api   84
      Boundaries   85
      Domain   86
      Persistence   86
      Service   86
   Monitoring the server   86
   Testing   88
   Banking-client   90
      Authentication endpoint client   91
      Account balance endpoint client   92
The clients   92
   JavaFX client   93
   Android client   94
   Thin client   96
Summary   97
Chapter 5: Model-View-Controller Architectures   99
MVC   100
The Model (M)   100
The View (V)   101
The Controller (C)   101
Benefits of using MVC   103
Common pitfalls   104
Implementing applications using MVC   106
Spring MVC   106
Testing   109
   Test coverage   112
UI frameworks   115
   Thymeleaf   116
Securing an MVC application   120
   Basic authentication   121
   Implementing basic authentication   123
Summary   126

Chapter 6: Event-Driven Architectures   127
   Underlying concepts and key aspects   127
     Command   128
     Event   128
   Patterns of event-driven architectures   130
     Event notification   130
     Event-carried state transfer   136
       Improving application performance   137
       Reducing the load on the source application   137
       Increasing the availability of the system   138
     Event sourcing   140
     CQRS   150
       Complex domain models   151
       Distinct paths to query and persist information   152
       Independent scaling   154
   Summary   155

Chapter 7: Pipe-and-Filter Architectures   157
   Introducing Pipe-and-Filter concepts   157
     Filters   158
     Pipes   159
   Boarding Pipe-and-Filter architectures   159
   Use cases for Pipe-and-Filter architecture   160
   Spring Batch   161
   Implementing pipes with Spring Batch   168
   Summary   180

Chapter 8: Microservices   181
   Principles of microservices   182
     Size   182
     Autonomous   182
     Working well together   183
     Advantages   183
       Alignment to the single responsibility principle   184
       Continuous releases   184
       Independent scalability   184
       Increased adoption of new technologies   185
     Drawbacks   186
       Too many options   186
       Slow at the beginning   186
       Monitoring   186
       Transactions and eventual consistency   187
   Modeling microservices   187
   Speeding up   189
     Accelerating the development process   189
     Embracing tests   190
     Going to production   191

Implementing microservices   191
  Dynamic configuration   192
    Implementing a configuration server   194
    Implementing a configuration client   194
  Service discovery and registration   196
    Introducing Eureka   197
    Implementing a Netflix Eureka service registry   198
    Implementing a service registry client   199
    Netflix Ribbon   201
  Edge services   202
    Introducing Zuul   204
  CAP theorem   208
    Consistency   208
    High availability   208
    Partition tolerance   208
  Circuit breaker   209
    Hystrix   210
  Summary   211
Chapter 9: Serverless Architectures   213
  An introduction to serverless architecture   214
  Infrastructure and file storage   215
  Benefits and pitfalls   216
  Backend as a service   217
  Function as a service   218
  Concerns about serverless architectures   219
    Vendor lock-in   219
    Security   220
    Framework support   220
    Troubleshooting   221
  Examples and common use cases   221
    Adopting serverless architectures for SPA   222
  Implementing FaaS with Spring Cloud Functions   223
  Functions with Spring   225
    Coding the example   226
  Adapters   231
  AWS Lambda adapter   231
  Azure adapter   237
  Summary   246
Chapter 10: Containerizing Your Applications   247
  Containers   248
  Basic concepts   249
    Containers and images   249
  Basic commands   250
    Running containers   250
    Working with containers   252
    Working with images   253

Building your own images   253
  FROM command   254
  MAINTAINER command   254
  RUN command   254
  ENV command   255
  EXPOSE command   255
  CMD command   255
Containerizing applications   256
  Docker Gradle plugin   259
Registries   260
  Publishing images   261
Provisioning multiple-container environments   264
  Docker Compose   265
    Linking containers   266
      links   267
      depends_on   267
Container orchestration with Kubernetes   269
  Pod   269
  Labels   271
  Replication controllers   272
  Services   274
Summary   275
Chapter 11: DevOps and Release Management   277
Silos   278
  How to break silos   279
DevOps culture   279
  Motivations   280
  DevOps adoption   281
Embracing automation   282
Infrastructure as code   283
  Spring application and DevOps practices   285
    Supporting different environments   286
    Selecting profiles   287
  Vagrant   288
    Working with Vagrant   288
Release management   291
  pipelines   291
    Continuous integration   292
    Continuous delivery and continuous deployment   293
    Automating pipelines   293
    Jenkins   296
Summary   301
Chapter 12: Monitoring   303
Monitoring   304
  Monitoring Spring applications   304

Application Performance Management (APM) tools   308
  New Relic   309
Summary   314

Chapter 13: Security   315
  Why security is important as a part of an application's architecture   315
    Key security recommendations   317
      Authentication and authorization   317
      Cryptography   320
      Data input validation   320
      Sensitive data   320
      Social engineering   320
      OWASP Top 10   321
      Penetration testing   321
  Authentication and authorization as a service   322
  Summary   325

Chapter 14: High Performance   327
  Why performance matters   327
    Scalability   328
      Horizontal scalability   328
      Vertical scalability   328
    High availability   329
    Performance   329
  The key recommendation to avoid performance issues   330
    Identifying bottlenecks   331
    Profiling applications   332
      Visual VM   332
    SQL query optimizations   336
    A load test example   337
  Summary   346

Other Books You May Enjoy   347

Index   351

Preface

Today we count on different software architecture styles that can be applied in different scenarios. In this book, we will review the most common software architecture styles and how they can be implemented using Spring Framework, which is one of the most widely adopted frameworks within the Java ecosystem.

At the beginning, we'll review some key concepts inherent to software architecture in order to understand the fundamental theory before diving into technical details.

Who this book is for

This book is aimed at experienced Spring developers who are aspiring to become architects of enterprise-grade applications and at software architects who would like to leverage Spring to create effective application blueprints.

What this book covers

Chapter 1, *Software Architecture Today*, provides an overview of how software architectures are managed today and why they are still important. It discusses how the most recent needs of the software industry are handled by the new emerging architecture models and how they can help you to solve these new challenges.

Chapter 2, *Software Architecture Dimensions*, reviews the dimensions associated with software architectures and how they influence the building process of your applications. We will also introduce the C4 model used to document software architectures.

Chapter 3, *Spring Projects*, speaks about some of the most useful Spring Projects. It's important to know which tools are inside your toolbox because Spring provides a wide variety of tools that fit your needs and can be used to boost your development process.

Chapter 4, *Client-Server Architectures*, covers how client-server architectures work and the most common scenarios where this style of architecture can be applied. We will go through various implementations, starting from simple clients such as desktop applications to modern and more complex usages such as devices connected to the internet.

Chapter 5, *MVC Architectures*, speaks about MVC, which is one of the most popular and widely known architecture styles. In this chapter, you will get an in-depth understanding of how MVC architectures work.

Chapter 6, *Event-Driven Architectures*, explains the underlying concepts related to event-driven architectures and which issues they handle using a hands-on approach.

Chapter 7, *Pipe-and-Filter Architectures*, focuses heavily on Spring Batch. It explains how to build pipelines, which encapsulate an independent chain of tasks aimed to filter and process big amount of data.

Chapter 8, *Microservices*, provides an overview about how to implement microservice architectures using the spring cloud stack. It details every component and how they interact with each other in order to provide a fully functional microservice architecture.

Chapter 9, *Serverless Architectures*, speaks about many services on the internet that are ready-to-use and can be used as part of software systems, allowing companies to just focus on their own business core concerns. This chapter shows a new way to think about building applications around a series of third-party services to solve common problems such as authentication, file storage, and infrastructure. We will also review what FaaS approach is and how to implement it using Spring.

Chapter 10, *Containerizing Your Applications*, explains that containers are one of the most handy technologies used in the last few years. They help us to get rid of manual server provisioning and allow us to forget the headaches related to building production environments and the maintenance tasks for servers. This chapter shows how to generate an artifact ready for production that can be easily replaced, upgraded, and interchanged eliminating the common provisioning issues. Through this chapter, we will also introduce container orchestration and how to deal with it using Kubernetes.

Chapter 11, *DevOps and Release Management*, explains that Agile is one of the most common approaches to organizing teams and making them work together to build products more quickly. DevOps is an inherent technique of these teams, and it helps them to break unnecessary silos and boring processes, giving teams the chance to be in charge of the whole software development process from writing code to deploy applications in production. This chapter shows how to achieve this goal by embracing automation to reduce manual tasks and deploy applications using automated pipelines in charge of validating the written code, provisioning the infrastructure, and deploying the required artifacts in a production environment.

Chapter 12, *Monitoring*, explains that once the application is published, unexpected behaviors are not uncommon and that it's essential to notice them so that they can be fixed as quickly as possible. This chapter gives some recommendations regarding techniques and tools that can be used to monitor the performance of an application bearing in mind technical and business metrics.

`Chapter` 13, *Security*, explains that often security is one of the fields that teams do not pay close attention to when they are working on developing their products. There are a few key considerations that developers should keep in mind when they are writing code. Most of them are pretty obvious, while others aren't, so we will discuss all of them here.

`Chapter` 14, *High Performance*, explains that there is nothing more disappointing in a job than dealing with issues in production when an application is behaving in an unexpected way. In this chapter, we'll discuss some simple techniques that can be applied to get rid of these annoying problems by applying simple recommendations on a daily basis.

To get the most out of this book

A good understanding of Java, Git, and Spring Framework is necessary before reading this book. A deep knowledge of OOP is desired, although some key concepts are reviewed in the first two chapters.

Download the example code files

You can download the example code files for this book from your account at `www.packtpub.com`. If you purchased this book elsewhere, you can visit `www.packtpub.com/support` and register to have the files emailed directly to you.

You can download the code files by following these steps:

1. Log in or register at `www.packtpub.com`.
2. Select the **SUPPORT** tab.
3. Click on **Code Downloads & Errata**.
4. Enter the name of the book in the **Search** box and follow the onscreen instructions.

Once the file is downloaded, please make sure that you unzip or extract the folder using the latest version of:

- WinRAR/7-Zip for Windows
- Zipeg/iZip/UnRarX for Mac
- 7-Zip/PeaZip for Linux

The code bundle for the book is also hosted on GitHub at `https://github.com/PacktPublishing/Software-Architecture-with-Spring-5.0`. We also have other code bundles from our rich catalog of books and videos available at `https://github.com/PacktPublishing/`. Check them out!

Download the color images

We also provide a PDF file that has color images of the screenshots/diagrams used in this book. You can download it here: `https://www.packtpub.com/sites/default/files/downloads/SoftwareArchitecturewithSpring5_ColorImages.pdf`.

Conventions used

There are a number of text conventions used throughout this book.

`CodeInText`: Indicates code words in text, database table names, folder names, filenames, file extensions, pathnames, dummy URLs, user input, and Twitter handles. Here is an example: "This object is represented by a `Servlet` interface."

A block of code is set as follows:

```
@RunWith(SpringRunner.class)
@SpringBootTest
public class ContextAwareTest {

    @Autowired
    ClassUnderTest classUnderTest;

    @Test
    public void validateAutowireWorks() throws Exception {
        Assert.assertNotNull(classUnderTest);
    }
}
```

When we wish to draw your attention to a particular part of a code block, the relevant lines or items are set in bold:

```
@Service
public class MyCustomUsersDetailService implements UserDetailsService {

    @Override
    public UserDetails loadUserByUsername(String username)
        throws UsernameNotFoundException {
        Optional<Customer> customerFound = findByUsername(username);
        ...
    }
}
```

Any command-line input or output is written as follows:

```
$ curl -X POST http://your-api-url:8080/events/<EVENT_ID
```

Bold: Indicates a new term, an important word, or words that you see onscreen. For example, words in menus or dialog boxes appear in the text like this. Here is an example: "Select **System info** from the **Administration** panel."

 Warnings or important notes appear like this.

 Tips and tricks appear like this.

Get in touch

Feedback from our readers is always welcome.

General feedback: Email `feedback@packtpub.com` and mention the book title in the subject of your message. If you have questions about any aspect of this book, please email us at `questions@packtpub.com`.

Errata: Although we have taken every care to ensure the accuracy of our content, mistakes do happen. If you have found a mistake in this book, we would be grateful if you would report this to us. Please visit `www.packtpub.com/submit-errata`, selecting your book, clicking on the Errata Submission Form link, and entering the details.

Piracy: If you come across any illegal copies of our works in any form on the Internet, we would be grateful if you would provide us with the location address or website name. Please contact us at `copyright@packtpub.com` with a link to the material.

If you are interested in becoming an author: If there is a topic that you have expertise in and you are interested in either writing or contributing to a book, please visit `authors.packtpub.com`.

Reviews

Please leave a review. Once you have read and used this book, why not leave a review on the site that you purchased it from? Potential readers can then see and use your unbiased opinion to make purchase decisions, we at Packt can understand what you think about our products, and our authors can see your feedback on their book. Thank you!

For more information about Packt, please visit `packtpub.com`.

Software Architecture Today 1

In this chapter, we will review what software architecture is and why it's still relevant today. We will also discuss the new business demands that have been guiding the world of software development in the last few years, and how they have affected the software industry as a whole.

Software and technology are evolving daily, introducing new demands that businesses must meet in order to remain relevant in a competitive market. Regardless of their core business, every competitive company has had to turn to technology. Online transactions and clients around the world are just some of the challenges that have to be mastered in order to stay ahead.

In order to support these new demands, we have been discovering new ways to do our work. Drastic changes have been made and adopted, directly affecting our **software development life cycle (SDLC)**. Some examples of these changes are reflected in how we work on the following phases:

- Gathering requirements
- Organizing teams
- Designing software architectures
- Writing code
- Deploying applications

In this chapter, we will start by revisiting the underlying concepts of software architecture, which have been present for a long time and are still relevant today.

This chapter will cover the following topics:

- Defining software architecture
- Common mistakes that are made when creating architectures
- Architecture and architects
- Software architecture principles

- Applying high cohesion and low coupling in order to create components
- SOLID principles
- Conway's law
- Choosing the right technology for you
- New technology tendencies

Defining software architecture

No matter whether or not someone holds the software architect role in a team, every application has an architecture that somebody needs to take care of. This is an important step as it helps us to avoid writing entangled code, which makes a software system impossible to evolve in the future.

First things first: In order to know why you need to remember software architecture, we first need to understand what it is and why it is important.

In software, the term *architecture* is hard to define. Authors often borrow the definition from the construction industry, which is wrong. Software architecture is not all about diagrams, such as plans for buildings or houses—it's more than that. It's about the shared knowledge that technical and even nontechnical people have about the application that the whole team is creating, how the modules are connected to shape it, and all the complicated and vital elements surrounding it. Good software architectures are heavily focused on business requirements rather than on frameworks, programming languages, diagrams, and programming paradigms. Of course, we need these because we create applications using them. However, they don't have to define the underlying principles that dictate how we conceive the software. Instead, this role should be played according to business requirements.

The long-term success of an application is mainly based on its architecture, which must be created to support a well-defined set of business requirements, as mentioned earlier. Since an application needs to resolve these specific requirements, they must guide the architecture of the application. However, there are two main scenarios in which we guide software architecture decisions based on technology instead of business requirements:

- I know my land
- I want to stay ahead

I know my land

This scenario occurs when we create software architectures using frameworks and programming languages that we already know about, without paying close attention to business needs.

Let's say that the ABC company needs an application for manipulating text from large log files. If someone were to ask to work on this requirement, then they will choose a programming language that they are comfortable with during the development process, instead of looking for the best approach elsewhere.

Imagine that the person in charge of creating this application has already mastered JavaScript. In this case, do you think it's a good idea to write code using Node JS or another JavaScript framework running on the server in order to write an application to manipulate log files? I'm not saying that this is impossible—you can do it. However, do you think an application created using this approach will be able to perform and scale better than a system written in Perl, Python, or C, for example? This is not to say that JavaScript is terrible—it is simply important to know that this approach is not a good fit for JavaScript.

I want to stay ahead

We all want to stay ahead with technology, using the latest trends in the programming world to have a better technological background and consequently land cool jobs. Some people tend to write applications, keeping this idea in mind. Let's explain this scenario using the application example for manipulating log files that we mentioned in the previous section.

Suppose you're asked to solve the problem that we mentioned in the *I know my land* section. In this scenario, your only concern is technology. For instance, let's say you want to try the newest features in the latest PHP release. In this case, you will build this application using PHP. While this programming language has been improving over the last few years since Facebook started to add new features to it, the idea behind writing an application to manipulate large log files using PHP is crazy. As you may know, this programming language is intended to create other kinds of applications—mainly those that have to be accessed using a web browser and without high transactional requirements.

Again, you can write an application using PHP to manipulate large log files, but what will happen when more features are needed? Do you think a software architecture created with this approach in mind will be able to respond quickly to new requirements and the inherent characteristics of the application used in this example?

Predicting the future

While we can't predict each detail of an application when we are creating it, we can keep some apparent assumptions in mind to avoid glaring mistakes, like the ones exposed in the preceding sections. Even if you have created an application using the wrong approach, one part of the software architecture process is to evaluate the code base from time to time and take corrective actions based on this. This is important because the existing software architecture needs to evolve in order to avoid becoming useless. During the development process—and because we do not want to miss the established project deadlines—we often use the FIXME and TODO tags. However, we should pay close attention to these and take action as soon as we can, as they represent a technical debt that gets worse as time passes. Imagine how easy it is to get rid of a recently introduced debt in the next iteration. Now, imagine how hard it would be if the developer who added that debt is no longer working on the project or even within the same company.

 Remember that these tags represent a debt, and debts are paid with interest that increases with time.

The process of improving the existing software architecture sometimes tends to be even more interesting than creating a new one from scratch. This is because you now have more information about the business requirements and how the application was performing at the time that it was in production.

When you are adding new features to an existing application, you will figure out how good the initial idea was. If the process of adding new features is simple and requires only a few changes in its structure, then we can conclude that the software architecture is doing its job well. Otherwise, if we need to make substantial changes to the underlying parts of the original design, we can say that the initial idea and assumptions were all wrong. However, at this point, the team in charge of the product should be responsible enough to make it evolve instead of writing additional patches to support new features.

Even though patching something sounds similar to making it evolve, it isn't. This idea is explained clearly in the book *Building Evolutionary Architectures*, written by Neal Ford, Rebecca Parsons, and Patrick Kua.

Proactive teams continually apply changes that make it possible to better support preexisting and new features rather than simply sitting and waiting for chaos when things get out of control. There's nothing wrong with changing an initial design, and it's always worth doing this. The following diagram illustrates this process, as applied to a geometric shape:

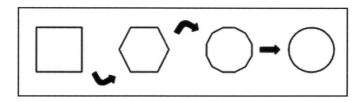

Evolving original designs

Now that we know that business needs must guide the application architecture, we can conclude that if it is unable to support new features, then new business opportunities will be missed, making the application and its architecture useless.

Architecture and architects

Before the agile and DevOps approaches appeared, architects used to focus on creating standards and rules to write code. In the past, it was common to find architects who wrote code, but this approach is currently outdated with regards to programming. Over the last few years, the idea of architects has been disappearing, all thanks to the new emerging models for creating teams. Agile movements have been in the software industry for a while, helping us to rethink how we are building software and organizing teams.

Nowadays, it's almost impossible to find software teams that have an architect working with them. Moreover, the idea of having different groups of people as part of an organization that collaborates using a silo style (where one task has to be finished before starting a new one) is disappearing. A few years ago, we had well-defined roles and even specialized departments for the following roles:

- Business analysts
- Developers
- QA engineers
- Architects
- DBAs

- People working on infrastructure
- Operations
- Security

The following graphic shows how teams work using a silos style:

Teams working as silos

The preceding list also grows in specific cases. Teams working using a silo style used to work on producing defined artifacts, such as documentation, UML diagrams, and other things that are usually incomplete.

This approach is changing, and having small and multidisciplinary teams in charge of taking care of every single detail of an application is now more common. This approach has helped to create proactive teams with strong skills that allow us to ensure that software architecture is still happening all the time.

It's evident that not every team member has the full set of skills required to work on every stage, from gathering requirements to deploying the application in production, but the communication among all of them allows us to reduce the technical gaps and have a better understanding of the bigger picture of the application. This is one of the most important aspects of software architecture.

This shared knowledge helps the team to continue improving the existing software architecture, overcoming the most complex problems. All of the teams in charge of writing software can understand the details of the system under development instead of delegating this responsibility to only one person or even to a department. This approach can lead us to rely on people or teams that would be slightly out of the business context of why the application was being created. This is because people that worked on the project in the past but no longer participate actively due to working on more than one project can't fully understand all of the details of every system.

Software architecture principles

Software architecture should improve by following two simple principles that are often difficult to achieve:

- Low coupling
- High cohesion

No matter what programming language, paradigm, or tools you are using to architect your applications, these two principles should guide you when building your software architecture components.

In order to build the components that will shape your architecture, it's always worth following the guidelines. These are still relevant, even after many years of existence, and they should always be considered when components are being created. In this section, I'm talking about SOLID principles and Conway's law, which we will discuss in more detail later in this chapter. It is now time to look at what components are in more detail.

Components

A component is a set of functions, data structures, and algorithms that solve one problem. This means that all the code and artifacts that are used to build the component have a high cohesion with each other; the rule here is that the classes or files that create a component should change at the same time and for the same reason.

Software architecture is built using many components, and you should not be worried about having an excessive quantity of these. The more components you write, the more freedom there is to assign them to different developers or even to different teams. Large software architectures can be created using many smaller components that can be developed and deployed independently of each other.

Once we connect these components to each other, they allow us to create the desired software architecture.

As shown in the following diagram, we can see the components as pieces of a puzzle that come together to form an application:

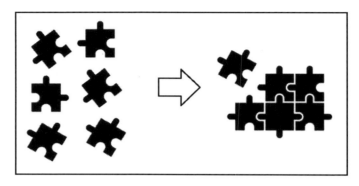

Components forming a larger application

The connected components define application architectures, and their designs describe how each component has been created internally. It's here that pattern designs and SOLID principles must be used to create good designs.

Low coupling

Low coupling refers to the degree to which components depend on each other by their lower structures instead of their interfaces, creating a tight coupling among them. Let's make this easier to understand by using a simple example. Imagine that you need to work on the next user's story:

As a bank customer, I want to receive my bank statement by email or fax in order to avoid having to open the bank application.

As you may discover, the developer should work on two things to solve this problem:

- Adding the ability to save the user's preferences in the system
- Making it possible to send the bank statement to the customer by using the requested notification channels

The first requirement seems quite straightforward. To test this implementation, we would use something fairly simple, such as the following code:

```
@Test
public void
theNotificationChannelsAreSavedByTheDataRepository()
```

```
throws Exception
{
  // Test here
}
```

For the second requirement, we will need to read these preferred notification channels and send the bank statement using them. The test that will guide this implementation will look like the following:

```
@Test
public void
theBankStatementIsSendUsingThePreferredNotificationChannels()
  throws Exception
{
  // Test here
}
```

It is now time to show a tightly coupled code in order to understand this problem. Let's take a look at the following implementation:

```
public void sendBankStatement(Customer customer)
{
  List<NotificationChannel> preferredChannels = customerRepository
  .getPreferredNotificationChannels(customer);
  BankStatement bankStatement = bankStatementRepository
  .getCustomerBankStatement(customer);
  preferredChannels.forEach
  (
    channel ->
    {
      if ("email".equals(channel.getChannelName()))
      {
        notificationService.sendByEmail(bankStatement);
      }
      else if ("fax".equals(channel.getChannelName()))
      {
        notificationService.sendByFax(bankStatement);
      }
    }
  );
}
```

Note how this code is tightly coupled with the implementation of the `NotificationService` class; it even knows the name of the methods that this service has. Now, imagine that we need to add a new notification channel. To make this code work, we will need to add another `if` statement and invoke the correspondent method from this class. Even when the example is referring to tightly coupled classes, this design problem often occurs between modules.

We will now refactor this code and show its low-coupled version:

```
public void sendBankStatement(Customer customer)
{
  List<NotificationType> preferredChannels = customerRepository
  .getPreferredNotificationChannels(customer);
  BankStatement bankStatement = bankStatementRepository
  .getCustomerBankStatement(customer);
  preferredChannels.forEach
  (
    channel ->
    notificationChannelFactory
    .getNotificationChannel(channel)
    .send(bankStatement)
  );
}
```

This time, the responsibility to get a notification channel is passed to the `Factory` class, no matter what kind of channel is needed. The unique detail that we need to know from the `channel` class is that it has a `send` method.

The following diagram shows how the class that sends notifications was refactored to send notifications using different channels and support an interface in front of the implementations per notification channel:

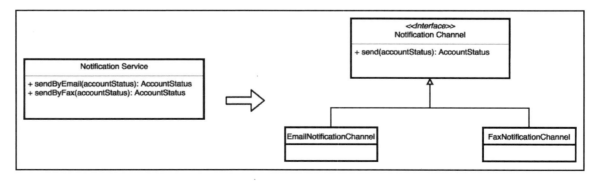

Classes after refactoring

This small but significant change has to lead us to encapsulate the details of the mechanism used to send notifications. This exposes only one well-defined interface that should be used by the other classes.

Although we have shown this example using classes, the same principle is applicable to components, and the same strategies should be used to implement them and avoid coupling among them.

High cohesion

The principle of high cohesion also has a pretty simple definition: one component should perform one and only one well-defined job. Although the description is pretty simple, we often tend to get confused and violate this principle.

In the previous example, we had `NotificationService`, which was in charge of sending notifications by email and fax. The word and can be helpful for us when it comes to identifying the violation of this principle. Now that we have two different classes (one per notification channel), it's fair to say that our classes only have one responsibility.

Again, the same is true for components, and another reason to keep the same idea with them is that you will likely have each component accomplishing only one specific requirement. For example, what would happen if all our customers just wanted to receive their bank statements by email; do you think it's okay to depend on a class that has the ability to send faxes too?

Although the previous question may seem unimportant, imagine that you solved an existing issue related to sending notifications using faxes as a notification mechanism, and a new issue was then introduced into the mechanism in order to send email notifications by mistake.

Remember that components shape your software architecture, and architects should design them in a way that maximizes team productivity. Aligning your components to the high-cohesion principle is an excellent way to separate them and allows teams to work independently on different parts of your application. This ability to create various components with clear responsibilities will make it easier when solving other issues and adding new features, and will also make you less prone to introducing bugs.

With regards to the previous example, you are probably wondering why the `NotificationChannel` class is apparently sending notifications with a `BankStatement` parameter.

Common sense leads us to believe that we need to replace this class with any other generic type. It can be helpful to allow the application to send different kinds of notifications, and not only bank statements: this may include drawbacks, or when a new deposit is received in the account. Even though the idea of supporting incoming requirements looks like something you might want to include in the program at this stage, the application doesn't currently need this ability. This is why it is not necessary for us to add this feature right now. Instead, this design should evolve when this becomes necessary; in this way, we are sticking to the KISS principle (`https://www.techopedia.com/definition/20262/keep-it-simple-stupid-principle-kiss-principle`) and following the directions of only building the most basic features to make the application work.

SOLID principles

SOLID is an acronym that represents the five underlying principles that guide a good software design. The design is related to the creation of components that shape your software architecture.

In 2004, Michael Feathers suggested this acronym to Robert C. Martin, the author of these principles. The process for creating them took him around 20 years, and during this period, many of them were added, removed, and merged to achieve a robust set of principles named SOLID. Let's review each one of the principles and provide a brief and clear explanation that will be helpful for getting a precise idea of how we can use them.

We will use the term *module* in tandem with the idea of modules shaping components, and we will make reference to the **object-oriented programming** (**OOP**) world using terms such as *classes* and *interfaces* in order to provide a more precise explanation of modules.

The single responsibility principle (SRP)

The SRP is very closely related to the high cohesion that we reviewed earlier. The idea behind this principle is that a module should be changed for one reason only.

This definition leads us to conclude that a module should have only one responsibility. One way to verify whether this principle is achieved in your design is to answer the following questions:

- Does the module's name represent its exposed functionality?

  The answer should be yes. For example, if the module's name refers to the domain, then the module should contain domain classes and some functionality around the domain objects related to the module's name itself. You won't want to have code to support audit elements or any other aspect out of the scope of the module you are working with, for example. If the module is supporting additional features, the code supporting those additional features should probably need to be moved to an existing audit module, or a new audit module should be created.

- When a new change is required, how many parts of the module are affected?

  The answer to this question should be many of them; all classes in the module are highly connected, and a new change will change them for this reason. The desired behavior is prevented from being changed through the exposed interface, but the background implementation is often volatile.

The Open–Closed Principle (OCP)

The OCP is simple to write, but difficult to explain. For this reason, I'll write the following definition first and describe it later:

New features can be added to an existing module by extension and not by modification.

It sounds simple, doesn't it? In order to understand this concept from a practical viewpoint, it is necessary to revisit our last example. Let's check that we are accomplishing this principle by answering the following questions:

- What do we need in order to support a new notification channel?

  We need to write a new class (module), and this should implement an existing interface. Note how the open-closed principle makes sense with the provided answer. To support a new notification channel in our application, we need to create a new class, but we don't need to modify the existing code. According to the previous refactoring that we made, if we needed to support this requirement, we had to adjust the existing service to send notifications.

A few questions to validate how well this principle is achieved are as follows:

- Do I add a new IF statement to my code?

No. If you're looking to add a new feature, you will write a new class instead of modifying an existing one. This is because you are adding and not changing features.

- How much code do I modify in order to support a new feature?

Hopefully, just a little bit. In a perfect world, you won't need to modify anything, but sometimes a few sections should be changed to support new features in the real world. The rule here is that if you are adding a new feature, your original design should be able to support this requirement with minimal changes. If this is not true, refactoring or changing your initial design is recommended.

- How big should my source code files be?

Big source code files are a bad idea, and there is no reason for them to be large. If your source code file has hundreds and hundreds of lines, revisit your functions and think about moving code to a new file in order to make the source code files smaller and easy to understand.

- Should I use abstractions within my code?

This is a tricky one. If you only have one concrete implementation for something, you won't need to have an abstract class or interface. Writing code and inventing new possible scenarios is not desirable at all, but if you have at least two concrete implementations that are related to each other, you have to think about writing an abstraction for them. For example, if we only need to send email notifications, there would be no reason to write an interface for this. However, since we are sending notifications via two different channels, we certainly need an abstraction to deal with them.

The Liskov substitution principle

The **Liskov substitution principle (LSP)** has a fancy definition:

Module A can be replaced by module B as long as B is a subtype of A.

Well-defined contracts heavily support this definition and help us reduce the coupling between modules. The following questions can help you figure out how well this principle is achieved:

- Are the modules interacting using abstractions or concrete implementations?

  Here, the answer should be that the modules should not be interacting with either option. There is no reason to establish interactions among modules by using their concrete implementations instead of their interfaces.

- Should I be casting objects in order to use them?

  I hope not. If so, it's because the interface is not well-designed, and a new one should be created to avoid this behavior. The use of the instanceOf function is also not desirable at all.

- Is the interaction between modules guided by IF statements?

  There is no reason for this to be the case. Your modules should be connected in a way that can be taken care of by the use of an interface and the correct dependency injection to solve their concrete implementations.

The interface segregation principle (ISP)

The principal motivation of the interface segregation principle is aligned with the lean movement where creating values with fewer resources is essential. Here's a short definition for it:

Avoid things that you don't use.

You may have already seen classes (modules) implementing interfaces with some method implementations, such as the following:

```
public   class Abc implements Xyz
{
  @Override
  public void doSomething(Param a)
  {
    throw new UnsupportedOperationException
    ("A good explanation here");
  }
  // Other method implementations
}
```

Alternatively, another option called *comment as implementation* tends to be used, as shown in the following code:

```
public   class Abc implements Xyz
{
   @Override
   public void doSomething(Param a)
   {
     // This method is not necessary here because of ...
   }
   // Other method implementations
}
```

The preceding examples successfully describe the problem that this principle was created to address. The best way to deal with this issue is by creating more consistent interfaces that conform to the other explained principles. The main problem with this issue is not related to having empty method implementations, but having additional functionality that is not used at all.

Suppose that an application depends on an *XYZ* library and the system is only using 10% of the available functionality. If a new change is applied to solve an issue that was present in the other 90%, that modified code represents a risk to the part that the application is using, even when it's not directly related to it.

The following questions will help you identify how well you are doing:

- Do I have empty or silly implementations like the ones mentioned earlier?

  Please don't answer YES.

- Does my interface have a lot of methods?

  Hopefully not, as this will make it more difficult to implement all the abstract methods in concrete implementations. If you have many methods, please refer to the next question.

- Are all the method names consistent with the interface name?

  The method names should be consistent with the interface name. If one or more methods don't make sense at all, then a new interface should be created to place them.

- Can I split this interface into two instead of only one?

  If yes, go ahead and do it.

- How many functions am I using from the whole set of exposed functions?

  If the modules interacting with an interface are only using a few of the exposed functions, then the other ones should probably be moved to another interface, or even to new modules.

The dependency inversion (DI) principle

It is now time to define the dependency inversion principle:

Modules should depend on abstractions rather than on concrete implementations.

Abstractions represent the high-level details of a module, and the interaction among modules should be done at this level. Low-level details are volatile and ever-evolving. We previously stated that there are no problems with evolved modules, but of course, we don't want to break module interactions because of low-level details, and an excellent way to do this is to use abstractions rather than concrete implementations. The following questions will help you identify how well you are doing:

- Do I have abstractions as part of my modules?

  As discussed earlier in this chapter, many concrete implementations should have an abstraction in front of them. However, when it comes to one specific implementation, this is probably not the case.

- Am I creating new instances by myself every time?

  The answer here should be no. Your framework or mechanism that is in charge of the dependency injection inside your application is responsible for doing this.

Conway's law

Mel Conway published a paper in 1968 that is still relevant today, stating the direction that companies should move in. For a long time, we focused on defining rules for everything, such as the following:

- What time you should arrive at the office
- The minimum hours that people should work
- How many days per week are used for working
- What type of clothing is appropriate to wear during working hours

These rules apply to any type of company, and, in many cases, they are still relevant today. Within the IT world (and particularly the software industry), we created another set of rules to guide our teams (feel free to avoid reading these rules if you don't want to get bored):

- Business analysts should create use cases with a well-defined structure, allowing the developer to ignore the business details and focus on the technical part of the process.
- Developers should follow the standard document created by the software architect of the product that was written many years ago.
- The lines of code written per day should indicate how productive a developer is.
- When you create a new database object, you have to update the existing trustable database dictionary.
- As soon as your code is ready to be pushed, use an email template to ask for revision by the QA team. After their approval, repeat this process with the design team and later again with the architecture team.
- Any change to the pushed code will force you to repeat the process that was explained in the preceding rule.
- Don't forget UML diagrams when you finish coding your assigned use case. Not all of them are required—only the most important ones, such as those listed here:
  - Class diagram
  - Object diagram
  - Package diagram
  - Component diagram
  - Sequence diagram
  - Deployment diagram

The preceding list of diagrams will be larger in some cases. Fortunately, things have changed nowadays, and crazy processes that force us to write huge documents and create different diagrams that pay no attention are no longer used. With these premises in mind, Mel Conway wrote the following as part of his paper:

"Any organization that designs a system will inevitably produce a design whose structure is a copy of the organization's communication structure."

Conway's thesis is still relevant and has been affecting the way we structure our teams to create successful projects and avoid wasting resources ever since.

People comprise teams, and the question of how these people should be arranged in order to create successful teams has been answered in many ways in the last few years. All of these answers have suggested building small and multidisciplinary teams that should be small enough to be fed using one pizza and multidisciplinary enough to avoid creating silos during the SDLC.

In this way, companies are promoting a culture of sharing and continuous learning within teams. Teams are continually learning from their successes and failures. They are interacting with each other directly instead of using intermediaries or other protocols of communication.

Business boundaries are defined by teams that allow them to communicate using well-defined interfaces, and since the communication is directly managed by themselves, rapid feedback will enable them to fix issues and take corrective actions when necessary.

Choosing the right technology for you

Earlier in this chapter, we defined what software architecture is and what the relevant elements surrounding it are. We also mentioned that frameworks, programming languages, paradigms, and so on are not the underlying elements that should guide your software architecture. Many people defend the idea of deferring as much of your technical decisions as possible in order to have your design open to new options, and that's worth doing. However, you can't postpone these choices forever.

There are a lot of frameworks available on the market. Many of them are new, but old frameworks are also still available. Even at the beginning of the process, when all this stuff is just a detail, you need to carefully choose the framework that you will use to build your software architecture, since this detail will make your life easier (or more difficult) depending on the features that you implement in order to solve the business requirements. I'll show you some considerations that you need to bear in mind when you're deciding which framework to use:

- How much documentation is available?

  This is an important factor to consider. Here, you must think about how much documentation has been written for the vendor, and how many courses are available online (not only by the vendor but by other developers, as well). If you can find books, articles, and showcases, it's always worth exploring these as they will allow you to learn about the tool that you have decided to use.

- How big is the community around your choice?

Having a lot of people working on improving a product is something that you should appreciate. Your choice should be supported not only by the vendor but also by other developers and companies using the product to solve their needs.

- Is it difficult to write tests using a defined technology that you have in mind?

No matter what your programming style is, you will always benefit from including tests as part of your SDLC. You will also benefit from including tests for another aspect of your software (or at least unit tests, integration tests, functional tests, and load tests). If your framework makes this task difficult, it is better to choose another one. If you are using a framework, ABC, for dependency injection, this should be tested, but if these tests are difficult to write, you won't want to waste your time with them. With this idea in mind, Spring has excellent support for testing, and we'll cover this in subsequent chapters by using a hands-on approach.

- Can I plug components to add more features?

You are probably thinking "if I want to add a new component, I can simply include a JAR". In some cases, this is true, and in other cases, you'll need to discover a whole set of dependencies for making it work. This is a painful procedure because sometimes you need specific versions of specific libraries, which is more challenging to figure out by ourselves, and this is not something you should spend too much time on. Spring includes Spring Boot, which has an excellent method for adding dependencies to your project in a straightforward way. You should only indicate to Spring that you want to work with JPA (for example) during the application creation process, and Spring itself will be able to figure out all the required dependencies to make it work by itself.

It is common to struggle with Maven a bit when you're looking for the right artifact to bootstrap your application for the first time. The good news with Spring is that you have Spring Initializer, which is a friendly website for bootstrapping your application in a few clicks. You can refer to `https://start.spring.io` for more details.

- What are companies using the product for?

Even when the market is crowded with new tools that look promising, you will not want to gamble when it comes to choosing technologies and frameworks. Before choosing a framework or technology, I encourage you to watch some videos of conferences on YouTube. It would be even better if you can go and attend one of them if you have the chance. You'll also benefit from reading papers, showcases, and case studies about a specific technology, as well as which companies are working with these. You can even start creating analogies based on this information in order to figure out how well a particular technology will fit for you.

However, for many years, I have seen how people have been working with Spring to accomplish their business requirements in different industries.

This framework is mature and is constantly evolving to embrace new programming styles and emerging techniques in the software industry. For example, the latest release of Spring includes support for the most recent features introduced within the Java world and the industry in general, such as reactive programming, the latest Java version, and even support for other programming languages that are becoming popular, such as Kotlin and Groovy.

New trends

In the last few years, a lot of programming languages have been emerging to solve new business requirements, and many of these run on the JVM, which gives a significant advantage to Java developers, making embracing new programming languages less difficult.

It's not a coincidence that new emerging software architectures have been created. Business has expanded around the world, which makes it more challenging to scale old applications. This approach has forced us to rethink how to split business boundaries in order to deliver scalable services to solve business needs. Since we needed to offer services to clients around the world, the cloud appeared, and nowadays we can even select regions to reduce the latency of our applications.

With the cloud ready to be used, the X appeared as a service paradigm. We now have services that are created to deal with specific requirements, such as online payments, authentication, data storage, and so on. This leads us to the creation of serverless architectures; with these, companies are focusing more on their businesses requirements rather than on details that were solved by other companies and are offered as ready-to-consume services.

Having clients around the world means that there is more data to store, and improved data storage is replacing old relational models. NoSQL was forced to be conceived, and recommended techniques such as normalization have been replaced with these models, making practices and recommendations that were previously good entirely useless now. This movement even forced the creation of new careers around it. We are currently studying this data and making it worthwhile. Data scientists are becoming popular today, and their role is to identify what other business opportunities are hidden behind the data, as well as what actions IT people need to take based on this.

Allowing customers to consume services quickly is the functionality that companies are looking for, and conversational interfaces are guiding us to the right path. Devices that contain software to allow people to establish conversations using their voice (such as Alexa, Cortana, and Siri, among others) are offering new possibilities to consume services easier and faster. SDK tools are currently available for developers in many programming languages, since polyglot developers are the most common nowadays.

Not all businesses need to embrace these new trends. However, these new options are introducing companies to a world of opportunities that will provide them with an advantage over those that are not embracing them.

Summary

In this chapter, we looked at the underlying concepts inherent to software architecture. Even when the exposed principles have been in the industry for a while, they are still relevant, and it's worth considering them when working on architectural aspects. Something to remember is that high cohesion and low coupling refers to how you connect your components to shape your software architecture, and the SOLID principles apply to the design of each one of them.

To wrap this up, in this chapter, we have talked about how the software industry is evolving to embrace the new business challenges that companies are currently facing. In the next chapter, we will review what software architecture dimensions are in depth, and we will also learn how to use the C4 model to document software architectures.

Software Architecture Dimensions

2

In the previous chapter, you learned that a software's architecture is made up of a team's shared knowledge when building a product or service, as well as other important aspects surrounding this concept. An architect's job is to share this knowledge with the entire team. Even when a team doesn't have somebody assigned to the specific role of the architect, individuals often end up becoming responsible for the system's architecture.

In this chapter, we will review software architecture dimensions and how they influence our applications. We will also introduce a model for documenting software architectures and making the process of sharing and understanding an architecture less difficult for teams. Ultimately, this will allow them to understand the bigger picture of software architecture.

This chapter will cover the following topics and subtopics:

- Software architecture dimensions:
    - Business dimension
    - Data dimension
    - Technical dimension
    - Operations dimension
- The C4 model:
    - Context diagram
    - Container diagram
    - Components diagram
    - Class diagram

Dimensions

According to Google, the word *dimension* has a few meanings. Let's use the following definition, which fits into the context that we will discuss in this section:

"An aspect or feature of a situation, problem, or thing."

Starting with this definition, we will consider dimensions as the aspects or features that will influence and guide the software architectures that we build.

In the previous chapter, we talked about the importance of understanding the business domain when crafting our solutions. Of course, this knowledge is not enough when it comes to generating a system that is able to address all business needs. You will also need to think about the mechanisms for supporting these solutions from a technical viewpoint, without forgetting the business requirements. As technical people, we need to provide a solution that can evolve with the passage of time, in order to accomplish new business needs and efficiently achieve goals.

The following list is comprised of the most common dimensions in the process of crafting a software architecture:

- Business
- Data
- Technical
- Operations

Depending on the context of the solution that you are working on, you can add some extra points to this list. These four dimensions are highly connected when you are looking at a product from a technical viewpoint, and they should be understood by the whole team in charge of the system.

The business dimension

This is the most crucial aspect to consider when we are building software, and that's why the software industry has been inventing new ways to collect requirements. Within this dimension, two relevant activities should be accomplished efficiently, as follows:

- Managing user requirements and gaining a clear idea about the domain model of the business
- Identifying and tracking business metrics

Managing user requirements

Some years ago, we used to write use cases, which have been renamed as **user stories** in the last few years. However, the names are not the key to success here, and it makes no difference whether you are using old-fashioned methods (such as the **Ration Unified Process** (**RUP**) or the most cutting-edge frameworks (such as Scrum) to build your projects. Understanding the domain of the business and owning a product will allow teams to develop successful projects.

As you probably know, RUP is a software development framework that defines a set of phases and has a tremendous amount of documentation associated with each stage. The idea here is to determine what artifacts to generate at each stage. This task is tedious, and teams have often ended up defining a large quantity of useless and time-consuming documentation, without providing any added value to the product. As an alternative to creating documentation, we will discuss the C4 model later in this chapter.

Over time, many books have been written to explain how to manage user requirements. Two of these include *Writing Effective Use Cases* by Alistair Cockburn and *User Stories Applied* by Mike Cohn. These books are the most relevant, and you should consider reading them and making them a part of your library, in order to use them as a reference source whenever necessary.

An efficient process for gathering user requirements should be a part of the vision and the goals that the project should accomplish. Having brainstorming meetings with as many people involved in the project as possible is beneficial for allowing the team in charge of the software implementation to distinguish between the **Minimum Viable Product** (**MVP**) and the desired and expendable features that will be implemented as part of a new release once the MVP version has been accomplished.

Understanding the MVP for the software under construction is paramount; it should give you the minimum features possible to satisfy the user requirements. Once these features are identified, it is also necessary to define the acceptance criteria for them. The products built from here will be used as the base for retrieving feedback from the business people (in order to correct any misconceptions) and also to add new features (in order to grow the solution).

Today, we also count on bug tracking systems to write user requirements as tickets with different classifications, such as bugs, user stories, and spikes, among others. These tickets are used to gain a better understanding of how long a feature takes to be implemented, and how many bugs are involved in it.

Dealing with business requirements in this way gives us useful information that can be analyzed later, in order to improve the performance of a team, as well as the way it is organized. There are a bunch of explanations of how to manage tickets, but if you want a better idea of the principles of bug tracking, I encourage you to read a useful article written by Yegor Bugayenko, which is available at `http://www.yegor256.com/2014/11/24/principles-of-bug-tracking.html`.

Identifying and tracking business metrics

Once the business requirements have been collected, another part of the business dimension emerges, including a way to identify the essential metrics around the business problems that you're solving. These metrics should be determined and expressed concerning the business domain, in order to understand how well an application addresses the business requirements that it was designed for.

Let's revisit an example that we used in the previous chapter. Suppose that the bank is currently using the post office to send monthly bank statements to its clients. In this case, you know a priori, how much money it costs, and the tasks involved in accomplishing the goal. In addition, you even know how many clients you have and how much paper should be printed, according to specific dates. After the implementation of your system, you will want to know that all of your clients are receiving their bank statements. Consequently, you will want to implement a mechanism to identify how many bank statements are being sent by the application, and which notification channels are preferred. This information will be used in the near future, in order to identify new business opportunities, discover when the system has problems, and monitor the ROI of the application. After all, the implementation of a system is guided by a business's needs, and you have to verify that those needs are met.

Once the application is in production, an excellent technique for assessing the business health of your application in the wild is to build bots. These bots exercise your application as a regular user; you'll want to at least create bots around the most important functionalities of your application. If not, how will you know if your application is working?

This goal can be achieved by executing scheduled checks that will send you notifications with the obtained results. This simple technique will give you confidence that the application is working as expected, and is providing a service to your clients—who are the purpose of the system.

The data dimension

Data is considered one of the most critical assets of any business, and that is why you have to invest a considerable amount of time in figuring out the best approach for dealing with it.

Nowadays, we have many options when it comes to choosing our approach to data. In the last few years, many kinds of databases and data storage have been created, including the following:

- File cloud storage
- Relational databases
- Document-oriented databases
- Real-time databases
- Graph databases
- In-memory databases

Your choice should depend on the problem that you're solving, and not on the option used by influential online companies, such as Facebook, Google, and Amazon.

 Remember that different business requirements require different methods of approach.

You may now be wondering what kind of data storage you should choose. The most common answer to that question is that it depends on the context.

However, a dependence on the context may not be the ideal answer here, as it does not provide you with much guidance. With this in mind, the best advice that can be given is to try to make as many analogies as you can, in order to figure out the best data storage method for you. One consideration to bear in mind is this: don't get scared because of the eventual consistency inherent in NoSQL databases. I have seen a lot of people get rid of this kind of database for that reason. You have to understand that eventual consistency is not a technical concern at all, but a business one. Let me explain why.

Considering the example presented in Chapter 1, *Software Architecture Today*, assume that you have been tasked with implementing a new feature in a system with the following description:

> *"We noticed that the notification channels do not always work as expected, and we decided to use an alternative channel when this happens. For example, if the user has configured the email as the preferred channel, then the SMS channel should be used if it fails. On the other hand, if the user has configured SMS as the preferred notification channel, the email notification should be used as an alternative if it fails."*

Notice that this requirement doesn't follow the standard user story format:

> *"As a < type of user >, I want < a goal > so that < reason >..."*

However, the requirements are easy to understand and implement for the team in charge of working on them. For that reason, I mentioned earlier that even if you're still working with use cases or user stories, the matter of business requirements is the most important aspect.

An example of where eventual consistency is not a big deal is with the ordering of Facebook posts, in which each post is timestamped. Here, when a person adds a comment to a post, they think that they are seeing the last comment above theirs, but a few seconds later, they see that other comments did, indeed, get added before their comment. When this happens, it can be confusing. However, not imposing atomicity requirements on the comment order allows Facebook to scale the database globally, covering millions of posts per second. In contrast, it is important that a money transferring transaction require atomic transactions, in order to maintain consistency and avoid fraud or wasting money.

In summary, you first have to understand the business requirement that you want to accomplish, make as many analogies as you can with the options available on the market, and then, make your choice from those options. Once your decision has been made, it's always worth counting on frameworks that will allow you to interact with the data storage of your choice. Fortunately, Spring Data supports a bunch of data storage options. We will discuss the benefits of using this Spring project in the next chapter.

The technical dimension

This dimension involves deeply exploring technical details. Let's discuss some useful questions that you will have to answer in order to accomplish this goal, as follows:

- What style of software architecture should I choose?

  Currently, there are many options for this. Subsequent chapters of this book will explain many of them in detail, and you'll probably find your answers there.

- What programming language is right for my application?

  Many programming languages in the market promise to be the best. For that reason, you have to avoid choosing one just because it's the newest or the latest one. Instead, you must choose a widely known one that suits you.

  The possibility of counting on a vast ecosystem of tooling is always essential, and should be part of your decision. Another part of your decision should be how difficult it is to find people to work with. It is unlikely that you will want to build your software using a programming language that not many people are familiar with. After all, you'll want to create an application that will live for a long time, and this implies that many people will be involved in writing code to make it evolve over time.

  Since this book is intended to be focused on the Spring platform, I'll be discussing the benefits of using Java and the **Java Virtual Machine (JVM)**.

  We all know that Java is a widely supported programming language that has been used to build tons of enterprise applications; this fact gives us the confidence to say that it's mature enough to write almost any kind of enterprise software. On the other hand, the JVM is built on the premise of *write once, run anywhere.* This is important, because a significant part of enterprise applications are currently running on Linux servers; however, this doesn't mean that you need to force your team to use Linux. Instead, they can keep using their preferred OS, since the JVM can run on Windows, Linux, and Mac.

Over the last few years, many programming languages have been written and widely adopted to solve different kinds of problems. Many of them run on JVMs, such as Scala, Groovy, Kotlin, and Jython, because of the benefits that this offers. All of the compiled code of these programming languages check into bytecode, which can interact with Java code, introducing a new world of opportunities. It's always a good idea to give new programming languages a try, to see how they work in different scenarios, and to accomplish different demands. For example, Groovy is a friendly programming language that is simple and easy to use. In subsequent chapters, we will develop some example applications using different programming languages that run on the JVM. These examples will help you to embrace Groovy as a part of your toolbox.

- What framework is right for me?
  Even when a massive list of frameworks crowds the Java world, we encourage you to use Spring, not only because this book is about it, but because it offers the following benefits:
    - Many of the programming languages listed previously are supported
    - Spring offers the chance to build almost any kind of application that you want
    - The learning curve is not a big deal
    - It has great support for unit and integration testing
    - Spring projects make it possible to grow your solution (we will discuss these in the next chapter)
    - It has excellent integration with the IDE of your choice
    - It has a great community
    - Tons of resources to learn about Spring are available on the internet
    - It provides for smooth integration with the most common Java frameworks, such as Hibernate, iBatis, Atomikos, Vaadin, and Thymeleaf

If this list is not enough for you, feel free to type *"why should I use Spring"* into Google; you will get a pleasant surprise, and will have the confidence to use the Spring framework.

The operations dimension

This dimension refers to mapping your architecture components to servers. These servers can live on-premise or in the cloud. The cloud has been becoming increasingly important over the past few years, and now, we can say that it's almost vital for every single business to count on services on the cloud.

The mapping of your software architecture components will depend on what they do and how the interaction occurs among your components.

How to deploy an application

This point is crucial because deploying a Rest API is not the same as deploying a distributed database or a big monolith application. In order to have a better understanding of the best approach for deploying a component, you will need to research the products supporting it. This can be quite simple; for example, by deploying a Spring Boot application that can run like a conventional Java application using the following widely-known command:

```
java -jar artifact_name.jar
```

However, in other cases, some products offer the chance to be deployed as clusters, where you will need to consider all of the options available and what your needs are. Depending on how in-demand your software is, you will need to have fewer or more nodes serving your users' demands. As you have probably noticed, even this dimension is derived from the business.

How interaction occurs among your components

Let's imagine that we have a regular web application persisting information in a database. This web application is deployed in server A, and the database is deployed in server B. Common sense leads us to realize that the latency won't be the same, whether both servers are located in the same or different data centers. Another consideration is, of course, where the end users are located. Today, the cloud offers the chance to choose where you want to deploy your components, depending on your needs, which is helpful when it comes to providing a better user experience.

Dealing with infrastructure

Once these points have been considered, another aspect to bear in mind is how to manage the infrastructure.

We all know that provisioning new servers is always a headache when we need to start from scratch because we will need to install the OS and all of the required tooling to make our application work. Some of these require specific files, directories, environmental variables, and other artifacts in order to work, which makes this process even more complicated. Fortunately, the Infrastructure as Code approach, discussed in the following section, will help us reduce the effort of provisioning new servers, and will give us other benefits, such as the following points:

- Understanding the infrastructure
- Versioning
- Testing

Understanding the infrastructure

Files are used to store the required configuration and steps needed to provision a server in the form of executable scripts. When a new adjustment to an existing server is necessary, the idea is to make these changes using the script files, instead of directly on the server. This will allow us to get the following benefits:

- Immutable servers
- Easy application of changes
- Having more than one identical server
- Rebuilding a new server from scratch very quickly, without errors

Moreover, technical people will be able to read and understand these scripts, allowing for an increase of shared understanding around the process of provisioning new infrastructure, which is excellent.

Versioning

Keeping the written scripts versioned using a **Version Control System** (**VCS**) will allow us to track changes in the script files; this is helpful for increasing the audibility of the written code that is being used to shape your infrastructure. During the versioning process, builds can (and should) be triggered to validate the written code.

Another benefit of versioning is that you can revert changes when needed. Imagine that you are writing code to make upgrades to your servers; if an issue is introduced during this process, you can always make a rollback and keep using the last stable version while the problem is solved.

Testing

There is no way of knowing whether something is working as expected if it has not been tested. Treating the Infrastructure as Code offers us the ability to test the code used to accomplish this goal, to validate and be sure that it works as expected. Otherwise, you will need to do these validations manually, and think about the debugging process involved at this level to identify where the errors are. Even when you could have Infrastructure as Code without testing, it's highly recommended to run tests on the scripts that have been created.

Embracing the Infrastructure as Code approach will help us to take full advantage of computers and systems, in order to make the process less tedious for us, and people should only be working in front of a data center when an issue occurs. This will also help you to keep your infrastructure up to date in a quick and easy manner. If you want an in-depth understanding of how to embrace this approach effectively, I encourage you to read the *Infrastructure as Code* book by Kief Morris.

Cloud versus on-premise

The choice between using servers on the cloud and using them on-premise is a big decision, governed by the restrictions and needs of your business. For security reasons, some companies are restricted to use on-premise infrastructures, which is probably due to a misconception about how security is managed in the cloud. Regardless, this restriction invalidates any attempt to move the infrastructure to the cloud.

On the other hand, if you have the chance to choose between these two options, I encourage you to use the cloud. It offers many benefits, such as pay as you go, which will allow you to save a significant amount of money during the first releases of your application. Some services charge you a few cents per hour, depending on what you need and the licensing model of the software that you use. For example, using free and proprietary software is not the same as using a server with Windows or Linux. In the same way, it is not the same as using an RDBMS, such as MariaDB or Oracle.

Even when you made the choice to use the cloud, there are a few considerations that you need to bear in mind in order to choose the right cloud provider for you, according to the set of features required. Some cloud providers, like AWS, provide a bunch of services for computing, storage, management tools, analytics, and so on, while others, like Heroku, offer a lower quantity of features that are good enough, depending on your demands. It isn't a good idea to choose a provider just because it gives you more services, because this also implies a higher cost. Even when the number of services provided by different vendors is similar, the simplicity of the process of deploying an application using the providers mentioned earlier is significant.

Deploying your application

There is no point in writing code that won't be brought to production. Regardless of whether you deploy your application to the cloud or in your on-premise environment, you can use some techniques and tools to automate the deployment process. This will help you to reduce the amount of effort required.

During the deployment process of a software system some years ago, the whole team writing the application had to sit with the operations team, just in case something went wrong. Consequently, the deployment date used to be scary for both technical and business people involved in the project. Fortunately, this has changed. Let's review how this change occurred.

Automation is a must when we are entering this field. There are many CI tools available for creating pipelines that will help you to automate deployments. The most widely used of these are Jenkins, Travis CI, Go CD, Codeship, and Bamboo, among others. With the help of these tools, you can create a pipeline that often involves the following:

1. Downloading the source code
2. Compiling the code
3. Running a defined set of tests
4. Deploying the code

The main step is the third one, which involves different sorts of tests, such as those listed here:

- Unit tests
- Integration tests
- Functional tests
- Performance tests

The more tests you include as a part of your application, the more confidence you'll gain. This is the only way to get rid of the fear caused by deployment. After all, if your tests verify that the functionality is working as expected, there is no reason to be worried about the deployment.

These CI tools also include support for sending notifications about the pipelines, generating metrics around the code, executing configuration scripts, and completing some other steps inherent to deployment. These pipelines are often triggered by commits, and they can also be scheduled.

The adoption of a CI tool is the first step toward automating and managing your deployments in a better way. At this point, you will want to adopt practices like Continuous Integration, Continuous Delivery, and DevOps, which we will explain in depth in `Chapter 11`, *DevOps and Release Management*.

The C4 model

In general, if something is not visible, it won't provide the desired effect. Even the most advanced software, produced with the most cutting-edge technology, is entirely useless if the team that works on it is unable to understand it. All of the efforts applied by the team will be a waste of time.

Simply designing a software architecture isn't enough. It has to be shared with the whole team in a way that allows them to use it correctly when fulfilling their activities. The documentation made by the architects speaks for them today, when they should be doing things other than answering a hundred questions about software architecture, and it speaks for them tomorrow when they have left the project and someone else is in charge of its evolution and maintenance.

The second principle of the agile manifesto (`http://agilemanifesto.org`) is that *"teams should value working software over comprehensive documentation."* This is often interpreted incorrectly by people believing that no documentation should be produced at all. Instead, the idea behind this principle is to encourage teams to only produce valuable documentation, and that's precisely what the C4 model looks for.

This model provides an easy way to communicate the design of the system to the whole team. It starts from a high-level viewpoint, and it can be used to delve into the smallest details of the software that is (or will be) produced. This model proposes four diagrams, as follows:

- Context diagram
- Container diagram
- Components diagram
- Class diagram

Context diagram

The context diagram provides the big picture of the users and the other software systems that it interacts with. All technical elements should be avoided in order to keep it simple and easy to understand. A context diagram should be straightforward enough to be understood by non-technical people.

The following shows a diagram contextualized for the example proposed in `Chapter 1,` *Software Architecture Today*:

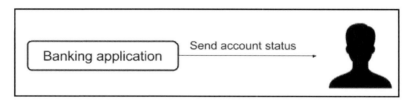

Context diagram

Container diagram

Containers are units that are in charge of hosting code or data. Consequently, this diagram shows the containers involved in the application, providing high-level details about how they interact with each other, as well as some other technical details to illustrate how the system works. Let's look at this diagram as it applies to our example:

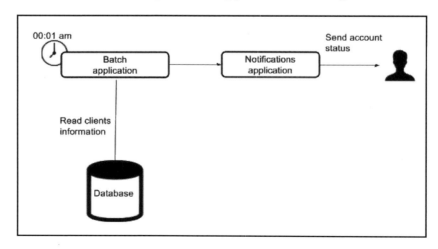

Container diagram

Components diagram

The idea behind this diagram is to show you how a container is shaped by components and the interactions among them. The components diagram for our example is as follows:

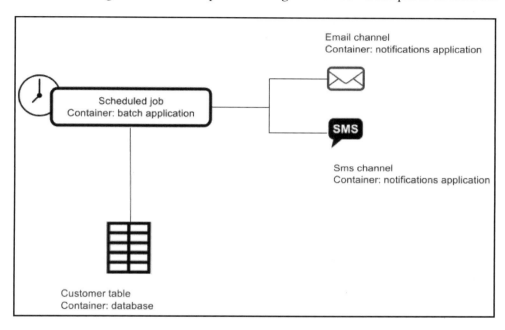

Components diagram

Class diagram

Since the main idea behind the C4 model is to remove unnecessary diagrams, the class diagram should be avoided, and should only be used when it's vital to illustrate specific details of an application. This diagram is intended for technical people, and it can be used when there is an element of your application that people should pay close attention to; it can also be used to clarify some specific parts in the code that might cause confusion.

Although this diagram is not necessary for our example, we will show it for illustrative purposes:

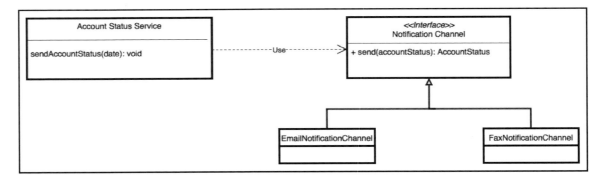

Class diagram

As you may have noticed, the four diagrams that we have presented are not difficult to create, and they are helpful when it comes to acquiring a better understanding of a system. Even when they are simple, it's always a good idea to review these diagrams from time to time to ensure that they are updated. Outdated documentation can lead to misconceptions, instead of improving the understanding of the system.

 Feel free to avoid creating any diagrams that you do not find helpful. Investing time in building unnecessary artifacts is something that you should avoid.

Summary

In this chapter, we discussed the four main dimensions associated with software architecture and looked at how they affect the way we build our applications. We also reviewed the C4 model that's used to document system architectures, using a lean approach that helps us to avoid wasting time in creating unnecessary documentation.

In the next chapter, we will review Spring Projects and how they can be used to create applications that satisfy different business demands.

3
Spring Projects

In this chapter, we will review some Spring projects, looking at a brief explanation of each of them as we explore some scenarios in which they may be used.

The following topics will be covered in this chapter:

- Why Spring appeared
- Spring projects:
  - Spring Initializr
  - Spring Boot in a Nutshell
  - Avoiding redeployment with developer tools
  - Spring Data
  - Supporting EIPs with Spring Integration
  - Spring Batch
  - Securing applications with Spring Security
  - Embracing (Spring) HATEOAS
  - Spring Cloud and the microservices world
  - Reactive and Spring
  - Reactive Spring Data
  - Reactive REST services

Why Spring appeared

As you probably know, Spring was created with the intention of simplifying all of the complexity of the J2EE world. It was created as a dependency injection framework and as an alternative to the EJB stack with distributed objects, which was unnecessary in most applications. The traditional approach to J2EE introduced a lot of complexity when it was used to bootstrap an application, and this involved even more complexity when used to accomplish the business requirements it had to solve. Consequently, we were left with applications that were difficult to test and were too costly to develop and maintain.

Spring and J2EE were created when Java didn't have annotations, so big XML files were necessary for wire classes. Fortunately, annotations became available in version 1.5 of the **Java Development Kit (JDK)**, and that helped to reduce the need for such descriptor files.

Spring evolves faster than JEE, since it doesn't have to satisfy the formality of talking with a large committee, as required for JEE. When a new feature has to be incorporated as part of the JEE specification, a JSR document has to be created and approved by the JCP. The main motivation for this is that it guarantees backward and forward compatibility among the different versions of the specification. On the other hand, Spring is a project that is always evolving, considering the constantly changing nature of the software industry.

When a new feature is required, it is either embraced as a part of an existing project, or a new project is created and supported by the Spring project umbrella. There is no reason to be worried about compatibility, since Spring is designed to run on any servlet container, such as Apache Tomcat, Jetty, and so on. This is contrary to JEE applications, which only run on servers that implement the Java EE specifications and provide the standard Java EE services.

Spring projects

Spring projects make use of an ecosystem of tools that can be used to create different kinds of applications in order to accomplish different goals. All of these projects are built around Spring, which is a legitimate modular framework that makes it possible to plug separate Spring projects to allow applications to deal with more technical requirements. If you're interested in the complete list of Spring projects, you can visit their home page at `https://Spring.io/projects`.

We will review the most commonly used Spring projects to build enterprise applications, but first, we will introduce Spring Initializr, one of the preferred websites for Spring developers.

Spring Initializr

When we plan to create a new project from scratch, we tend to think about which build tool we will use, which framework we will use, and so on. One of the most difficult tasks is finding the right dependencies to make the projects work. That is what Spring Initializr was created for. This excellent Spring initiative makes it possible to bootstrap applications in minutes, or even seconds, no matter what version you prefer. Spring Initializr can be used on the web or in your favorite IDE (Eclipse or IntelliJ), and it even has a cool CLI tool. My preferred approach is the web, and the following screenshot illustrates why:

Spring Initializr home page

At the top of the page, you have the option to specify your favorite build tool. The available options for this are Maven and Gradle. The next option allows you to choose the programming language of your choice (at the moment, Java, Groovy, and Kotlin are supported). The last option at the top of the web page asks which Spring Boot version you want to use. In this section, even snapshot and milestone versions are included. In the **Project Metadata** section, you specify the group and artifact name of your project. The **Dependencies** section has the **Search for dependencies** text field, which is helpful for defining what Spring projects you want to include as a part of your application. If you want to see more, go ahead and click on the **Switch to the full version** link; this will show you a big list of all of the available dependencies.

All of these projects are created using the Spring Boot framework, which makes it easy to create standalone applications that are ready for production. Now, let's quickly go over Spring Boot.

Spring Boot in a Nutshell

The Spring Boot framework intends to make the following tasks easier:

- Servlet container integration
- Autoconfiguration
- Dependency management

Servlet container integration

Previously, we created `.war` files and then dropped them into the corresponding servlet container's deployment directory. However, Spring Boot includes an embedded servlet container, which ensures that this is no longer necessary. The idea is to generate a JAR file with all involved dependencies, and then execute the JAR file as a regular Java application. It's possible, but not recommended, to keep using the old approach of generating WAR files.

Autoconfiguration

Spring Boot always attempts to automatically configure your application, based on the dependencies that you have added. For example, if H2 is a part of your dependencies, a data source to use an in-memory database will be configured automatically. You can always override these default configurations by using annotations, environment variables, configuration files, and even arguments when you're running the `.jar` file.

Dependency management

Each Spring Boot version includes a curated list of dependencies. Because of this, you don't even have to know what artifacts and versions are required as a part of your application. You will always have the option to override these dependencies if you have to, but that is often unnecessary. This approach allows us to easily upgrade our Spring Boot applications.

Let's create a simple Spring Boot application by running the following `curl` command:

```
curl https://start.Spring.io/starter.zip -o Spring-boot-demo.zip
```

The preceding command will download a `.zip` file containing the following file structure:

```
.
├── mvnw
├── mvnw.cmd
├── pom.xml
└── src
    ├── main
    │   ├── java
    │   │   └── com
    │   │       └── example
    │   │           └── demo
    │   │               └── DemoApplication.java
    │   └── resources
    │       └── application.properties
    └── test
        └── java
            └── com
                └── example
                    └── demo
                        └── DemoApplicationTests.java
```

Spring Boot project structure

Let's quickly review these files.

mvnw and mvnw.cmd

These first two files are a part of the Maven wrapper (`https://github.com/takari/maven-wrapper`). Here, the idea is to avoid forcing the developers to install Maven from scratch, instead of providing a built-in script that is able to download the right version and make it ready to work.

pom.xml

This file contains the necessary dependencies to run a Spring Boot application. Let's review the file's content, as follows:

```xml
<?xml version="1.0" encoding="UTF-8"?>
...
<parent>
  <groupId>org.springframework.boot</groupId>
  <artifactId>Spring-boot-starter-parent</artifactId>
  <version>1.5.8.RELEASE</version>
  <relativePath/>
</parent>
...
```

```
      <dependencies>
        <dependency>
          <groupId>org.springframework.boot</groupId>
          <artifactId>Spring-boot-starter</artifactId>
        </dependency>
        <dependency>
          <groupId>org.springframework.boot</groupId>
          <artifactId>Spring-boot-starter-test</artifactId>
          <scope>test</scope>
        </dependency>
      </dependencies>
      ...
    </project>
```

The `parent` pom section provides the necessary dependency and plugin management for the application.

The `Spring-boot-starter` dependency contains all of the dependencies that you need to get the project up and running, using a curated set of managed transitive dependencies. There are also other starters that you may want to use, depending on what you need for your project (for example, JPA, queues, security, and so on).

The `Spring-boot-starter-test` dependency includes the whole set of dependencies for testing. It will allow you to write not only unit tests, but integration tests as well.

DemoApplication.java

This is a simple class with a `main` method, which is in charge of running the application. This `main` class can be executed in this way because of the `@SpringBootApplication` annotation, which enables all of the required autoconfiguration, as follows:

```
@SpringBootApplication
public class DemoApplication
{
  public static void main(String[] args)
  {
    SpringApplication.run(DemoApplication.class, args);
  }
}
```

The application.properties file

Within this file, you have to define all of the configuration properties for your application. For example, if you are interacting with an SQL database, this file will have properties such as the JDBC URL, database username, password, and more. If you want to, you can change its extension from `.properties` to `.yml`, in order to make it more expressive by using a YAML format (`http://www.yaml.org/start.html`).

DemoApplicationTests.java

As a bonus, the following is an example of a simple integration test that you can use as a guide, to keep writing tests for your new code. Thanks to annotations, writing this kind of test is relatively simple:

```
@RunWith(SpringRunner.class)
@SpringBootTest
public class DemoApplicationTests
{
  @Test
  public void contextLoads()
  {
  }
}
```

The preceding explanations should be enough to provide you with a brief overview so that you can understand what Spring Boot is and what its benefits are. Now, it's time to review other Spring projects that you'll love.

Avoiding redeployment with developer tools

This module is awesome because it's meant to help you avoid redeployment when you're working on a Spring Boot application. It is similar to JRebel, but this product is absolutely free, and you can include it as a part of your application by simply adding the following dependency:

```
<dependency>
  <groupId>org.springframework.boot</groupId>
  <artifactId>spring-boot-devtools</artifactId>
  <optional>true</optional>
</dependency>
```

Once the dependency has been added, you just have to recompile the classes to trigger an application restart. Depending on your IDE configuration, this process will be done either automatically or manually.

Spring Data

This project offers you an additional abstraction layer for accessing data storage; it has a bunch of interfaces that you need to extend, in order to take advantage of the built-in functionalities offered by Spring Data. When you extend these interfaces, all of the standard operations surrounding data storage will be ready to use.

Spring Data supports technologies such as relational and non-relational databases, map-reduce frameworks, and cloud-based data services. These technologies are supported by modules; if you are interested in the whole list of existing modules, you can visit `http://projects.Spring.io/Spring-data/`.

Let's play with Spring Data by using an SQL database, such as H2. Suppose that you want to build a **Create, Read, Update, Delete (CRUD)** operation for a country database table. With this framework, you only need to create the entity class and an empty interface extending the `CrudRepository` interface provided by Spring Data, as follows:

```
@Component
public interface CountryRepository extends CrudRepository<Country, Integer>
{
}
```

Since the `CrudRepository` interface has all of the CRUD operations in it, you won't have to implement anything; you will only have to use its functionality. Let's see this in action, as follows:

```
@SpringBootApplication
public class SpringDataDemoApplication
{
  @Bean
  InitializingBean populateDatabase(CountryRepository
  countryRepository)
  {
    return () ->
    {
      countryRepository.save(new Country(1, "USA"));
      countryRepository.save(new Country(2, "Ecuador"));
    };
  }
  @Bean
  CommandLineRunner queryDatabase(CountryRepository
  countryRepository)
  {
    return args ->
    {
      countryRepository.findAll()
```

```
      .forEach(System.out::println);
    };
  }
  public static void main(String[] args)
  {
    SpringApplication.run(SpringDataDemoApplication.class,args);
  }
}
```

We have two **Beans** that use the repository interface created previously. The first method will run, and it will insert two rows into the table. The second method will query all of the rows in the table and then print them in the console. After running this application, you will see the following output in the console when the application starts:

```
...
Country [id: 1 name: USA ]
Country [id: 2 name: Ecuador ]
...
```

Spring Data has more features; it also gives you the chance to create queries in a fascinating way. Let's suppose that you want to filter the countries by name. In that case, you will need to add the method to your interface repository, as follows:

```
@Component
public interface CountryRepository extends CrudRepository<Country, Integer>
{
    List<Country> findByName(String name);
}
```

Then, we can use the preceding method in the following way:

```
countryRepository.findByName("USA")
```

There's no implementation at all for this method, which is a great advantage. Spring Data uses the method's name to generate the required implementation, allowing us to forget trivial implementations for these kinds of queries. There are many interfaces that provide more functionalities, such as pagination, sorting, and reactive extensions.

Supporting EIPs with Spring Integration

Integration is important because applications are intended to interact with each other. Forcing them to work in isolation makes them useless.

It's common to find companies that have their own software, developed in-house, to solve their specific business requirements; but, since certain scenarios tend to be common for more than one company, there are third-party services that can fulfill these needs. Since the functionality offered by these systems is ready to use, we have to find a way to make these applications work as a single system, and that's where **Enterprise Integration Patterns (EIP)** come into play.

EIPs provide proven solutions to recurring problems that can be applied in different contexts with slight modifications, depending on particular business needs. There is a vast catalog of these patterns available on the internet, and a must-read within this field is the book *Enterprise Integration Patterns*, by Gregor Hohpe and Bobby Woolf. This book explains a large list of patterns, along with example scenarios, by using a technology agnostic approach.

Once you understand the theory around EIPs, you will find Spring Integration pretty handy for implementing them; it will have all of the benefits inherent to the Spring Framework, as discussed previously.

When we discuss integration, we can consider the concept using a three-step approach. Let's start reviewing the following diagram which shows these three steps:

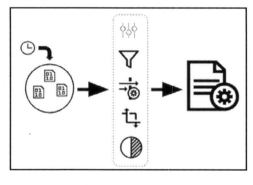

EIPs

The following is a list of steps that are executed as a part of the preceding process:

1. There is a data source where the information is extracted; a poll is sometimes needed, in order to ask for data.
2. The ingested data is filtered, transformed, composed, decomposed, routed, and so on, depending on what's required. It's here that the EIPs are used.
3. The processed data is ready to be delivered or stored, depending on what is needed.

Spring Integration provides built-in support for retrieving or sending information from or to queues, databases, system files, FTP servers, and many other options. Moreover, if needed, you can write your own implementation and plug it in, in order to make it work as a part of your process. The DSL provided by Spring makes it easy to read and implement the EIPs.

Spring Batch

No matter what type of architecture we are using, sometimes we will need to work with a great amount of data and apply some transformations to make it useful. This kind of processing usually happens when we need to consolidate (or simply process) data from one or many data sources, making it available for certain business purposes.

These batch processes require a well-defined set of steps for accomplishing the required goal. Using Spring Batch, you can implement them by using jobs that are composed of steps to read, process, and write the processed data. One job can have as many steps as required, as shown in the following diagram:

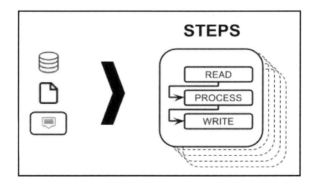

Spring Batch – Job structure

The read step

In this case, the information is read from an external data source using a built-in `ItemReader` object that is part of Spring Batch. The `ItemReader` object will serve a `<T>` object, which will be consumed later.

The process step

Here, the data processing is done by an `ItemProcessor` object that can transform and manipulate the `<T>` data that has been read from the `ItemReader` object. An `ItemProcessor` can return the same `<T>` object that was read, or another `<O>` object that is completely different if that's the desired behavior.

The write step

Once the processing step has finished, an `ItemWriter` object is available to use, writing the `<O>` transformed object obtained in the processing stage.

Spring provides the ability to interact with traditional data sources, such as the following:

- Files
- JMS providers
- Databases

With Spring Batch, one cool feature is that it offers the chance to rerun and skip jobs, since it has its own database where the state to executed jobs is stored.

Since Spring Batch is designed to deal with huge amounts of data, in order to accelerate the processing, the framework offers the chance to process the information as chunks of data. This also makes it possible to reduce the server resources required for processing.

Securing applications with Spring Security

Spring Security is an extensible framework that can be used to secure Java applications. It can also be used to handle authentication and authorization, and it uses a declarative style that is not at all intrusive of the existing code.

The framework supports different approaches to authentication, such as the following:

- LDAP
- JDBC
- In-memory

You can also add your own custom authentication mechanism by implementing the AuthenticationProvider interface, as follows:

```
@Component
public class CustomAuthenticationProvider
implements AuthenticationProvider
{
  @Override
  public Authentication authenticate(Authentication
  authentication)
  throws AuthenticationException
  {
    // get the entered credentials
    String username = authentication.getName();
    String password = authentication.getCredentials().toString();
    // check the entered data
    if ("user".equals(username) && "password".
    equals(password))
    {
      return new UsernamePasswordAuthenticationToken(
      username, password, new ArrayList<>());
    }
    ...
  }
  ...
}
```

In the preceding example, the user and password hardcoded strings are expected as credentials in order to have a successful authentication process, and you should replace that verification with the necessary logic.

The aforementioned authentication mechanisms follow the **Basic Authentication** model, which is the preferred model for web applications. However, when you're writing APIs, you will need other approaches to deal with security. A good option is to use a model based on tokens, such as JWT or OAuth, which we will review and implement in subsequent chapters.

Embracing (Spring) HATEOAS

When talking about the REST subject, it's always worth discussing the Maturity Model, created by Leonard Richardson, which establishes three steps that a REST API should accomplish in order to be considered mature:

- Resources
- HTTP verbs
- Hypermedia controls: HATEOAS

In this section, we will focus on the last element. **HATEOAS** is intended to provide information about what we can do next, using additional **Uniform Resource Identifiers** (**URIs**) that are included as part of the resource.

Let's revisit our banking example, in order to explain HATEOAS from a practical view. Suppose that you have the following URI to query the customer's bank statements: `http://your-api/customer/{customer_id}/bankStatements`.

```
[
  {
    "accountStatusId": 1,
    "information": "Some information here"
  },
  {
    "accountStatusId": 2,
    "information": "Some information here"
  }
]
```

Also, let's suppose that the API has the ability to resend the bank statements or mark them as failed. With the information provided by the previously mentioned payload, there is no way to know about these operations. It's here that HATEOAS can be used, to let our API users know about the existence of these additional features. After applying HATEOAS, the payload will look as follows:

```
{
  "_embedded":
  {
    "bankStatementList":
    [
      {
        "bankStatementId": 1,
        "information": "Some information here",
        "_links":
        {
```

```json
      "markAsFailed":
      [
        {
          "href": "http://localhost:8080/customer/
          1/bankStatements/1/markAsFailed"
        },
        {
          "href": "http://localhost:8080/customer/
          1/bankStatements/1/markAsFailed"
        }
      ],
      "resend":
      [
        {
          "href": "http://localhost:8080/customer/
          1/bankStatements/1/resend"
        },
        {
          "href": "http://localhost:8080/customer/
          1/bankStatements/1/resend"
        }
      ]
    }
  },
  ...
    }
   }
  ]
 }
}
```

Note how easy it is to learn about the existence of these operations, which were hidden before applying HATEOAS as part of the API.

Spring Cloud and the microservices world

This project provides a set of tools to deal with distributed applications. Spring Cloud is mainly used within the microservices world, which we will review in depth in Chapter 8, *Microservices*. This project is composed of modules that offer different functionalities, which can be embraced all at once or one by one, depending on your needs. Let's briefly review some of the most common modules available in Spring Cloud, and look at how they work.

Configuration server

This module provides a centralized tool for storing all of the configurations that your applications need in order to work. Within the Java world, it's quite common to have `.properties` and `.yml` files that store all of the required configurations.

Spring offers the ability to create different profiles, in order to deal with different environments, using files with the previously mentioned extensions. However, it also has the option to keep all of the configuration centralized in a server, where you can store values and even encrypted information. When clients need to access this secret information, the configuration server has the ability to decrypt the information and make it available to the client. Furthermore, you can change the configuration values on the fly. The files storing this configuration reside inside of a Git repository, which gives us the additional benefit of accounting for the changes applied in the configurations.

Service registry

A service registry works like a phone book for the Cloud, which makes it possible to find out where the services are and how many instances of them are available for handling incoming requests.

Spring offers support for most of the common service registries, including the following:

- Zookeeper
- Consul
- Netflix Eureka

Using a service registry offers the following benefits:

- Sophisticated load balancing, such as availability zone awareness
- Client-side load balancing
- Request routing

Edge services

An edge service acts as a proxy. It is designed to take all incoming requests and do something useful with them, before sending them to the services that are behind the load balancers, firewalls, and so on.

There are two main types of edge services:

- Microproxy
- API gateway

One of the benefits of using an edge service is that you can manage all of the specific client details in a centralized place instead of writing code to deal with these details in each service individually. For example, if you need to make a particular consideration for mobile clients, this is the perfect place to do it.

Microproxy

A microproxy is a kind of edge service that retrieves an incoming request only, and then redirects the request to the corresponding service.

A classic example of this type of edge service involves dealing with **Cross-Origin Resource Sharing (CORS)**, as defined at `https://en.wikipedia.org/wiki/Cross-origin_resource_sharing`. As you probably know, CORS restricts access to specific resources when they are requested from a domain different from where they reside. You can allow access to the resources on each service, or you can take advantage of an edge server, in order to allow services to be requested from other domains.

API gateway

The use of an API gateway transforms incoming requests before redirecting them to the corresponding services. Not only can the requests be modified, but the responses are also provided.

A gateway can also work as a facade, which should orchestrate some services before sending the responses to the clients. When we are working with this particular use case, we can implement the circuit breaker pattern in order to be more defensive.

Circuit breaker

A circuit breaker is a pattern used to deal with failed calls. If an error occurs, you can usually throw an exception and let the user know that something went wrong, but you can also use an alternative path to serve an alternative response. For example, let's suppose that service A has failed. Now, instead of returning a failed response, you can invoke an alternative service, B, which acts similarly to service A, in order to provide a valid response to the client, hence improving the user experience.

Reactive and Spring

Reactive programming is a paradigm built around a simple concept that proposes propagating changes using events. This programming style has been used for a while in programming languages such as JavaScript, and one of its main benefits is its asynchronous and non-blocking behavior.

In order to embrace this programming paradigm within the Java world, the Reactive Stream specification was created, following the goals declared in the Reactive Manifesto (https://www.reactivemanifesto.org), which was written a few years ago.

This specification is mainly composed of four interfaces, as follows:

- Publisher
- Subscriber
- Subscription
- Processor

Let's briefly review these interfaces.

Publisher

This interface has a simple method, which makes it possible to register subscribers that will eventually receive the data when it is available to consume. The following is the code for the `Publisher` interface:

```
public interface Publisher<T>
{
  public void subscribe(Subscriber<? super T> s);
}
```

Subscriber

This interface is where the action happens. The following methods have names that are self-describing:

```
public interface Subscriber<T>
{
  public void onSubscribe(Subscription s);
  public void onNext(T t);
  public void onError(Throwable t);
  public void onComplete();
}
```

With each of the previously mentioned methods, you can register a callback that will be invoked under the appropriate circumstances, as follows:

- onSubscribe: This method is executed when the subscription process happens
- onNext: This method is executed when a new event is received
- onError: This method is executed when an error occurs
- onComplete: This method is executed when the producer has finished and there are no more results to receive

Subscription

This interface is intended to be used when you want to request a subscription to the Publisher interface, specifying the number of elements to request to the upstream; the cancel method should be called when the subscriber is no longer interested in receiving data:

```
public interface Subscription
{
  public void request(long n);
  public void cancel();
}
```

Processor

The processor interface implements two additional interfaces: Publisher and Subscriber. This interface is used to subscribe to and publish events.

Project reactor

This project is an implementation of the Reactive Streams specification, which is preferred by Spring Framework. There are also adapters that make it possible to use other implementations if required, but that is often unnecessary.

 Project reactor can also be used to implement Reactive applications without using Spring.

When we're registering functions to handle events, we tend to nest callbacks that make it difficult to understand the written code. In order to simplify these kinds of requirements, Reactor has its own set of operators (visit https://goo.gl/y7kcgS to see the whole list of available operators). These operators allow us to interact with the API in a cleaner way, without having to chain callback functions together.

There are two main producer classes that deal with results where the operators can be applied:

- Mono
- Flux

Mono

Mono represents the asynchronous result of a single or empty value (0...1).

The following diagram was taken from the Project Reactor documentation, and it indicates how an item is emitted by a Mono object:

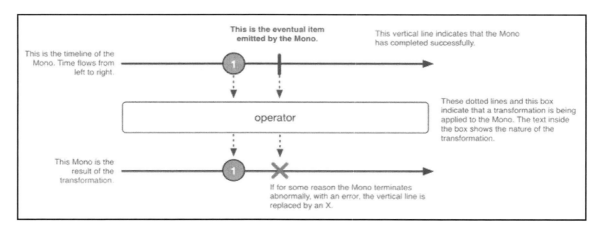

Item emitted by a Mono object

The preceding diagram illustrates the following flow:

- A new value is produced
- An operator is applied to the produced value
- The result is delivered

The following example shows how to work using an empty value:

```
@Test
public void givenAnEmptyMono_WhenTheDefaultIfEmptyOperatorIsUsed_
ThenTheDefaultValueIsDeliveredAsResult() throws Exception
{
  String defaultMessage = "Hello world";
  Mono<String> emptyMonoMessageProduced = Mono.empty();
  Mono<String> monoMessageDelivered = emptyMonoMessageProduced
  .defaultIfEmpty(defaultMessage);
  monoMessageDelivered.subscribe(messageDelivered ->
  Assert.assertEquals(defaultMessage, messageDelivered));
}
```

Flux

Flux represents an asynchronous sequence of 0 to *n* items.

We will again borrow a diagram from the Project Reactor documentation, which explains how a `Flux` object emits items:

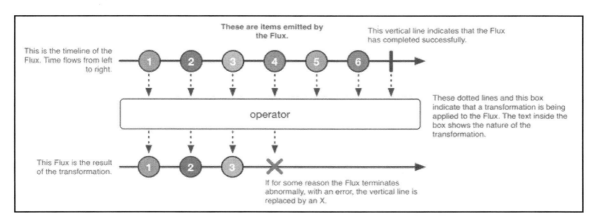

Item emitted by a Flux object

The preceding diagram illustrates the following process:

- At least six values have been produced
- An operator is applied to the produced values
- The result is delivered

In the following example, we will first convert each produced value to uppercase, in order to deliver the values:

```
@Test
public void givenAListOfCapitalizedStrings_WhenThe
FlatMapConvertsToUpperCaseTheStrings_ThenTheStringsAre
InUpperCase() throws Exception
{ .
  List<String> namesCapitalized = Arrays.asList("John",
  "Steve", "Rene");
  Iterator<String> namesCapitalizedIterator = namesCapitalized.
  iterator();
  Flux<String> fluxWithNamesCapitalized = Flux.fromIterable
  (namesCapitalized);
  Flux<String> fluxWithNamesInUpperCase = fluxWithNamesCapitalized
  .map(name -> name.toUpperCase());
  fluxWithNamesInUpperCase.subscribe
  (
    nameInUpperCase ->
    {
      String expectedString =namesCapitalizedIterator.
      next().toUpperCase();
      Assert.assertEquals(expectedString, nameInUpperCase);
    }
  );
}
```

Back pressure

Back pressure is a mechanism that allows us to specify the required number of elements to be read at once. It is used when you're interested in chunks of data with a defined quantity of n elements. The data is delivered in chunks until the whole dataset is reached.

Suppose that you want chunks of data with three elements, from a `Flux` object with ten elements. In this case, you will retrieve the data four times, as shown in the following example:

```
@Test
public void givenAFluxWith10Elements_WhenBack
PressureAsksForChunksOf3Elements_ThenYouHave4Chunks()
throws Exception
{
  List<Integer> digitsArray = Arrays.asList(1, 2, 3, 4,
  5, 6, 7, 8, 9, 0);
  Flux<Integer> fluxWithDigits = Flux.fromIterable
  (digitsArray);
```

```
fluxWithDigits.buffer(3)
.log()
.subscribe
(
  elements ->
  {
    Assert.assertTrue(elements.size() <= 3);
  }
);
}
```

The following is the generated output from the log:

```
[ INFO] (main) onSubscribe(FluxBuffer.BufferExactSubscriber)
[ INFO] (main) request(unbounded)
[ INFO] (main) onNext([1, 2, 3])
[ INFO] (main) onNext([4, 5, 6])
[ INFO] (main) onNext([7, 8, 9])
[ INFO] (main) onNext([0])
[ INFO] (main) onComplete()
```

As mentioned previously, Spring 5 supports reactive programming by using the Reactor project. We have the ability to use it as a part of Spring MVC and Spring Data, as well.

Reactive Spring Data

Since Reactor can be used with Spring Data, we can take full advantage of the reactive programming model at this stage. This means that you can persist data represented as Flux or Mono objects. Let's review the following example, implemented with MongoDB:

```
@Test
public void findAllShouldFindTheTotalAmountOfRecordsInserted()
{
  int quantityOfEntitiesToPersistAsFlux = 100;
  // Saving a Flux with 100 items
  repository.saveAll
  (
    Flux.just(generateArrayWithElements
    (quantityOfEntitiesToPersistAsFlux))
  )
  .then()
  .block();
  // Saving a Mono
  repository.saveAll(Mono.just(new Customer("Rene")))
  .then()
  .block();
```

```
        List<String> customerIds = repository.findAll()
        .map(customer -> customer.getId())
        .collectList()
        .block();
        int totalAmountOfInserts = quantityOfEntitiesTo
        PersistAsFlux + 1;
        Assert.assertEquals(totalAmountOfInserts, customerIds.size());
    }
```

Note that the provided information is represented as `Flux` and `Mono` objects, and the queried data is obtained as a `Flux` object, which is manipulated using the map operator to recover only the IDs as `List<String>` to verify the number of entities created.

Reactive REST services

Reactive REST services have been added by using `WebFlux` as a part of the Spring web stack. This allows us to implement endpoints that are capable of delivering information as streams.

Let's review how this works from a practical viewpoint. Suppose that you want to retrieve notifications that are often pushed by users. Without using the reactive approach, you can retrieve all of the notifications created until the request is made; but, with the reactive approach, you can keep receiving new notifications, which means that if a new notification is created, you will receive it at that exact moment. Let's analyze the following code snippet:

```
@GetMapping(value = "/{singer}/comments", produces =
MediaType.TEXT_EVENT_STREAM_VALUE)
public Flux<Comment> querySingerComments(@PathVariable
String singer)
{
    // generate one flux element per second
    Flux<Long> intervalToGenerateComments =
  Flux.interval(Duration.ofSeconds(1));
    Flux<Comment> comments = Flux.fromStream(Stream.generate(()
    ->new Comment(composeComment(singer), new Date())));
    return Flux.zip(intervalToGenerateComments, comments)
    .map(fluxTuple -> fluxTuple.getT2());
}
```

First of all, pay attention to the produced content. This is a stream value, rather than JSON, XML, or any other content type. Next, we are simulating that a new comment is created every second (check the code in bold). At the end of the process, that information is delivered by the endpoint. You can give this a try with the following `curl` command:

```
curl http://localhost:8080/jlo/comments
```

Now, you can see how a new comment is being retrieved each second. This feature opens up a new world of opportunities and functionalities that can be implemented in our applications.

Summary

In this chapter, we reviewed some of the most common projects available in Spring, along with a brief explanation and use case for each of them. We also looked at the Spring Reactor project and the features associated with it, which can be implemented using Spring Data. We then looked at writing RESTful web services.

With all of the knowledge that you have acquired, it's time to dive into the subsequent chapters to review some architectural styles and learn how to implement them using the Spring Framework.

Client-Server Architectures

4

The client-server architecture is one of the most common architectural styles applied today, and it has been used in many different ways.

When we hear the term client-server architecture, we often think of old applications that provide a UI for editing complex databases in which the major part of the business logic resides. However, the truth is that this architectural style offers underlying support for almost every single modern architectural style, including microservices, event-driven architectures, or any distributed computing system.

In this chapter, we will review how the client-server architecture works, as well as how it can be implemented. We will use the Spring Framework to build the server side, and then we'll code clients interacting with the server using Java.

This chapter will cover the following points:

- Understanding client-server architectures
- Where to apply client-server architectures
- Implementing client-server architectures:
    - Writing a server with Spring
    - Introducing Spring actuator
    - Monitoring the health of an application
    - Writing clients with Java FX and Android
- Testing the implemented code

Understanding client-server architectures

In client-server architectures, each running process is either a server or a client. They interact with each other using requests that are sent through a defined communication channel, in a network that connects them together. We have all used an email service, and we understand how such a service works; that is the quintessential example of a client-server architecture, illustrated in the following diagram:

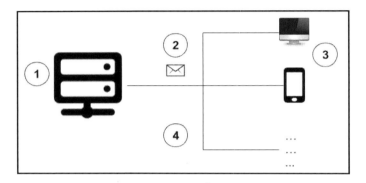

Email service components

We will now provide a brief overview of each component in the preceding diagram, in order to explain how it fits within the client-server architectural style. The precedingdiagram is comprised of the following parts:

- The server (**1**)
- The request payload (**2**)
- The clients accessing the server resources (**3**)

Server

The server is in charge of processing the received requests (which should comply with a predefined format), and then producing results.

Once the data is retrieved, a whole process begins, checking the requests before processing them. This process begins by authenticating and authorizing checks that verify the client's identity. A validation process then starts, to review the input provided by clients, and the provided body request is tested to verify its structure. After that, checks to validate that the data complies with the business logic constraints are executed. To finish, the requests are processed by the server.

These steps make it possible to achieve a certain level of reliability within the application, since ill-intentioned or corrupt requests that would eventually destroy the data or convert the system into an inconsistent state are not processed at all.

The responses offered by the server are often services or resources that will be consumed by the clients later. When the requests are not processed successfully, a response, including reasonable information, is remitted to the client.

A high-performance server is used to support the required processing. The servers are located in an on-premise or cloud-based infrastructure.

Scaling

Once the server is in production, it's a good idea to monitor its resource consumption and business metrics associated with the application. If we identify any anomalies or high traffic, we should consider scaling the server to offer a better user experience.

Since a client can be any device that is able to connect to the server, including separate computers, we might suddenly have millions of clients accessing the server. When the application ran on one machine, the balance of resource consumption between the client and server parts of the application was fixed. However, as soon as clients and servers could be scaled independently, it became easy for clients to scale way out of proportion to the server's capacity. Today, clients only need to interact with one user. Because of this, it is easy for them to have adequate resources. However, servers may be asked to support numbers of clients across a wide, dynamic range. It's in this situation that scaling becomes an important technical requirement.

We have two options for scaling a server, as follows:

- Vertical
- Horizontal

We can think about vertical scaling for services that cannot be deployed on more than one node, because of its own nature. A node can be represented by a computer or process running the service.

In this scaling option, we can only scale a service by adding more resources, such as RAM, CPU, hard-disk, and so on, as shown in the following diagram:

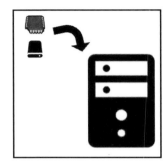

Vertical scaling

An explicit limitation that we have is that we can only increase the power of the unique process that is running the service.

On the other hand, if you have a stateless service, like a REST API, it can be deployed on more than one node, making it possible to scale the service horizontally. This approach allows us to scale applications in a better way, but a load balancer should be in front of them, in order to route the request appropriately, using an algorithm for it. A typical algorithm to use is round-robin, which distributes the requests equally among all of the available nodes.

The following diagram shows servers arranged behind a load balancer, using a horizontal scaling approach:

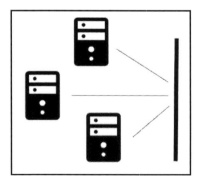

Horizontal scaling

Request

A request is a piece of information that is sent to the server by a client. The client and the server have to agree on the protocol that they use to communicate, in order to allow them to interact with each other.

In order to facilitate the exchange of data, it is recommended that an SDK (or some sort of library) be provided by the product vendors. For example, if you're interested in interacting with a database from a Java application, there are drivers coded in the form of libraries that can be used for that. Furthermore, the database vendors also provide drivers for different programming languages, desktop applications, or UIs, to interact with servers such as pgAdmin or MySQL Workbench.

Providing an SDK is not a must; even when an SDK is provided, an easy to understand document will avoid introducing a conformist relationship between the server and clients.

Conformist relationship is a term coined by domain driven design. It suggests that a service has a complex and large model that forces the downstream dependencies to be modified when the server introduces new changes or releases new features. The modification should happen, because the effort required to write their own model adaptations or mechanisms to interact with the server is extremely high and is difficult to achieve.

Client

There are a plenty of options that can be used for application clients. For the email example, it's well known that there are native applications included as part of the computers' operating systems, and also in mobile devices like smartphones, iPads, or tablets, that can be configured to interact with existing email servers. There are two types of clients, as follows:

- Fat clients
- Thin clients

Fat clients have implemented logic that is in charge of performing some validations, formatting data, and fulfilling other related duties. They are designed to make the interaction between the end users and the server easier.

Think about a Windows PC running Outlook. This represents a classic example of a fat client. In contrast, a web browser talking to a webmail site is a good example of a thin client.

We can also compare fat clients with regards to the native applications running on our mobile phones that can partially work when they are unable to establish communication with the server; meanwhile, a thin client, like a web browser, is absolutely useless.

Within the fat client category, we also have middleware, which often consumes more than one service and orchestrates the requests to accomplish a business goal. The most common examples are the **enterprise service buses** (**ESB**) commonly used as part of SOA architectures.

Thin clients are quite simple, and they count with a simple mechanism that makes it possible to interact with the server. A common example of this is `curl` commands, used to interact with Rest-APIs through the HTTP(S) protocol.

Network

A network is a medium that supports communications between servers and clients, following the request-response messaging pattern in which a client sends a request to the server and the server responds to the request by using this medium. A typical example of a network is the internet, which enables us to communicate with all devices connected to it. Today, there are tons of devices that can be connected to the internet, including computers, tablets, smartphones, Arduino, Raspberry PI, and others. The use of these devices has enabled the growth of the **Internet of Things** (**IoT**), giving us the chance to innovate and create a new era of applications. There are also other sorts of networks, such as Bluetooth, LiFi, LAN, and so on, that can be used to allow interaction between clients and servers, depending on business needs.

Where to apply client-server architectures

There are a bunch of situations where the client-server architectural style can be used. Let's review some typical examples, in order to better understand this approach.

As mentioned previously, databases commonly fit this architectural style. Currently, we have many database vendors available in the market, and the majority of them only offer the chance to scale vertically. Two classic examples of this approach are SQL Server and PostgreSQL. However, there are options to scale horizontally, as well. The most well-known database following this model is Cassandra, which is a database created by Facebook that was later adopted as an Apache project. This database uses a ring model to connect different nodes, where the data is stored. In this manner, you can add as many nodes as you need to, in order to support high-availability.

Chat services, like Slack, are a classic example of client-server architectures that use the cloud. This chat has clients for almost any computer operating system, and for mobile platforms, as well; you can even use it directly on the browser, if you don't want to install a native application on your device.

Agents are also an interesting application of this architectural style. An agent is a piece of software in charge of sending information from the clients to the server, without needing human interaction attached to it. For example, New Relic (`https://newrelic.com/`) is an **Application Performance Monitoring and Management (APM)** used to monitor the health of servers and applications using agents.

Let's suppose that you want to monitor your existing Java application. To achieve this goal, you only need to add the New Relic agent when the application is started, using the `javaagent` option. In this way, the agent will continually be sending information to New Relic, which will give us information related to the memory and CPU consumption, response time, and so on. In this case, the server that processes the data sent by the agents is also in the cloud.

The IoT also relies heavily on the use of client-server architectures, where small devices with sensors (or some other mechanisms) used to gather data are constantly sending information to servers in charge of analyzing that data, in order to execute operations, depending on what is needed.

Implementing client-server architectures with Spring

Now that you have a better comprehension of client-server architectures, we will code an example that follows this diagram:

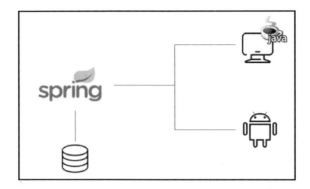

Example of client-server architecture

The functionality of our application will be simple. The server will expose an endpoint with the customer's bank statement, and then we will code a few clients to consume that information.

The server

There are a bunch of options to build the server side using the Spring Framework, including the following:

- SOAP web services
- RESTful Web Services
- **Common Object Request Broker Architecture (CORBA)**
- Sockets
- AMQP

SOAP web services

SOAP web services were widely implemented by developers before the REST style appeared, and they are heavily based on the use of XML. There are also a bunch of libraries available to deal with them, including Apache CXF, and JAX-WS. The following screenshot represents a request payload for a simple addition operation:

```
POST /calculator.asmx HTTP/1.1
Host: www.dneonline.com
Content-Type: application/soap+xml; charset=utf-8
Content-Length: length

<?xml version="1.0" encoding="utf-8"?>
<soap12:Envelope xmlns:xsi="http://www.w3.org/2001/XMLSchema-instance" xmlns:xsd="http://www.w3.org/2001/XMLSchema" xmlns:soap12="http://www.w3.org/2003/05/soap-envelope">
  <soap12:Body>
    <Add xmlns="http://tempuri.org/">
      <intA>int</intA>
      <intB>int</intB>
    </Add>
  </soap12:Body>
</soap12:Envelope>
```

Request payload

The following screenshot shows how the response looks:

```
HTTP/1.1 200 OK
Content-Type: application/soap+xml; charset=utf-8
Content-Length: length

<?xml version="1.0" encoding="utf-8"?>
<soap12:Envelope xmlns:xsi="http://www.w3.org/2001/XMLSchema-instance" xmlns:xsd="http://www.w3.org/2001/XMLSchema" xmlns:soap12="http://www.w3.org/2003/05/soap-envelope">
  <soap12:Body>
    <AddResponse xmlns="http://tempuri.org/">
      <AddResult>int</AddResult>
    </AddResponse>
  </soap12:Body>
</soap12:Envelope>
```

Response payload

The preceding examples were taken from `http://www.dneonline.com/calculator.asmx?op=Add`.

These XML files are following the **Web Services Description Language** (**WSDL**) format used by SOAP web services.

RESTful web services

The RESTful style, on the other hand, is currently preferred, and there are a bunch of public APIs that use it. Common examples are companies such as GitHub and Yahoo. This style bases its functionality on the use of HTTP verbs, making it easy to understand how they work. For example, the following HTTP request makes it possible to query the repositories from GitHub:

```
GET https://api.github.com/users/{{GITHUB_USERNAME}}/repos
```

This style appeared in 2000, with Roy Fielding's doctoral dissertation that explains the REST principles and dictates how well-designed web applications should behave. The use of HTTP verbs is described in the following table:

HTTP Method/Verb	Usage
GET	Lists all of the resources available under the specified URI
POST	Creates a new resource in the specified URI
PUT	Replaces the existing resource under the specified URI with another one
DELETE	Deletes the resource specified in the URI
PATCH	Partially updates a resource that resides in the specified URI

CORBA

The CORBA is a really old standard, designed to allow applications written in different programming languages to interact with each other. It is hard to use this standard because of all of the required plumbing code to achieve the goal. CORBA is not popular nowadays, but some legacy applications still use it to interact with old code, written mainly in Cobol, which was one of the preferred programming languages to write banking cores.

Sockets

Sockets are a common protocol that became even more popular with the emergence of WebSockets, which establishes a full-duplex communication channel among the server and clients. A typical scenario wherein this protocol is used includes messenger applications, such as Slack.

AMQP

Applications using the AMQP, or any similar messaging protocol, are designed to allow for interoperability among heterogeneous applications, with an asynchronous approach. There are a bunch of commercial and open source implementations, such as AWS-SQS/SNS and RabbitMQ, among others, that can be used to implement applications using this model. We are going to review how this works in detail in Chapter 6, *Event-Driven Architectures*. The basic concept of this approach is to use a messaging broker in charge of receiving messages, and then distribute them to their subscribers.

For our example, we are going to choose RESTful web services, which is a popular choice nowadays. In order to accomplish our goal, we will use Spring Boot (to bootstrap our application) together with Spring Data (to persist the information using H2, which is an in-memory database). Our app will be secured using the JSON Web Tokens RFC (`https://tools.ietf.org/html/rfc7519`).

JWT is an open standard, intended to allow for authenticating clients with servers. Another use case is to validate the integrity of the messages. In order to use JWT as an authentication mechanism, the clients should send their credentials to the server, and it will respond to them with a token in the form of a string. This token should be used for the subsequent requests. When they are executed, if the provided token is invalid or expired, we will receive a **401 UNAUTHORIZED** status code from the server. Otherwise, the request will be successful:

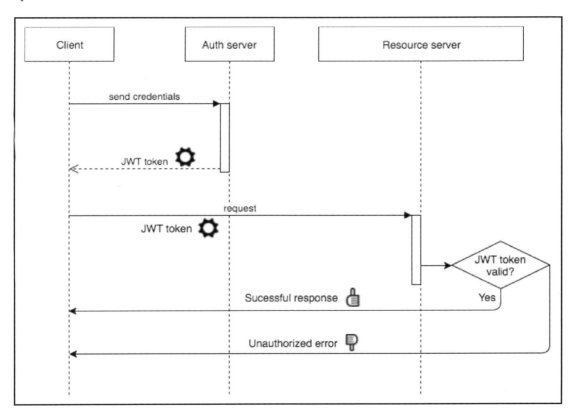

JWT authentication flow

Since the functionality of this application doesn't require a considerable amount of computing or real-time processing, we used Groovy as the programming language. Groovy has a pretty similar syntax to Java, but with tons of built-in functionalities that allow us to avoid writing verbose code. In conjunction with Groovy, we will use Spock as a testing framework. This will enable us to write highly expressive tests using a **Behavior Driven Development (BDD)** approach, with the `given`, `when`, and `then` syntax. The main idea behind BDD is to reduce the uncertainty about what a test method is testing, using expressive test names that are helpful for understanding what goes wrong when a test fails.

The BDD approach is based on the structure of user stories, and the idea is to write tests that make it clear what they are testing. A classic example, used to explain this concept, is provided by Dan North (the BDD creator) and starts with the following user story related to how an ATM works:

Title – Customer withdraws cash	Scenario 1 – Account is on credit	Scenario 2 – Account is overdrawn past the overdraft limit
As a customer, I want to withdraw cash from an ATM so that I don't have to wait in line at the bank.	Given that the account is in credit, the card is valid and the dispenser contains cash, when the customer requests cash, then ensure that the account is debited, cash is dispensed, and the card is returned.	Given that the account is overdrawn and the card is valid, when the customer requests cash, then ensure a rejection message is displayed. Ensure that cash is not dispensed and the card is returned.

The preceding validation can be easily expressed with code by using Spock. Let's check one of our implemented tests to understand how it works:

```groovy
def "when the credentials are not found, an UNAUTHORIZED code is
returned"()
{
  given:
  def nonExistentCredentials =
  new Credentials(username: "foo", password: "bar")
  def loginService = Mock(LoginService)
  loginService.login(nonExistentCredentials) >>
  {
    throw new LoginException()
  }
  def securityController = new SecurityController(loginService)
  when:
  def response = securityController.auth(nonExistentCredentials)
  then:
  response.statusCode == HttpStatus.UNAUTHORIZED
}
```

As you can see, the test explains itself well, using the `given`, `when`, and `then` syntax provided by Spock.

Spock also allows for using mocks, without needing additional libraries such as Mockito, because this feature is built in. If you are interested in knowing more about Spock, I encourage you to visit `http://spockframework.org/`.

Implementing the server

Let's implement the server project for our example. We are going to organize its functionalities in modules, in order to make it easy to evolve and understand. For the sake of simplicity, we are going to add a simple functionality that will later be consumed by different application clients. The server example will have three modules, as follows:

- Banking-domain
- Banking-api
- Banking-client

Banking-domain

This module contains all of the domain objects required to build our application; it's a good idea to keep them separated, as another module. By doing this, you can later include the module as a dependency of other modules, which will help to avoid writing the same code twice. The following diagram shows the contents of this module:

```
src/
├── main
    ├── java
        └── com
            └── packtpub
                └── bankingapplication
                    └── balance
                        └── domain
                            ├── BalanceInformation.java
                            └── Credentials.java
```

The banking-domain module

As you can see, this module contains only two classes. The `Credentials` class is used as the payload, to authenticate a user and retrieve the JSON web token, and the `BalanceInformation` class contains the payload resultant of querying the customer account balance.

Banking-api

The banking-api module contains the functionality exposed by the server that will later be consumed by different application clients; the functionality will be made available for RESTful web services. Let's review the project structure for this API:

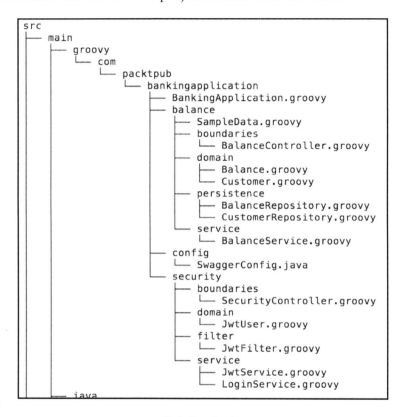

```
src
├── main
    ├── groovy
        └── com
            └── packtpub
                └── bankingapplication
                    ├── BankingApplication.groovy
                    ├── balance
                    │   ├── SampleData.groovy
                    │   ├── boundaries
                    │   │   └── BalanceController.groovy
                    │   ├── domain
                    │   │   ├── Balance.groovy
                    │   │   └── Customer.groovy
                    │   ├── persistence
                    │   │   ├── BalanceRepository.groovy
                    │   │   └── CustomerRepository.groovy
                    │   └── service
                    │       └── BalanceService.groovy
                    ├── config
                    │   └── SwaggerConfig.java
                    └── security
                        ├── boundaries
                        │   └── SecurityController.groovy
                        ├── domain
                        │   └── JwtUser.groovy
                        ├── filter
                        │   └── JwtFilter.groovy
                        └── service
                            ├── JwtService.groovy
                            └── LoginService.groovy
    ├── java
```

The banking-api module

As mentioned previously, this module is implemented entirely using Groovy, and that's why all of the files have a `.groovy` extension. The project structure is more important here, as the project is separated into `balance`, `config`, and `security` packages, which makes it fairly simple to understand their purposes. It's always worth organizing the code in this way, in order to make it easy to understand.

We mentioned previously that not only should an SDK be provided, but proper documentation is also highly recommended. The tedious part of writing documentation is that you need to keep it in sync with the new features added to the project. To achieve this goal, we have integrated Swagger into our application. This is a helpful tool that generates a website with examples to consume the endpoints of an application. Furthermore, it also creates payload demos for each one of them when it's required, as shown in the following screenshot:

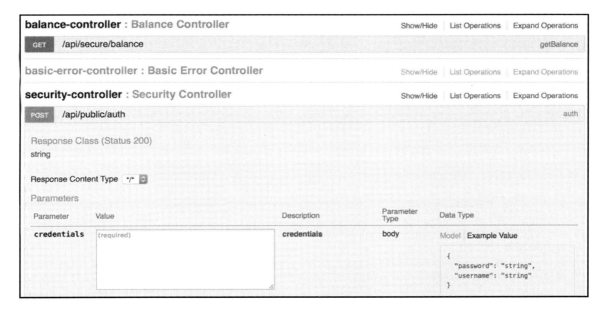

Autogenerated Swagger UI

This portal is available at `http://localhost:8080/swagger-ui.html`.

Now, let's briefly review the packages listed in the screenshot for each module.

Boundaries

The `boundaries` package contains the functionality exposed by the application that will be used to allow for the interaction with the clients. In this case, we are placing the endpoints of our service here.

Domain

The domain package has the domain objects that are required only by this module. The classes placed here won't be used in any other place, and that's why it doesn't make sense to place them in the banking-domain module, which is intended to be shared.

Persistence

As the name suggests, we are going to write the required code to persist information in this package. Since the persistence storage of our application is a database, and we defined that we are going to use Spring-data for it, we have our Spring-data repositories here.

Service

We have put the required business logic for our service into this package. This is where the interaction with many classes happens, in order to achieve the business requirements.

Monitoring the server

We mentioned earlier that monitoring is quite important to understanding how an application performs in the wild. Fortunately, Spring has `actuator`, which is a library that can be easily attached to an existing Spring Boot application by adding the following dependency:

```
compile("org.springframework.boot:spring-boot-starter-actuator")
```

Spring Boot Actuator provides a bunch of endpoints that are ready to be consumed and provide useful information about the application. Let's review some of them in the following table:

Endpoint	Brief Description
`/health`	This provides brief information about the application status and its main dependencies, such as databases or messaging systems.
`/autoconfig`	This provides information about the auto-configuration provided for the app by the Spring Framework. Remember that Spring prefers convention over configuration, so you'll find tons of default values here.
`/beans`	This shows the list of Spring beans configured as a part of the application context.
`/dump`	This performs a thread dump at the exact moment that the endpoint is requested.

/env	This lists all of the variables configured in the server. Values provided as a part of `.properties`/`.yml` files and arguments provided to run the application are listed, as well.
/metrics	This shows some metrics around the available endpoints exposed in the app.
/trace	This gives information regarding the last 100 (by default) requests, including details about the requests and responses.

If you are interested in a complete list of the endpoints available by default, I encourage you to visit `https://docs.spring.io/spring-boot/docs/current/reference/html/production-ready-endpoints.html`.

All of the preceding endpoints can mainly be configured with three parameters:

- `id`: This is the endpoint identification
- `sensitive`: This indicates whether or not Spring Actuator should enforce security
- `enabled`: This indicates whether or not the Spring Actuator endpoints are available

If you want to configure the endpoints, you have to use the following entries as a part of your configuration (`.properties`/`.yml`) file:

```
endpoints.endpoint_name.property
```

The following bullet points expand upon this idea:

- `endpoints`: This is a constant value.
- `endpoint_name`: This should be replaced with the desired endpoint.
- `property`: This can be `id`, `sensitive`, or `enabled`.

For example, let's suppose that you want to enable the `health` endpoint, rename it to `status`, and not enforce `security`. To achieve this requirement, the configuration should look as follows:

```
endpoints.health.id = status
endpoints.health.sensitive = false
endpoints.health.enabled = true
```

All of the endpoints are enabled by default, except for `/shutdown`, which is intended to stop the application gracefully.

Furthermore, Spring actuator can be configured to generate business metrics, as well. This is an excellent feature that can be integrated with other tools, which makes it possible to visualize the collected metrics using graphical interfaces. We will review this feature in detail in Chapter 12, *Monitoring*.

Testing

Up until now, we have introduced unit tests to validate that the code is working as expected. However, we would like to add even more tests. After all, the more tests we include in our system, the more confidence we will gain.

Since we are writing a rest API, we will create a simple script that will exercise our endpoints from time to time, giving us the confidence that the app is always working. To achieve this goal, our tests will follow a simple process:

1. Authenticate the user using the endpoint.
2. Validate the status code from the response.
3. Take the token from the response body.
4. Hit the balance endpoint using the token.
5. Validate the status code from the response.

The easiest way to achieve this goal is by using Postman (https://www.getpostman.com/). This is a handy tool that allows for trying RESTful web services, and creating tests for them, as well.

Let's discuss the test generated for the endpoint to authenticate a user, as shown in the following screenshot:

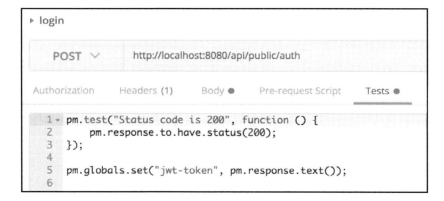

Test for the authentication endpoint in Postman

The first three lines of the preceding code check the retrieved status code, and line 5 stores the retrieved body response as a variable named `jwt-token`.

Using the preceding code, we can later inject the value of this variable into the subsequent requests and perform whatever validations we want.

Once all of the tests have been created, we can generate a link referring to the collection that contains them, as shown in the following screenshot:

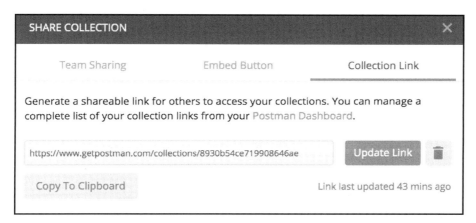

Postman collection link

With this link, the collection of tests can be executed over and over again, using a command-line integration runner named Newman (`https://www.npmjs.com/package/newman`) and the following command:

```
newman run https://www.getpostman.com/collections/8930b54ce719908646ae
```

The following screenshot shows the results of the Newman command's execution:

```
demo-server-client

→ login
  POST http://localhost:8080/api/public/auth [200 OK, 409B, 19ms]
  ✓  Status code is 200

→ query-balance
  GET http://localhost:8080/api/secure/balance [200 OK, 199B, 16ms]
  ✓  Status code is 200
```

	executed	failed
iterations	1	0
requests	2	0
test-scripts	2	0
prerequest-scripts	0	0
assertions	2	0

```
total run duration: 314ms

total data received: 289B (approx)

average response time: 17ms
```

The results of the Newman command execution

This tool can be integrated with any CI server, such as Jenkins, to schedule jobs in charge of verifying the health of the application regularly, which will give us the confidence that our app is always working.

Banking-client

Since our server is implemented using RESTful web services, there are a bunch of options for writing clients and consuming them with libraries, such as Netflix Feign, OkHttp, Spring Rest Template, and Retrofit.

Because of this, the clients can have their own implemented mechanisms to consume the services. This approach is not bad at all; actually, we should keep it open, and the decision of writing our own tool to interact with the server should be a client choice, in order to avoid the conformist relationship described earlier. However, it's always a good idea to provide a built-in SDK or library to interact with the server and reduce the amount of effort required for it, and that's the reason we have the banking-client module.

It's quite common to find SDKs provided by product vendors. For example, AWS provides SDKs with support for a bunch of programming languages, in conjunction with a developer guide document that explains how to use them. This is helpful for accelerating and encouraging the adoption of products to build applications by other developers. Another example is Google Firebase, which is a real-time database that provides SDKs that are ready to use in different platforms; it has a website with excellent demos that make it possible for developers to understand how it works and how to use it.
This banking-client module is implemented using a library named Retrofit (`http://square.github.io/retrofit/`), which makes it possible to write type-safe HTTP clients that can be used for almost any kind of Java application. This also offers many benefits, such as the following:

- Support for mobile apps, like Android
- Code that is easy to read and explains itself well
- Support for synchronous and asynchronous resource consumption
- Smooth integration with converters, such as GSON

Let's take a look at the implemented clients, in order to consume the endpoints.

Authentication endpoint client

In order to consume a RESTful web service, we only have to create an interface with a few annotations to provide some metadata:

```
public interface SecurityApi
{
  @POST("/api/public/auth")
  Call<String> login(@Body Credentials credentials);
}
```

It's fairly simple to understand that the authentication endpoint uses the POST HTTP verb. This is available in the URI /api/public/auth, and it needs a Credentials object as the request body.

Account balance endpoint client

In this case, we will consume an endpoint, available in the URI `/api/secure/balance`, that uses the GET HTTP verb and requires that the token be used as a header in the request:

```
public interface BankingApi
{
  @GET("/api/secure/balance")
  Call<BalanceInformation> queryBalance(@Header("x-auth-token")
  String token);
}
```

As you have probably noticed, this module uses the `BalanceInformation` and `Credentials` classes, so we don't need to write them again; we only need to add the banking-domain module as a dependency.

You're probably wondering where you have to specify the IP address and port for the server, and that is done in the `Retrofit` object, as follows:

```
Retrofit retrofit = new Retrofit.Builder()
        .baseUrl("http://IP:PORT")
        .addConverterFactory(GsonConverterFactory.create(gson))
        .build();
```

In the client's implementation, we will review how to use this `Retrofit` object in conjunction with the interfaces, in order to make the requests.

The clients

Now that we have implemented the server, we are going to build three clients, as follows:

- JavaFX client
- Android client
- Thin client, using CURL

These clients will use the HTTP protocol to send the requests and retrieve the responses. Since we have written a client module, the interaction with the server will be fairly simple.

JavaFX client

This client is a simple JavaFX application that has a dependency on the banking-client module to interact with the server. We can say that this client is a sort of fat client, since it has some code written to simplify the interaction with the server.

Let's review the project structure in the following screenshot:

```
├── main
│   ├── java
│   │   └── com
│   │       └── packtpub
│   │           └── bankingclient
│   │               ├── BankingClientApplication.java
│   │               ├── balance
│   │               │   └── ui
│   │               │       └── BalanceController.java
│   │               ├── security
│   │               │   └── ui
│   │               │       └── LoginController.java
│   │               └── ui
│   │                   ├── LayoutPane.java
│   │                   └── NavigableController.java
│   ├── resources
│   │   └── com
│   │       └── packtpub
│   │           └── bankingclient
│   │               ├── balance
│   │               │   └── ui
│   │               │       └── Balance.fxml
│   │               └── security
│   │                   └── ui
│   │                       └── Login.fxml
```

JavaFX client project structure

This project is fairly simple, and it has only two screens, which allow the users to enter their credentials and then query their account balance.

Retrofit offers the availability to make synchronous and asynchronous requests. In this client, we will use synchronous requests, as follows:

```
SecurityApi api = BankClient.getRetrofit().create(SecurityApi.class);
Call<String> call = api.login(
        new Credentials(username.getText(), password.getText()));
Response<String> response = call.execute();
// do something with the response
```

The `execute` method allows for making synchronous requests. The `Retrofit` object contains the base URI that will be used in conjunction with the partial URIs provided in the client interfaces, in order to form the full URI to hit the endpoints.

The process of this client application is shown in the following screenshot:

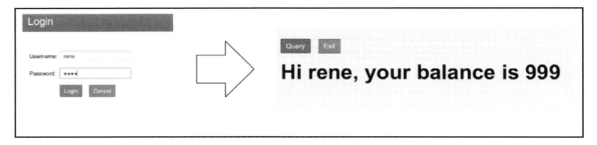

JavaFX client application

Android client

The Android client also uses the provided banking-client module to interact with the server, but in this case, it's necessary to use the asynchronous method to make requests (this requirement comes from the nature of how Android works). We can also say that this is a fat client, by looking at the definition provided earlier.

Let's review the structure of this project in the following screenshot:

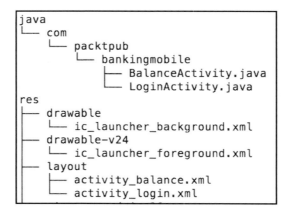

Android client project structure

The `Activity` classes have the code to make the asynchronous requests, as follows:

```
SecurityApi api = BankClient.getRetrofit().create(SecurityApi.class);
Call<String> call = api.login(new Credentials(username, password));
call.enqueue(new Callback<String>()
{
  @Override
  public void onResponse(Call<String> call,
  Response<String> response)
  {
    // do something with the reponse
  }
  @Override
  public void onFailure(Call<String> call, Throwable t)
  {
    // handle the error properly
  }
}
```

The `enqueue` method allows for hitting the endpoint asynchronously, and it registers two callbacks that will be executed, depending on whether the response fails or succeeds.

The execution flow for this client application is shown in the following screenshot:

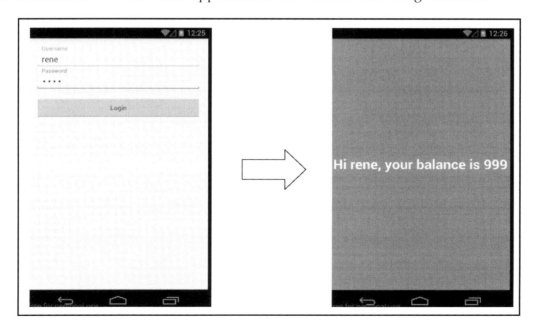

Android client application

Thin client

As mentioned previously, there are also thin clients, which don't include a lot of code to interact with the server; one good example of a thin RESTful web service client is `curl`.

In order to interact with the endpoints provided by the server example, we can use two `curl` commands, as follows:

- The following code provides for retrieving the authentication JWT token:

```
$ curl -H "Content-Type: application/json" \
-X POST -d '{"username":"rene","password":"rene"}' \
http://localhost:8080/api/public/auth
```

- The following code provides for using the JWT token to query the user's account balance:

```
$ curl -H "x-auth-token: JWT_TOKEN" \
-X GET http://localhost:8080/api/secure/balance
```

For these kinds of clients, we don't have to write our own code; the interaction with the server doesn't have a fancy frontend, which can be good (in cases where the API is used for other middleware, for example).

As you can see, our client-server architecture implementation is simple, but it uses all of the necessary pieces to make it work. In this case, we have used the HTTP protocol as the communication channel. However, depending on what kind of server you are implementing, it may be different, and it can also affect the authentication mechanism. For example, when you're using a message broker such as RabbitMQ to allow for the interaction between servers and clients, the protocol to establish the communication is AMQP, which is a different protocol (in comparison to HTTP).

The kinds of clients that your application will have also affects the way in which you will build the solution. Let's suppose that you're using agents as clients; a more secure authentication mechanism would be based on the use of certificates instead of tokens, as seen in the preceding example.

Summary

In this chapter, we reviewed what client-server architectures are and how to implement them using the Spring Framework. One important aspect to remember is that when we are building applications following this architectural style, it's always worth providing an SDK to make the server resources easy to consume.

Providing proper documentation can help clients to write their own code to interact with the server, if necessary. In this case, we will avoid introducing a conformist relationship among the server and clients. We also explored spring actuator, a library that can be used to add endpoints that provide information about the application. Furthermore, we reviewed how to use Postman to create tests that can regularly assess the application's health.

In the end, we created a couple of clients using a library implemented with Retrofit, which drastically reduced the effort required to consume the resources exposed by the server.

In the next chapter, we will review MVC architectures and how to write them using Spring.

5
Model-View-Controller Architectures

In this chapter, we will dive into one of the most common architectural patterns used by frameworks today.

The **Model-View-Controller** (**MVC**) architectural pattern was formulated in 1979 by Trygve Reenskaug. This was one of the first attempts to create an organized method for working on graphical user interfaces. Although many years have passed since then, this pattern continues to be quite popular even in the most modern UI frameworks. This is because it is designed to build almost any type of application, including the most common types of applications, such as mobile, desktop, and web applications.

The popularity of this pattern mostly comes down to the ease of understanding it. MVC provides an excellent way to separate applications into three different components, which we will review in this chapter.

In this chapter, we will cover the following topics:

- The elements of MVC:
    - Model
    - View
    - Controller
- The benefits of using MVC architectures
- Common pitfalls
- Implementing applications using MVC:
    - Spring MVC
    - Testing
    - UI frameworks: Thymeleaf

- Securing an MVC application:
  - Basic authentication
  - HTTP and HTTPS

MVC

The idea of supporting the MVC pattern was developed as a part of Trygve Reenskaug's research in which he concluded the following key idea:

> *"MVC was conceived as a general solution to the problem of users controlling a large and complex data set. The hardest part was to hit upon good names for the different architectural components. Model-View-editor was the first set. "*

> – http://heim.ifi.uio.no/~trygver/themes/mvc/mvc-index.html

One of the biggest problems in computer science is related to naming things, which is why the original name was Model-View-Editor. It later evolved into MVC, as mentioned in the preceding link:

> *"After long discussions, particularly with Adele Goldberg, we ended with the terms Model-View-Controller."*

MVC is a software architectural pattern that makes it possible to establish a clear separation between the domain objects of an application (where the business logic resides) and the elements that are used to build the UI.

With this concept in mind, the isolation and separation of concerns between these parts are quite important. They also constitute the underlying principles to build applications using this pattern. In following sections, let's review how the business logic and presentation layer of an application fits within the MVC pattern.

The Model (M)

Within this context, the **Model** represents the domain objects needed to express the business logic supporting the requirements inherent to the application. It's here that all of the use cases are represented as real-world abstractions and a well-defined API is made available to be consumed by any kind of delivery mechanism, such as the web.

Regarding traditional applications, all of the logic to interact with a database or middleware is implemented in the Model. However, the Model (the M in MVC) should expose functionalities (in terms of the business) that are easy to understand. We should also avoid building anemic models that only allow for interacting with the database and are difficult to understand for the rest of the team working on the project.

Once this part of the application has been coded, we should ideally be able to create any UI that allows the users to interact with the Model. Furthermore, since UIs can defer from each other (mobile, web, and desktop apps), the Model should be agnostic to all of them.

In a perfect world, an isolated team would be able to build this part of the application, but in real life, this assumption is entirely wrong. Interaction with the team in charge of building the GUI is required, in order to create an effective Model that is able to address all of the business requirements and expose a comprehensive API.

The View (V)

The **View** is a visual representation of the Model (M in MVC) but with some subtle differences. As a part of these differences, the View tends to remove, add, and/or transform specific Model attributes, with the aim of making the Model understandable for the users interacting with the View.

Since the Model is sometimes complex, many views can be used to represent one part of it, and, conversely, many parts of the Model can be included as only one part of the View.

The Controller (C)

A **Controller** is a link between the end user of an application and the business logic implemented by the Model. Controllers are objects in charge of taking user input and figuring out what part of the Model should be invoked to achieve defined business goals. As a result of this interaction, the Model is often changed, and these changes should be propagated to the views using Controllers.

 Direct communication between the View and the Model must never happen since it constitutes a violation of how this pattern works.

Keeping the preceding tip in mind, all communication should be done in a specific order from each part of the MVC pattern, passing the information from the View to the Controller and from the Controller to the Model, and never directly from the Model to the View, as illustrated in the following interaction diagram:

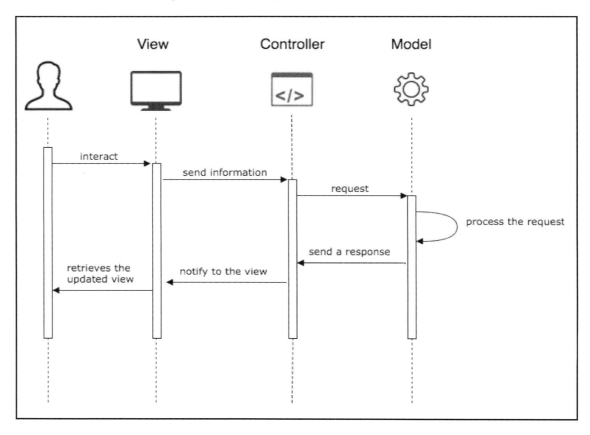

MVC interaction diagram

In order to propagate these changes, the View elements are bound to representations in the Controllers, which makes it possible to manipulate them as required. The process of updating a View occurs when the Model is updated, and it often involves reloading data or hiding/showing certain elements in the View.

When a change should be propagated to more than one element in the View, various Controllers can work together collaboratively to achieve the goal. In these cases, a simple implementation of the observer design pattern can often be useful for avoiding entangled code.

The following diagram is a graphical representation of how the pieces in this pattern are arranged, in either the presentation or business logic layer:

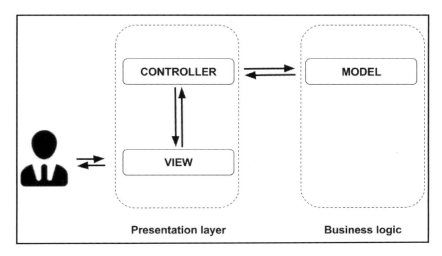

MVC graphical representation

Benefits of using MVC

MVC provides many benefits for applications that are implemented using it; the main benefit is the clear separation of concerns, with a single responsibility for each part of the application, thereby avoiding messing up the code and making the code easy to understand.

While Controllers and views are tied together to build the visual representation of the application using MVC, the Model is absolutely isolated. This makes it possible to reuse the same Model to create a different kind of application, including, but not limited to, the following:

- Mobile
- Web
- Desktop

You might be tempted to conclude that a project developed using this Model can count on teams working in parallel, but separately, during the development phase, which is true in some cases, but not a rule in general. As mentioned previously, effective communication across teams is still necessary for building the application as a whole.

Common pitfalls

When we work on applications using MVC, it's common to find projects structured following the MVC acronym, as the following diagram illustrates:

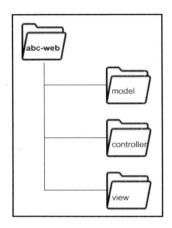

MVC project structure

This directory structure indicates the following:

- The project name is **abc-web**
- This is a web application
- The application uses the MVC architecture (structure)

Unfortunately, none of these points provide meaningful information for the team in charge of creating or maintaining an application. That is because a team working on a project is not interested in the file organization. Instead, it's much more useful to organize your code according to business rules, use cases, or other factors related to the business itself, rather than the technical aspects.

With this idea in mind, we will suggest that a much more useful directory structure is as follows:

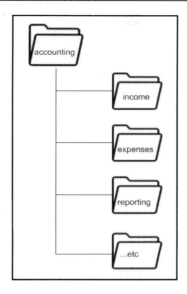

Understandable project structure

From this diagram, we can infer the following points:

- This is an **accounting** system.
- The main features of the project are related to the following, and more:
    - Income
    - Expenses
    - Reporting

Using the project layout shown in the preceding diagram, if we are tasked with fixing a report that is no longer working, we can think about reviewing the reporting folder. This approach is helpful for reducing the amount of time and effort required to accomplish project tasks.

We can conclude that the information provided by the second project structure is much more useful and practical, in comparison to the first one, since the first one does not provide information regarding the business at all.

 Every single part of the project should communicate information regarding the business, rather than concerning the delivery mechanism or pattern used.

These details are small, but they are essential. At the beginning of this book, we mentioned that a good architecture is built around business requirements, and any goal that an architecture pursues should be understood by the whole team. We should approach every single detail with an aim to achieve this goal. Remember: details matter.

Implementing applications using MVC

Now that you understand the theory behind MVC architectures, it is time to put the concepts that you have learned into practice and to see how the Spring Framework implements them. We are going to start by reviewing Spring MVC, which is the project that allows us to achieve this architectural style.

Spring MVC

Spring provides support for the MVC architectural pattern through Spring MVC. This Spring project allows for incorporating a vast set of UI frameworks, in order to build forms and related components that will enable users to interact with the application.

Spring MVC is built on top of the servlet API, which is designed to create web applications. There is no way to create a desktop, or any other kind of application, using this. Even though the MVC architectural pattern can be applied to all of them, Spring MVC is only focused on the web.

 Spring MVC is formally known as Spring Web MVC.

Despite the large number of View technologies supported by Spring MVC, the one most commonly used tends to be Thymeleaf, because of its smooth integration. However, you can also use another framework, such as the following:

- JSF
- FreeMarker
- Struts
- GWT

Spring MVC is designed around the front-Controller pattern, which relies on a single object to handle all of the incoming requests and provide the respective responses. In the case of Spring MVC, this object is represented by a `Servlet` implemented by the `org.springframework.web.servlet.DispatcherServlet` class.

This `Servlet` is in charge of delegating the requests to the Controllers and rendering the corresponding page on the screen, with the desired data. The following diagram shows how `DispatcherServlet` processes the requests:

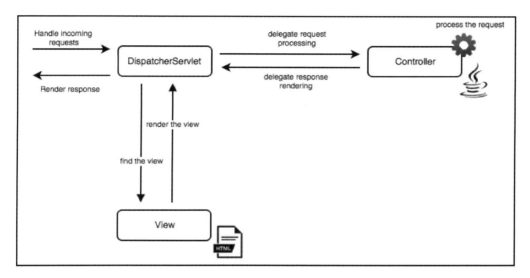

DispatcherServlet request processing

In the preceding diagram, we can see that **Controller** is a Java class and **View** is an HTML file. In the latter case, we can also use any `tag-library/template-engine` tag that will later be compiled as HTML code that is rendered in a web browser.

A Controller in Spring is created using the `@Controller` annotation over the class name, as shown in the following code snippet:

```
import org.springframework.stereotype.Controller;

@Controller
public class DemoController
{
    ...
}
```

Now that the class is marked as a Controller, we need to indicate what request mapping will be handled, and what actions need to be executed as a part of the request processing. In order to support this functionality, we need to write a simple method using the @RequestMapping annotation, as shown in the following code:

```
@RequestMapping(value = "/ABC", method = RequestMethod.GET)
public String handleRequestForPathABC() {
    // do something
    return "ui-template";
}
```

As you can see, the preceding method handles the incoming request from the /ABC path, and, once the processing is done, a ui-template is provided, to be rendered on the browser.

This operation is done by Spring MVC using View resolvers, which will look to render a file with the name ui-template.html. You can also write custom resolvers to add suffixes or prefixes to your views, if required.

When we need to pass data from the Controller to the View, we can use the Model object, enabled by Spring View resolvers. This object can be populated with any data that you want to use in your views. In the same way, when the user submits data from the views, this object is populated with the entered information, which the Controllers can use to perform any desired logic.

In order to send data from the Controller to the View, we need to include the Model object as an argument in the method that handles the request, as follows:

```
@RequestMapping(value = "/ABC", method = RequestMethod.GET)
public String passDataToTheView(Model Model) {
    Model.addAttribute("attributeName", "attributeValue");
    // do something
    return "ui-template";
}
```

All templates have the ability to read the attributes passed from the Controller using the ${...} syntax, known as expression language:

```
<!DOCTYPE html>
<html lang="en">
    <head>
        <title>Title</title>
    </head>
```

```
    <body>
        ${attributeName}
    </body>
</html>
```

Alternatively, if you want to pass data from View components to the Controller, you have to populate an object in the View (using a form, for example), as follows:

```
<!DOCTYPE html>
<html lang="en">
    <head>
        <title>Title</title>
    </head>
    <body>
        <form action="#" th:action="@{/process}"
        th:object="${myObject}">
            <label for="name">Name:</label>
            <input type="text" id="name" th:field="*{name}"/>
            <button type="submit">OK</button>
        </form>
    </body>
</html>
```

Once the object fields are populated and the submit button is pressed, the request will be sent, so that we can declare a method to handle the request:

```
@RequestMapping(value = "/process", method = POST)
public String processForm(@ModelAttribute MyObject myObject) {
    String name = myObject.getName();
    // do something
    return "ui-template";
}
```

In this case, you may have noticed that we are using @ModelAttribute to capture the data that was sent in the request.

Testing

Testing is crucial to our applications. When we use Spring MVC, we can count on the spring-test module to add support for unit and integration tests that are context-aware, which means that we can rely on annotations to wire dependencies. We can also use the @Autowired annotation to test a specific component.

The following is an example of how simple it is to write a test that is context-aware:

```
@RunWith(SpringRunner.class)
@SpringBootTest
public class ContextAwareTest {

    @Autowired
    ClassUnderTest classUnderTest;

    @Test
    public void validateAutowireWorks() throws Exception {
        Assert.assertNotNull(classUnderTest);
    }
}
```

Let's review the code in bold, in order to understand how it works:

- The first two annotations do all of the work for us; they will allow running our tests inside of a servlet container, and the Spring Boot annotations used for testing will wire all of the classes in the same way as the code running in production.
- Since we added the previously mentioned annotations, we can now wire the components that we want to test using the @Autowired annotation.
- The code validates that the class being tested has been successfully instantiated, and is ready to be used. This also means that all of the dependencies in the class have been successfully wired.

This is an easy way to test code that has to interact with databases, message broker servers, or any other middleware. The approach used to validate interactions with a database server uses an in-memory database, such as H2, for traditional SQL databases such as PostgreSQL or MySQL; there are also options for NoSQL databases, such as an embedded Cassandra or Mongo.

On the other hand, when you need to test integrations with other third-party software, an excellent approach to keep in mind is the use of sandboxes. A sandbox is an environment that is similar to the production environment, provided to software vendors for testing purposes. These sandboxes are often deployed in production, but they also have some restrictions. For example, operations related to payments are not processed in the last stage.

This testing approach is useful when you don't have any way to deploy applications in your own environments, but of course, you will need to test whether the integrations are working with your applications.

Let's suppose that you are building an application that has integration with Facebook. In this case, it's evident that no change is required in order to deploy a Facebook instance in your own staging area for testing purposes. This is a perfect example of when a sandbox environment is appropriate.

> Bear in mind that sandboxes test integrations using third-party software. If you're a software vendor, you need to consider providing sandboxes that allow your customers to try your products in a testing mode.

Spring MVC Test also has a fluent API that makes it possible to write highly expressive tests. This framework provides a MockMvc object that can be used to simulate end-user requests and then validate the provided responses. Common use cases include the following:

- Validating HTTP code statuses
- Verifying expected content in the responses
- URL redirection

The following code snippet uses the MockMvc object to test the previously described examples:

```
@RunWith(SpringRunner.class)
@SpringBootTest
@AutoConfigureMockMvc
public class RedirectionTest
{
    @Autowired
    private MockMvc mockMvc;
    @Test
    public void contentAndRedirectionTest() throws Exception
    {
        this.mockMvc.perform(get("/urlPage"))
        .andExpect(redirectedUrl("/expectedUrlPage")
        .andDo(print()).andExpect(status().isOk())
        .andExpect(
          content().string(containsString("SomeText")))
        );
    }
}
```

Let's quickly review the code in bold, in order to understand how it works:

- The AutoConfigureMockMvc annotation generates all of the required plumbing code to use the MockMvc object in the tests.

- The `MockMvc` object is autowired and ready to use.
- The fluent API provided by `MockMvc` is used to validate the expected status code from the response. We are also testing a simple redirection, as well as the content expected on the page once the redirection is done.

Test coverage

When we discuss tests, it's quite common to hear the term **test coverage.** This is a measure used to check how much code is being executed by the suite tests, and it's helpful for determining what alternative paths of code are not tested and are hence prone to bugs.

Let's suppose that you are writing a method that has an `if` statement. In that case, your code has two alternative paths to follow; so, if you want to achieve 100% coverage, you will need to write tests to validate all of the alternative routes that your code can follow.

There are many useful libraries available for measuring the coverage that code has. In this chapter, we are going to introduce one of the most popular libraries in the Java world; the library is called JaCoCo (`http://www.eclemma.org/jacoco/`).

In order to make JaCoCo a part of our application, we need to include it as a plugin, using our preferred build tool.

The following is the required configuration to include JaCoCo using Gradle:

```
apply plugin: "jacoco"
jacoco
{
  toolVersion = "VERSION"
}
```

The following is the required configuration to include JaCoCo using Maven:

```
<plugin>
  <groupId>org.jacoco</groupId>
  <artifactId>jacoco-maven-plugin</artifactId>
  <version>VERSION</version>
</plugin>
```

Once JaCoCo has been included as a part of the project, we will have new tasks that can be used to measure the coverage of our code. Let's generate a coverage report by executing the following Gradle task:

```
$ ./gradlew test jacocoTestReport
```

The coverage report that is generated will be available in HTML format, as shown in the following screenshot:

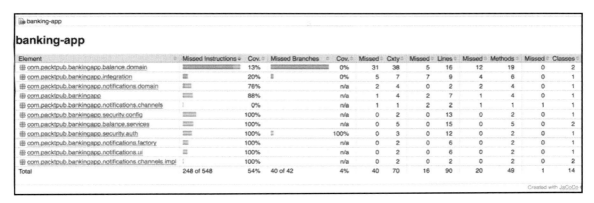

JaCoCo report

Although it is true that we want to achieve high coverage for our code, we need to be careful with what kinds of tests we are writing because, with this approach in mind, we may be tempted to write useless tests, just to achieve 100% coverage.

To fully understand what I'm talking about here, let's review the report generated by JaCoCo for one of the classes in the domain package:

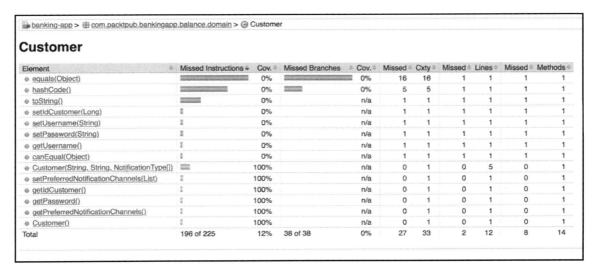

Test coverage report for a domain class

The report shows that there are no tests at all for some methods. Some of these methods are standard for any Java object, and the others are only getters and setters (accessors), which do not need to be tested. Writing getters and setters often leads to building anemic domain models, and, most of the time, this is only used to make the code compatible with frameworks relying on the Java Beans convention. For this reason, there is no need to write tests to cover getters and setters.

I have seen people writing tests for these methods only to achieve 100% coverage, but that is a useless and impractical procedure that should be avoided, as it doesn't add any value to the quality of the code or the written tests.

Now, let's review the report for one of the classes that has some logic worth testing:

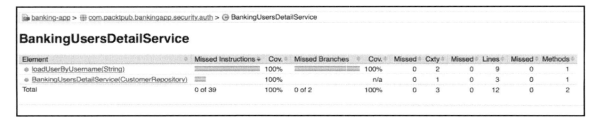

JaCoCo coverage report for a service class

Surprisingly, this class has 100% coverage. Let's review the associated tests for this class, as follows:

```java
@RunWith(MockitoJUnitRunner.class)
public class BankingUserDetailServiceTest
{
  @Mock
  CustomerRepository customerRepository;
  @InjectMocks
  BankingUsersDetailService bankingUsersDetailService;
  @Test(expected = UsernameNotFoundException.class)
  public void whenTheUserIsNotFoundAnExceptionIsExpected()
  throws Exception
  {
    String username = "foo";
    Mockito.when(customerRepository.findByUsername(username))
    .thenReturn(Optional.empty());
    bankingUsersDetailService.loadUserByUsername(username);
  }
  @Test
  public void theUserDetailsContainsTheInformationFromTheFoundCustomer
  () throws Exception
```

```
    {
      String username = "foo";
      String password = "bar";
      Customer customer =
      new Customer(username, password, NotificationType.EMAIL);
      Mockito.when(customerRepository.findByUsername(username))
      .thenReturn(Optional.of(customer));
      UserDetails userDetails = bankingUsersDetailService
      .loadUserByUsername(username);
      Assert.assertEquals(userDetails.getUsername(), username);
      Assert.assertEquals(userDetails.getPassword(), password);
      Assert.assertEquals(userDetails.getAuthorities()
      .iterator().next().getAuthority(), "ROLE_CUSTOMER");
    }
  }
```

We cannot always achieve 100% coverage, as we did in this example. However, a good measure tends to be 80%. You must think of the previously mentioned percentage not as a rule, but a recommendation; if you verify that your tests are exercising all of the logic needed, sometimes a value less than 80% will be fine.

You need to be smart, using the generated report to figure out what logic needs to be tested and then work on it, rather than feel frustrated by the results.

One of the good things about using this kind of tool is that you can integrate it as part of your continuous integration server, to generate reports that are visible all of the time. In this way, the reports can be used to continually check whether the coverage is growing or going down and take action. We will discuss this topic in more detail in `Chapter 11`, *DevOps and Release Management*.

UI frameworks

When you are working with Spring MVC, you have the option to choose from a huge set of technologies to build your web pages. Depending on what framework you have chosen, you will need to add the corresponding configuration, in order to let Spring know about your choice.

As we know, Spring supports configuration by code, so you will need to add a few annotations and/or configuration classes to make your frameworks work. If you want to avoid these steps, you can use Thymeleaf; this framework can be easily integrated as part of an existing Spring application including the Thymeleaf starter dependency. There are different lines of codes to be used depending upon the tools being used which are as follows:

- The dependency when Gradle is used is as follows:

```
compile('org.springframework.boot:spring-boot-starter-thymeleaf')
```

- The dependency when Maven is used is as follows:

```
<dependency>
  <groupId>org.springframework.boot</groupId>
  <artifactId>spring-boot-starter-thymeleaf</artifactId>
</dependency>
```

Once the application starts, Spring Boot will do all of the boring stuff for you, preparing your application for using Thymeleaf.

Thymeleaf

Thymeleaf is a relatively new template engine; the first version was released in 2011. Thymeleaf is pretty similar to HTML, which doesn't require any servlet containers to preview content in a browser. This is exploited in order to allow designers to work on the look and feel of the application, without deploying it.

Let's review how to convert a web template build, using HTML and Bootstrap, into a Thymeleaf template, in order to see that this template engine is not intrusive. The following code represents a very basic HTML template:

```
<!DOCTYPE html>
<html lang="en">
  <head>
    <meta charset="UTF-8"/>
    <title>Default title</title>
    <meta name="viewport" content="width=device-width,
    initial-scale=1"/>
    <link rel="stylesheet" href="https://maxcdn.bootstrapcdn.com/
    bootstrap/3.3.7/css/bootstrap.min.css"/>
    <script src="https://ajax.googleapis.com/ajax/libs/
    jquery/3.3.1/jquery.min.js"></script>
    <script src="https://maxcdn.bootstrapcdn.com/bootstrap/
    3.3.7/js/bootstrap.min.js"></script>
```

```
    </head>
    <body>
      <nav class="navbar navbar-inverse">
        <div class="container-fluid">
          <div class="navbar-header">
            <a class="navbar-brand" href="#">MVC Demo</a>
          </div>
          <ul class="nav navbar-nav">
            <li><a href="/index">Home</a></li>
            <li><a href="/notifications">My notification channels</a>
            </li>
          </ul>
          <ul class="nav navbar-nav navbar-right">
            <li>
              <a href="/login"><span class="glyphicon glyphicon-user">
              </span>  Login</a>
            </li>
            <li>
              <a href="/logout">
                <span class="glyphicon glyphicon-log-in"></span>
                  Logout
              </a>
            </li>
          </ul>
        </div>
      </nav>
      <div class="container">
        <div class="row">
          <div class="col-md-3"></div>
          <div class="col-md-6">
            Page content goes here
          </div>
          <div class="col-md-3"></div>
        </div>
      </div>
    </body>
</html>
```

Since this is a regular HTML file, you can open it in a browser to see how it looks:

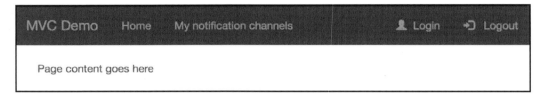

HTML and Bootstrap template

Now, let's implement a few requirements, to make our template work in a more realistic way:

- The **Logout** option should be present only when the user is logged in
- The **My notification channels** option should not be present if the user is not logged in
- The **Login** option should not be present once the user is logged in
- Once the user is logged in, the **Home** option should show a welcome message using their username

These requirements are trivial when we are creating web applications, and fortunately, they are also easy to implement using Thymeleaf.

In order to show/hide certain elements in a web page once the user is logged in, we need to include an additional library to deal with this stuff.

To include the library with Gradle, use the following command:

```
compile('org.thymeleaf.extras:thymeleaf-extras-springsecurity4')
```

To include the library with Maven, use the following command:

```
<dependency>
    <groupId>org.thymeleaf.extras</groupId>
    <artifactId>thymeleaf-extras-springsecurity4</artifactId>
</dependency>
```

Now, we need to add a tag declaration in the HTML file, in order to use Thymeleaf and the new extension that was added:

```
<html lang="en"
      xmlns:layout="http://www.ultraq.net.nz/thymeleaf/layout"
xmlns:sec="http://www.thymeleaf.org/thymeleaf-extras-springsecurity4">
```

Once we have included these tags, we will have the ability to use the provided built-in functionality. When you need to hide/show a certain element, depending on whether or not the user is logged in, you can use the isAuthenticated() condition, as follows:

```
<ul class="nav navbar-nav navbar-right">
    <li sec:authorize="!isAuthenticated()">
        <a href="/login"><span class="glyphicon glyphicon-user"></span>
Login</a>
    </li>
    <li sec:authorize="isAuthenticated()">
        <a href="/logout">
            <span class="glyphicon glyphicon-log-in"></span>
                Logout
        </a>
    </li>
</ul>
```

It's also quite common to restrict access, depending on the user roles assigned. These checks are also easy to implement using the added extension, as shown in the following code:

```
<li sec:authorize="hasRole('ROLE_ADMIN')"><a href="/a">Admins only</a></li>
<li sec:authorize="hasRole('ROLE_EDITOR')"><a href="/b">Editors
only</a></li>
```

To finish, if you need to show the username on a web page, you can use the following tag inside of your HTML file:

```
<p>Hello, <span sec:authentication="name"></span>!</p>
```

Alternatively, once the template has been created by our designers or frontend experts, we will want to use it across the whole application, to keep a consistent look and feel. In order to achieve this goal, we need to define which part of the page will be replaced by specific content in the template, using the layout tags:

```
<div class="col-md-6" layout:fragment="content">
    Page content goes here
</div>
```

The pages will then need to define the template name and the content that should be shown in the defined fragments, as follows:

```
<!DOCTYPE html>
<html lang="en"
    xmlns:layout="http://www.ultraq.net.nz/thymeleaf/layout"
    xmlns:sec="http://www.thymeleaf.org/thymeleaf-extras-springsecurity4"
    layout:decorator="default-layout">
<head>
```

```
        <title>Home</title>
</head>
<body>
<div layout:fragment="content">
    // Content here
</div>
</body>
</html>
```

We mentioned earlier that Thymeleaf is not intrusive at all, and we are going to show you why. Once all of the desired logic has been implemented using the Thymeleaf tags, you can open the template again using a regular browser, without deploying the application in a servlet container. You will get the following result:

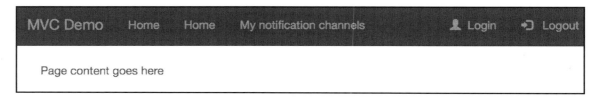

Thymeleaf and Bootstrap template

We have duplicate menu options, and we can still see the login and logout options, because the browser is not able to interpret the Thymeleaf tags. However, the good news is that the introduced code is not harming the template at all. This is exactly why your web designers can keep working and still have a preview in the browser. No matter how many Thymeleaf tags you have introduced in the template, these tags are not intrusive to the existing HTML code.

Securing an MVC application

Security is a key aspect in software development, and we need to take it seriously if we want to avoid exposing our applications to common attacks. Also, we may want to restrict access to non-authorized people. We will review some techniques to keep our software safe in Chapter 13, *Security*. In the meantime, you will learn how to secure an MVC application using Spring Security.

Up to this point, we have reviewed how to build a web application using Thymeleaf and Spring MVC. When working with web applications, one of the most common authentication mechanisms is basic authentication. Let's discuss this in more detail.

Basic authentication

Basic authentication, or basic access authentication, is a mechanism used to restrict or provide access to specific resources in the server. In a web application, the resources are often web pages, but this mechanism can be used to secure RESTful web services, as well. However, this approach is not common; a different mechanism, based on tokens, is preferred.

When a website is secured using basic authentication, the users need to provide their credentials before requesting the website's pages. The user credentials are merely a simple combination of a username and password that is encoded using a Base64 algorithm, to calculate the value that should be in the **Authentication** header. This will be used by the server later, to validate whether the user is authenticated and authorized to access the requested resource. If the user is authenticated, this means that the provided username and password combination is valid; being authorized means that the authenticated user has permission to execute specific actions or View individual pages.

One problem with using this authentication mechanism is that when the user sends the credentials to the server during the authentication process, the credentials are sent in plain text. If the request is then intercepted, the credentials are exposed. The following screenshot makes this problem evident; in this case, the request was intercepted using a tool called Wireshark (`https://www.wireshark.org`):

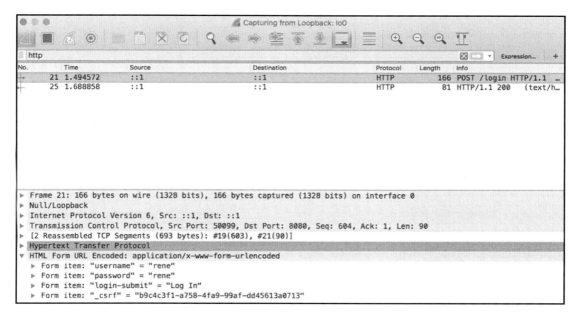

Intercepted HTTP request

This issue can be solved easily using a secure version of HTTP, in which a certificate is necessary for encrypting the data that is exchanged between the server and the browser. The certificate should be issued by a trusted **Certificate Authority (CA)** and should be located in the server. Browsers have a list of trusted CA root certificates that are validated when a secured connection is established. Once the certificate is validated, the address bar shows a padlock, as shown in the following screenshot:

Padlock shown in the address bar

As you can see in the following screenshot, the HTTPS protocol uses the 8443 port instead of the standard 80, which is intended for HTTP:

Address bar using HTTPS

For development purposes, you can generate your own certificates, but the browser will show you a warning indicating that the certificate could not be validated; you can add an exception to open the requested pages using HTTPS.

The following diagram shows how a connection is established using the HTTPS protocol:

HTTPS connection

The padlock located in the middle represents the encrypted data when it is going through the computer network, which makes it impossible to read. The following screenshot shows how the data looks when it is intercepted using Wireshark:

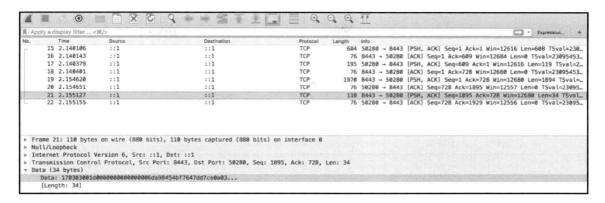

Intercepted HTTPS request

As you can see, this intercepted data is hard to understand. In this way, all of the information sent is protected, and, even if it is captured in transit, it can't be easily read. This attack is known as a man-in-the-middle attack, which is one of the most common types of attack.

Implementing basic authentication

Now that you know the basics related to Basic authentication and how it works, let's review how to implement it in a Spring MVC application.

To begin, we need to include the starter dependency for Spring Security.

It can be included in Gradle as follows:

```
compile('org.springframework.boot:spring-boot-starter-security')
```

It can be included in Maven as follows:

```
<dependency>
    <groupId>org.springframework.boot</groupId>
    <artifactId>spring-boot-starter-security</artifactId>
</dependency>
```

After adding this dependency, Spring Boot will do all of the boring stuff for us, and we won't have to do anything to secure the application. If we don't add any additional configurations, Spring will generate a user for testing, and the password will be printed in the console. This scenario is perfect when we are only in the early stages of development.

On the other hand, if we require a customized way to allow or restrict access to users, all that we need to do is implement the `loadUserByUsername` method, which is a part of the `UserDetailsService` interface.

The implementation is fairly simple; the method retrieves the `username` provided, and, using that username, you will need to return a `UserDetails` object with the user information.

Let's review an example, as follows:

```
@Service
public class MyCustomUsersDetailService implements UserDetailsService {

    @Override
    public UserDetails loadUserByUsername(String username) throws
UsernameNotFoundException {
        Optional<Customer> customerFound = findByUsername(username);
        if (customerFound.isPresent()) {
            Customer customer = customerFound.get();
            User.UserBuilder builder = User
                    .withUsername(username)
                    .password(customer.getPassword())
                    .roles(ADD_YOUR_ROLES_HERE);
            return builder.build();
        } else {
            throw new UsernameNotFoundException("User not found.");
        }
    }
}
```

The `findByUsername` method is responsible for finding the users that you need in a database or in any other storage. Once you have customized where your users are, you have to work on the authorization for the web pages. This can be done by implementing the `WebSecurityConfigurerAdapter` interface, as shown in the following code:

```
@Configuration
@EnableWebSecurity
public class SecurityConfig extends WebSecurityConfigurerAdapter {

    @Override
    protected void configure(HttpSecurity httpSecurity) throws Exception {
        httpSecurity.authorizeRequests()
                .antMatchers("/index").permitAll()
                .antMatchers("/guest/**").permitAll()
                .antMatchers("/customers/**").hasAuthority("ROLE_CUSTOMER")
                .anyRequest().authenticated()
                .and()
```

```
    .formLogin()
   .loginPage("/login")
   .failureUrl("/login?error")
   .successForwardUrl("/home")
    .usernameParameter("username").passwordParameter("password")
        .permitAll()
    .and()
    .logout().logoutSuccessUrl("/logout")
    .and()
    .csrf();
    }
 }
```

Let's review the code that has been highlighted in bold:

- We are configuring a path to grant access to any user, whether or not the request is authenticated
- A configuration for restricting access to only users with the CUSTOMER role is added for all of the pages under the customers path
- A login page is configured, as well as the pages to forward successful and failed authentication attempts to
- The URL /logout is provided, to redirect the user once the logout process has occurred

As you can see, once you have implemented the preceding configuration class, you will have all that you need to secure the web pages in your application.

We mentioned earlier that a good approach to follow is to use HTTPS to encrypt the data that is sent between the browser and the server. To achieve this goal, Spring Boot offers the ability to add the following configuration properties to the application.properties file:

```
server.port: 8443
server.ssl.key-store: keystore.p12
server.ssl.key-store-password: spring
server.ssl.keyStoreType: PKCS12
server.ssl.keyAlias: tomcat
```

Let's review the configurations in this file:

- As mentioned earlier, HTTPS uses the 8443 port.
- The next parameter allows for specifying the digital certificate name.

- The keystore password should also be provided. Note that this value can be provided when executing the application as a parameter. An even better method is to get these values from a configuration server, instead of having them hardcoded in the `application.properties` file.
- This parameter is used to specify the store type used when the certificate was generated.
- The last parameter corresponds to the alias for the digital certificate.

Note that the code should not be modified to enable HTTPS in the application.

For the sake of testing, a self-signed certificate can be created by using a key tool, which is part of a standard Java installation, as shown in the following screenshot:

```
MacBook-Pro-de-Rene:~ moe$ keytool -genkey -alias tomcat -storetype PKCS12 -keyalg RSA -keysize 2048 -keystore keystore.p12 -validity 3650
Enter keystore password:
Re-enter new password:
What is your first and last name?
  [Unknown]:
What is the name of your organizational unit?
  [Unknown]:
What is the name of your organization?
  [Unknown]:
What is the name of your City or Locality?
  [Unknown]:
What is the name of your State or Province?
  [Unknown]:
What is the two-letter country code for this unit?
  [Unknown]:
Is CN=Unknown, OU=Unknown, O=Unknown, L=Unknown, ST=Unknown, C=Unknown correct?
  [no]:  yes
```

Self-signed certificate creation

Summary

In this chapter, we explored the concepts related to MVC architecture and how they work. We also discussed the errors that people tend to make when building applications using this architectural style.

Then we reviewed how to create an application using Spring MVC, looking at different tests and how to implement them using features provided by Spring. We also reviewed how to use Thymeleaf with Spring MVC in order to build the UI for a web application. To finish this chapter, we discussed some security concepts, including how to apply them in a Spring MVC application.

In the next chapter, you will learn about event-driven architectures, which are becoming quite popular.

6
Event-Driven Architectures

Event-driven architectures (**EDA**) are based on commands and events that are created each time an application changes state. According to Martin Fowler, there are four patterns that are used to build software systems using this approach.

In this chapter, we are going to learn about these four patterns and look at how messaging can be tied together to take full advantage of a programming model based on messages. Even when it's not a requirement, messaging can be used to add more capabilities into applications that are built using an event-driven architectural style.

In this chapter, we will look at the following topics:

- Underlying concepts and key aspects associated with event-driven architectures:
  - Commands
  - Events
- Common patterns used within event-driven architectures:
  - Event notification
  - Event-carried state transfer
  - Event sourcing
  - CQRS

Underlying concepts and key aspects

Before looking into the details of event-driven architectures, we are going to start by learning about some key aspects surrounding them.

The applications created using this approach are developed with two different but related concepts in mind:

- Commands
- Events

Let's look at a brief definition of each of these concepts.

Command

A command is an operation performed within an application that emits one or more events as the result of a successful or failed execution. We can think about these as operations that are intended to modify the state of a system.

Commands are called actions. This makes a lot of sense if we take their intended use into consideration. The following list shows some examples of such commands:

- Transfer money
- Update user information
- Create an account

It's highly recommended that you use present tense verbs for naming commands, as demonstrated with these examples.

Event

An event is the result of a command execution within an application. These are used as a notification mechanism for subscribers who are interested in receiving them. Events are immutable and should not be modified, as they are designed to keep a log that keeps information on how the application state has mutated over time.

When it comes to naming events, the rule of thumb is to use past tense, such as the following:

- Money transferred
- User information updated
- Account created

Events are not concerned with what actions will be performed after their creation. This makes it possible to decouple a system but still notify the subscribers. In this way, we can decouple applications because the subscribers are responsible for executing one or more operations, depending on what is needed when they have been notified of an event's creation.

At this point, we can conclude that we can decouple applications because the subscribers are responsible for executing one or more operations, depending on what is needed when they have been notified of an event's creation. We can also infer that events are an excellent way to reverse dependencies by delegating responsibilities to other systems.

The following diagram shows how a command emits events and how the subscribers to these events are notified:

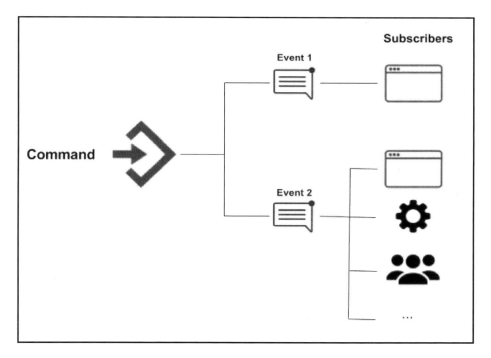

Events creation and propagation

Now that we have a better understanding of events, let's review the four patterns that we mentioned at the beginning of this chapter in order to create applications using an event-driven architectural style.

Patterns of event-driven architectures

When people talk about event-driven architectures, they often refer to one of the following patterns:

- Event notification
- Event-carried state transfer
- Event sourcing
- CQRS

At times, more than one of these are used together within the same system, depending on what the business requirements are. Let's review each of these patterns in order to identify the scenarios in which they can be used.

Event notification

The event notification pattern works by emitting events to subscribers once a command is executed. This can be compared to the observer pattern in which you observe a subject that has a list of many listeners or subscribers that are automatically notified when the state of the observed object changes.

This behavior is widely used by event bus libraries that allow publish-subscribe communication among the components that are part of an application. The most common use cases for these libraries are targeted towards the UI, but they are also applicable to other parts of the system in the backend. The following diagram demonstrates how an event is sent to the bus and then propagated to all subscribers, which were previously registered:

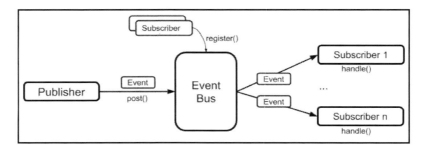

Event bus

There are two main benefits to using this event-notification mechanism:

- Decoupled systems and functionalities
- Inverted dependencies

To better understand these benefits, let's imagine that we need to work on the following requirement of our banking application:

> *The bank wants to offer customers who are using the mobile app the chance to transfer money. This will include either transferring between accounts owned by our bank or transferring to external banks. Once this transaction is executed, we need to notify the customers about the transaction status using their preferred notification channels.*
>
> *The bank also has an application that is used by the call center staff that notifies our agents of our clients' balance. When a client's account balance is higher than a predetermined amount of money, the call center system will alert the agents, who will then call the clients to make them aware of the possibility of investing their money in the bank. Finally, if a transaction involves an external bank, we need to notify them about the transaction status too.*

Using a classic approach to write an application, we can correctly build a system where all the following postconditions listed in the requirements are executed within the transfer application boundaries after the money transfer occurs, as demonstrated in the following diagram:

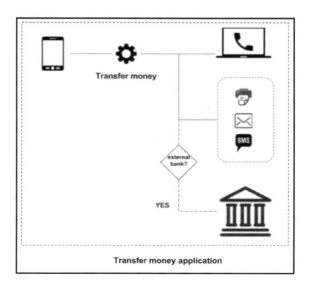

Coupled transfer money application

As we can see from the preceding diagram, the transfer money application needs to know about all the postconditions that have to be met once the transaction has occurred; using this approach, we will end up writing all the necessary code to interact with other systems, which leads us to couple the application with other systems.

On the other hand, using the event-notification pattern, we can decouple the transfer money application, as shown in the following diagram:

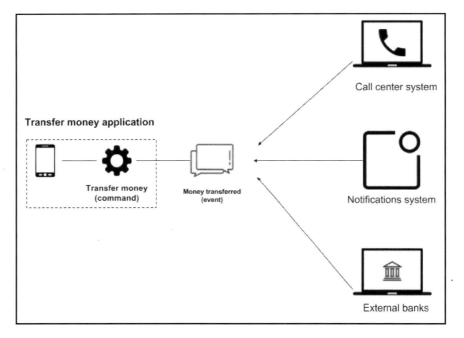

Decoupled transfer money application

In the preceding diagram, we can see that once the `<Transfer money>` command is executed, a `<Money transferred>` event is emitted, and all the subscribed systems are notified. By doing this, we can get rid of the coupling among the systems.

The important thing to note here is that the money transfer application doesn't even need to know about the existence of other software systems, and all the postconditions are met out of the boundaries of this application. In other words, decoupled systems lead us to invert dependencies.

Decoupled systems and inverted dependencies sound fantastic, but the implicit disadvantage of these is that you lose visibility. This is because the application emitting events doesn't know anything about the processes that are executed once the event is published, and there is no code for reading other systems.

It is often impossible to identify dependencies downstream, and some techniques for correlating events across different logs are commonly used to relieve this nightmare.

Coupled systems give all the information regarding downstream dependencies, and are hard to evolve. Conversely, decoupled systems know nothing about downstream dependencies, but they offer the chance to evolve systems independently.

Now that we have learned of the underlying concepts that are supporting the event-notification pattern, we can say that the most visible technology for implementing this kind of application is the use of messaging systems such as RabbitMQ, AWS SQS/SNS, MSMQ, and so on. These are supported by Spring under the Spring Cloud Stream project umbrella. In our case, we are going to use RabbitMQ, which can be supported by adding the following dependency:

```
<dependency>
    <groupId>org.springframework.cloud</groupId>
    <artifactId>spring-cloud-stream-binder-rabbit</artifactId> </dependency>
```

In order to make the setup process of RabbitMQ accessible, the code provided for this book in this chapter includes a Docker Compose file that should be executed using the docker-compose up command. We will look at what Docker Compose is and how it works in Chapter 10, *Containerizing your Applications*.

Spring Cloud Stream is built on the top of Spring Integration and offers the chance to produce and consume messages easily, as well as the chance to use all the built-in functionalities of Spring Integration. We are going to use this project to implement the example of the banking application mentioned earlier, so we will need to add the following dependency:

```
<dependency>
    <groupId>org.springframework.cloud</groupId>
    <artifactId>spring-cloud-stream</artifactId>
</dependency>
```

The transfer money application will expose an endpoint to allow the transferring of money. Once this transaction is done, an event notification needs to be sent to the other apps. Spring Cloud Stream makes it possible to define messaging channels with the use of the `@Output` annotation, as follows:

```
public interface EventNotificationChannel
{
    @Output
    MessageChannel moneyTransferredChannel();
}
```

This interface can be annotated and used wherever you want. Let's look at how to use this in the controller, which exposes the functionality to transfer money:

```
@RestController
public class TransferController
{
    private final MessageChannel moneyTransferredChannel;
    public TransferController(EventNotificationChannel channel)
    {
        this.moneyTransferredChannel = channel.moneyTransferredChannel();
    }
    @PostMapping("/transfer")
    public void doTransfer(@RequestBody TransferMoneyDetails
    transferMoneyDetails)
    {
        log.info("Transferring money with details: " +
        transferMoneyDetails);
        Message<String> moneyTransferredEvent = MessageBuilder
        .withPayload
        ("Money transferred for client with id: " +
        transferMoneyDetails.getCustomerId()).build();
        this.moneyTransferredChannel.send(moneyTransferredEvent);
    }
}
```

One thing to keep in mind when we are using the event-notification pattern is that the application that is emitting events simply provides very basic information regarding the executed command. In this case, the <Money Transferred> event contains the client ID that should be used later to query more information and determine whether or not additional operations need to be executed. This process always involves one or more additional interactions with other systems, databases, and so on.

The subscribers can take advantage of Spring Cloud Stream as well. In this case, the
@Input annotation should be used as follows:

```
public interface EventNotificationChannel
{
  @Input
  SubscribableChannel subscriptionOnMoneyTransferredChannel();
}
```

Using Spring Integration, a complete integration flow can be executed to process the
incoming message in this way:

```
@Bean
IntegrationFlow integrationFlow(
           EventNotificationChannel eventNotificationChannel) {
    return IntegrationFlows.from
        (eventNotificationChannel
         .subscriptionOnMoneyTransferredChannel()).
            handle(String.class, new GenericHandler<String>() {
            @Override
            public Object handle(String payload,
            Map<String, Object> headers) {

            // Use the payload to find the transaction and determine
            // if a notification should be sent to external banks

    }
        }).get();
}
```

Once the message is retrieved, it should be used to query additional information regarding
the transaction and determine whether a notification should be sent to external banks. This
approach is useful for reducing the size of the payload. It also helps to avoid sending
information that is often unnecessary and useless for other systems, but which increases the
traffic retrieved by the source application.

In worst-case scenarios, every single event produced will retrieve at least one additional request asking for the transaction details, as shown in the following diagram:

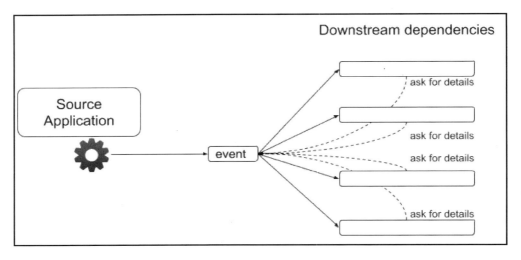

Downstream dependencies requesting transaction details

In our example, we will have at least three other requests from the dependent systems for each event produced.

Event-carried state transfer

The event-carried state transfer pattern has a minor variation in comparison to the event-notification pattern discussed earlier. Here, the event contains very basic information related to the executed command. In this case, the event contains all of the information regarding the executed command that is used to avoid contacting the source application to perform further processing by the dependent systems.

This pattern brings the following benefits to the table:

- Improves application performance
- Reduces the load on the source application
- Increases the availability of the system

Let's talk about each of these points in the following sections.

Improving application performance

In the previous example, once the event was produced and retrieved by the downstream systems, an additional operation needed to be executed in order to obtain the details associated with the transaction. This determined what action needed have to been performed as part of the process. This additional operation involved establishing a communication with the source application. This step could take only a few milliseconds in some cases, but the response time could take longer depending on the network traffic and latency. This would then influence the performance of the dependent systems.

As a result, the size of the payload provided by the source application increases, but less traffic is required.

Reducing the load on the source application

Since all the information associated with the executed command is included as part of the produced event, there is no need to ask for more information about the source application. Consequently, there are fewer requests, reducing the load retrieved by the source application.

The relationship between the produced events and the requests retrieved once the event is emitted is 1:1 in the best-case scenarios. In other words, one request will produce one event, but this could be even worse depending on how many dependent systems need to ask for additional information when the event is retrieved.

To avoid this extra load, all downstream systems often have their own data storage in which the events information is persisted, as shown by the following diagram:

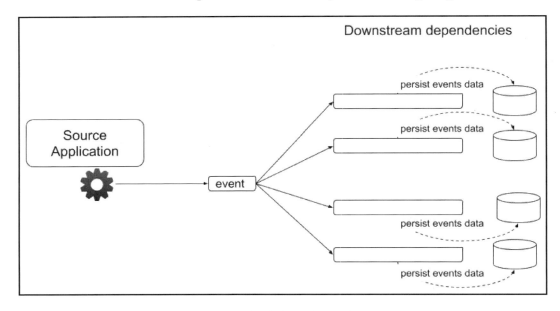

Downstream dependencies persisting events data

When using this approach, each one of the downstream systems only stores the data that is relevant to itself, and the rest of the information provided is ignored because it is useless for the system, and won't be used at all.

Increasing the availability of the system

After removing the need to ask for additional data once the event has been retrieved, it's natural to assume that the availability of the system has increased as, no matter whether the other systems are available or not, the event will be processed. An indirect consequence of introducing this benefit is the eventual consistency that is now part of the system.

Eventual consistency is a model that is used to achieve high availability in the systems where, if no new updates are made to the given data, once a piece of information has been retrieved, all instances of accessing that data will eventually return the last updated value.

The following diagram shows how a system changes its data without propagating these changes to the downstream dependencies:

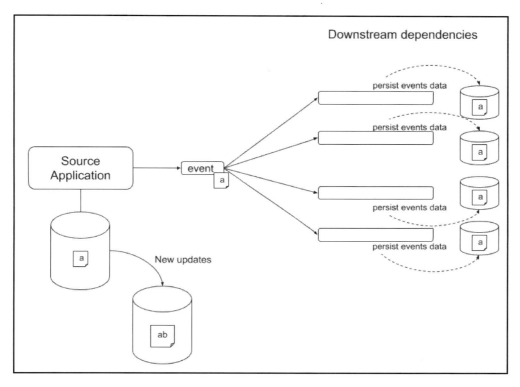

Data updates are not propagated

To change the preceding example so that it follows this approach, we only need to include additional information as part of the payload. Previously, we just sent a String with the clientId; now we are going to cover the complete TransactionMoneyDetails in the following way:

```
@RestController
public class TransferController
{
    private final MessageChannel moneyTransferredChannel;
    public TransferController(EventNotificationChannel channel)
    {
        this.moneyTransferredChannel = channel.moneyTransferredChannel();
    }
    @PostMapping("/transfer")
    public void doTransfer(@RequestBody TransferMoneyDetails
```

```
      transferMoneyDetails)
      {
        // Do something
        Message<TransferMoneyDetails> moneyTransferredEvent =
        MessageBuilder.withPayload(transferMoneyDetails).build();
        this.moneyTransferredChannel.send(moneyTransferredEvent);
      }
    }
```

The `Message` class can support any kind of object that should be specified within <>, since this class is implemented using the generic types feature from Java.

The downstream-dependent systems should also be modified to make them able to retrieve an object instead of a simple string. Since the `Handler` to process incoming messages also supports generics, we can implement this feature with a small change in the code, as follows:

```
@Bean
IntegrationFlow integrationFlow(EventNotificationChannel
eventNotificationChannel)
{
  return IntegrationFlows
  .from(eventNotificationChannel
  .subscriptionOnMoneyTransferredChannel())
  .handle(TransferMoneyDetails.class, new GenericHandler
  <TransferMoneyDetails>()
  {
    @Override
    public Object handle(TransferMoneyDetails payload, Map<String,
    Object> map)
    {
      // Do something with the payload
      return null;
    }
  }).get();
}
```

Event sourcing

Event sourcing is another way to implement applications using an event-driven approach, where the core of the functionality is based on the use of commands that produce events that change the system state once they have been processed.

We can think of a command as the result of a transaction executed within the system. This transaction would be different depending on factors such as the following:

- User actions
- Messages received from other applications
- Scheduled tasks performed

Applications created using an event-sourcing approach store the events associated with the executed commands. It's also worth storing the commands that produced events. This makes it possible to correlate all of them in order to get an idea of the boundaries that were created.

The main reason to store events is to use them whenever you want to rebuild the system state at any point in time. A way to make this task easier is by periodically generating backups for the database that stores the system state, which is helpful for avoiding the need to reprocess all the events that were created since the application started to work. Instead, we will just need to process the set of events that were executed after the database snapshot was generated.

Let's review the following set of diagrams to understand how this works. The first diagram shows that once Command A is executed, three Events are created, and a new State is generated after each one of them is processed:

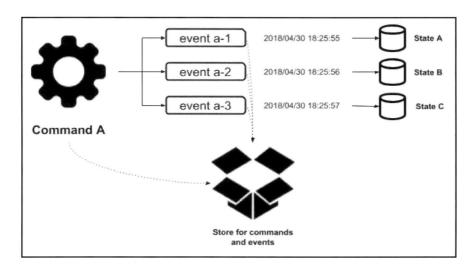

Events and application states generated once Command A is executed

The following diagram represents quite a similar process. In this case, two Events were created as a result of the Command B execution:

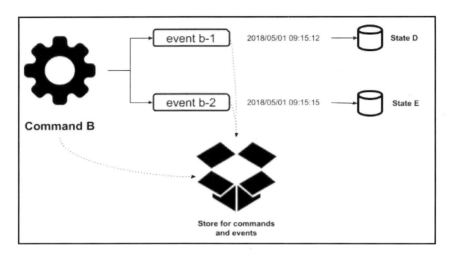

Events and application states generated as the result of the Command B execution

So far, our application has five states:

- State A
- State B
- State C
- State D
- State E

Let's say we are interested in debugging Event b-1 because, when it was executed, the application crashed. To achieve this goal, we have two options:

- Process the events one by one and study the application behavior during the Event b-1 execution, as shown in the following diagram:

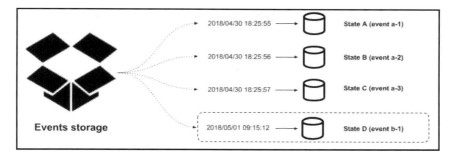

Rebuilding the application state processing all the events

- Process the rest of the events after restoring a database snapshot and study the application behavior during the `Event b-1` execution, as shown in the following diagram:

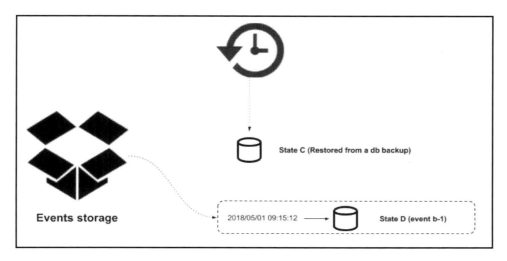

Rebuilding the application state from a database snapshot

Obviously, the second approach is much more efficient. Scheduled tasks are often in charge of creating database snapshots after a certain period of time, and a policy should be established to manage the existing snapshots. For example, you can establish a policy to create a new snapshot every single day at midnight and get rid of old snapshots after the most convenient period of time for your business.

As you may have realized, the source of truth for our system is the events storage, which allows us to rebuild the application state at any time. Since the events are being used to generate the system state, we can 100% rely on the events storage. However, we should also consider the fact that an event execution within a system would also require interaction with another application. In this case, if you replay that event, you should think about how the other system(s) will be affected. Here, we would end up with one of the two following scenarios:

- The operations executed in the other application(s) are idempotent
- The other application(s) will be affected because a new transaction will be generated

In the first case, since the operations are idempotent, we don't have to be worried at all. This is because another execution will not affect the other system(s). In the second case, we should consider a way to create compensation operations or a way to ignore these interactions to avoid affecting the other systems.

The inherent benefits that we are going to have after following this approach are as follows:

- A data store that can be used for auditing purposes
- An excellent logging level
- It will be easier to debug an application
- A historic state
- The ability to go back in time to a previous version of the state

The quintessential example for event-sourcing applications is version control systems (VCS) such as Git, Apache subversion, CVS, or any other version control system where all the changes that are applied in the source code files are stored. Furthermore, the commits represent the events that allow us to undo/redo changes when required.

In order to make it as simple as possible to understand, you can think of an event-sourcing application as something that manages data changes in the same way that a version control system manages file changes. You can also think about a `git push` operation as a command in an event-sourcing system.

Now that we have explained the underlying concepts behind event sourcing, it's time to dive into details that will allow us to understand how to implement a system following this approach. Although there are different ways to create event-sourcing applications, I'll explain a generic way to do it here. It is important that you keep in mind that this approach should be changed depending on the particular needs or assumptions that you need for your business.

We mentioned that an event-sourcing system should have *at least* two places in which to store the data. One of these will be used to save event and command information and the other one will be used to save the application state—we say *at least two* because more than one storage option is sometimes needed to persist the system state of an application. Since the input retrieved by the system to perform their business processes are very different from each other, we should consider using a database that supports the ability to store data using a JSON format. Following this approach, the most basic data that should be stored as part of a command that is executed within an event-sourcing system is as follows:

- Unique identifier
- Timestamp
- Input data retrieved in JSON format
- Any additional data to correlate commands

On the other hand, the recommended data that should be stored for an event is as follows:

- Unique identifier
- Timestamp
- Relevant data for the event in JSON format
- Identifier of the command that generated the event

As we mentioned earlier, depending on your business needs, you would need to add more fields, but the ones mentioned earlier are necessary in any case. The key here is to make sure that your data will be able to be processed later to recreate the application state when that's needed. Almost any NoSQL database has support to store data as JSON, but some SQL databases, such as PostgreSQL, can also deal with data in this format very well.

On the subject of the system state, the decision of choosing an SQL or NoSQL technology should completely depend on your business; you don't have to change your mind just because the application will be built using an event-sourcing approach. Furthermore, the structure of your data model should also depend on the business itself rather than on the events and commands that generate the data that will be stored there. It is also worth mentioning that one event will generate data that will be stored in one or more tables of the system state data model, and there are no restrictions at all in these terms.

When we think about commands, events, and states, a question that is usually raised is with regards to the order in which the information is persisted. This point would be an interesting discussion, but you don't have to worry too much about the order in which the data was persisted. You can choose to persist the data synchronously or asynchronously in any of the data storage instances.

An asynchronous approach sometimes leads us to think that we will end up having inconsistent information, but the truth is that both approaches could lead us to that point. Instead of thinking about synchronous or asynchronous processing, we should consider mechanisms to recover our app from these crashes, such as proper logging, for example. Good logging would be helpful for recovering the data of our systems in exactly the same way as we do for applications that are built using any approach other than event sourcing.

Now it's time to review some code to put the concepts that we discussed previously into practice. Let's build an application that allows us to open a new bank account. The input data required will be as follows:

- Customer name
- Customer last name
- An initial amount of money to open the account
- Account type (savings/current)

After creating the account, our application state should reflect one new customer and a new bank account that has been created.

As part of our application, we will have one command: `CreateCustomerCommand`. This will generate two events, named `CustomerCreated` and `AccountCreated`, as shown in the following diagram:

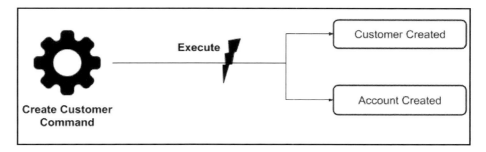

Command execution

Once this command is executed, a few things need to happen:

- The command should be saved
- The aforementioned events should be created with the relevant information for them
- The events should be saved
- The events should be processed

The relevant code for this process is shown in the following code:

```
public class CreateCustomerCommand extends Command {

    public void execute() {

        String commandId = UUID.randomUUID().toString();
        CommandMetadata commandMetadata
            = new CommandMetadata(commandId, getName(), this.data);
        commandRepository.save(commandMetadata);

        String customerUuid = UUID.randomUUID().toString();

        JSONObject customerInformation = getCustomerInformation();
        customerInformation.put("customer_id", customerUuid);

        // CustomerCreated event creation
        EventMetadata customerCreatedEvent
                = new EventMetadata(customerInformation, ...);
        // CustomerCreated event saved
        eventRepository.save(customerCreatedEvent);
        // CustomerCreated event sent to process
        eventProcessor.process(customerCreatedEvent);

        JSONObject accountInformation = getAccountInformation();
        accountInformation.put("customer_id", customerUuid);
        // AccountCreated event creation
        EventMetadata accountCreatedEvent
                = new EventMetadata(accountInformation, ...);
        // AccountCreated event saved
        eventRepository.save(accountCreatedEvent);
        // AccountCreated event sent to process
        eventProcessor.process(accountCreatedEvent);

    }
    ...
}
```

Once the events are handled, the system state should be generated. In this case, it means a new customer and a new account should be created, as shown in the following diagram:

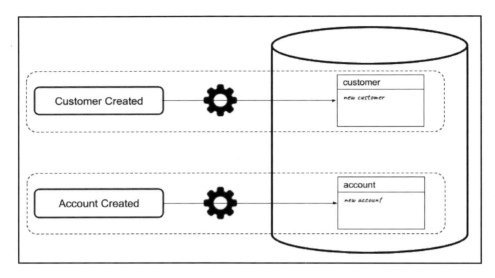

System state generated after processing the events

To achieve this goal, we have a pretty basic implementation that, depending on `event name`, executes code instructions, as shown in the following code:

```
@Component
public class EventProcessor {

    public void process(EventMetadata event) {
        if ("CustomerCreated".equals(event.getEventName())) {
            Customer customer = new Customer(event);
            customerRepository.save(customer);
        } else if ("AccountCreated".equals(event.getEventName())) {
            Account account = new Account(event);
            accountRepository.save(account);
        }
    }
    ...
}
```

If you want to see how the application works, you can execute the following CURL command:

```
$ curl -H "Content-Type: application/json" \
    -X POST \
    -d '{"account_type": "savings", "name": "Rene", "last_name": "Enriquez", "initial_amount": 1000}' \
    http://localhost:8080/customer
```

You will see the following messages in the console :

```
COMMAND INFORMATION
id: 8782e12e-92e5-41e0-8241-c0fd83cd3194 , name: CreateCustomer , data:
{"account_type":"savings","name":"Rene","last_name":"Enriquez","initial_amo
unt":1000}
EVENT INFORMATION
id: 71931e1b-5bce-4fe7-bbce-775b166fef55 , name: CustomerCreated , command
id: 8782e12e-92e5-41e0-8241-c0fd83cd3194 , data:
{"name":"Rene","last_name":"Enriquez","customer_id":"2fb9161e-
c5fa-44b2-8652-75cd303fa54f"}
id: 0e9c407c-3ea4-41ae-a9cd-af0c9a76b8fb , name: AccountCreated , command
id: 8782e12e-92e5-41e0-8241-c0fd83cd3194 , data:
{"account_type":"savings","account_id":"d8dbd8fd-fa98-4ffc-924a-
f3c65e6f6156","balance":1000,"customer_id":"2fb9161e-
c5fa-44b2-8652-75cd303fa54f"}
```

You can check the system state by executing SQL statements in the H2 web console available in the URL: `http://localhost:8080/h2-console`.

The following screenshot shows the result of querying the **Account** table:

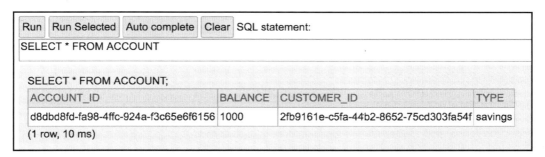

Query result from the Account table

The following screenshot shows the result of querying the **Customer** table:

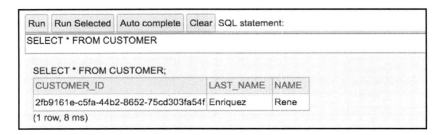

Query result from the Customer table

The most crucial test for an event-sourcing application is the ability to recreate the `state` once the data is deleted. You can run this test by deleting the data from the table using the following SQL statements:

```
DELETE FROM CUSTOMER;
DELETE FROM ACCOUNT;
```

After executing these operations in the H2 console, you can recreate the state by running the following CURL command:

```
$ curl -X POST http://localhost:8080/events/<EVENT_ID>
```

Note that you will need to replace the `<EVENT_ID>` listed in the preceding URL with the values listed in the console when the command was executed.

CQRS

Command-Query Responsibility Segregation (**CQRS**) is a pattern in which the main idea is to create separate data structures and operations to read and write data by creating segregated interfaces to interact with the system's data storage.

CQRS is not really based on events, but since it's often used in conjunction with event-sourcing implementations, it is worth mentioning the scenarios in which it would be applied. There are three main use cases where the segregation of interfaces to process and query information would be useful:

- Complex domain model
- Distinct paths to query and persist information
- Independent scaling

Complex domain models

This scenario refers to systems where the inputs retrieved are simple to manage and persist in the database. However, before delivering information to users, many transformations are needed to make the data useful and comprehensive for the business.

Imagine a system where the code is comprised of a large set of entity objects mapping database tables to persist information using an ORM framework. This kind of system involves many writes and read operations that are executed using the ORM and some operations that run as part of the system to transform the retrieved data—in the form of entity objects—into data transfer objects (DTOs) to provide information in a meaningful way for the business.

The following diagram shows the dataflow from the database to the business services that is designed to follow this approach:

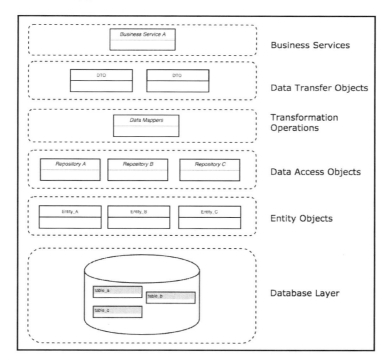

Dataflow using entity objects and DTOs

Transforming data is not a big deal. In systems using an ORM, the biggest problem arises when entity objects bring columns containing useless information that is ignored during the transformation process, introducing an unnecessary overhead on the database and the network. On the other hand, in the preceding diagram, we can see that a big process is needed to map the database tables as objects before actually getting the requested data. A good approach to getting rid of this problem is to replace the read operations executed by the ORM frameworks with stored procedures or plain query statements to retrieve only the required data from the database.

The following diagram shows how entity objects can be replaced with DOTs:

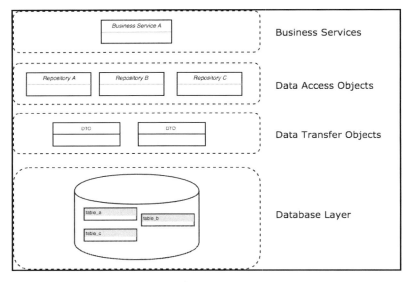

Data flow using DTOs

It's evident that this approach is much more simple and easy to accomplish. Even the amount of code required is drastically reduced. I'm not concluding that ORM frameworks are bad—actually, many of them are awesome, and projects such as Spring Data provide tons of built-in features. However, depending on the business requirements, plain JDBC operations are sometimes much more beneficial for the system.

Distinct paths to query and persist information

When we are building applications, it's quite common to find ourselves writing tons of validations on the retrieved input before using the provided information in the system.

Common validations applied to the retrieved data include the following:

- Verification for non-null values
- Specific text formats, such as emails
- Checks to validate string lengths
- The maximum quantity of decimals allowed in numbers

There are many mechanisms available for implementing this kind of validation within our code. The most popular of these are based on third-party libraries that rely on annotations that can be extended using regular expressions for specific scenarios. There is even a specification that is part of the platform that can be used to validate class fields called Bean Validation. This is currently part of the **Java Specification Request (JSR) 380** (`http://beanvalidation.org/`).

While it is essential to have all these validations when users or external systems provide the data, there is no need to keep performing these checks when the information is read from the database and returned to the user. Furthermore, in some cases, such as event sourcing, once the data is retrieved, some commands are executed, events are created, and at the end, the information is persisted.

In these scenarios, it is apparent that the processes to persist and read information are different, and they need separate paths in order to accomplish their goals.

The following diagram shows how an application uses different paths to persist and retrieve data:

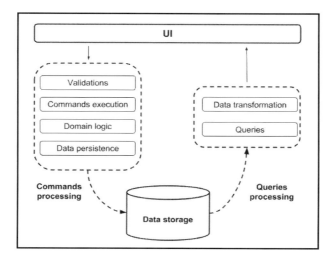

Data persisted and queried using different paths

From the preceding diagram, we can quickly note how much processing is avoided because it is absolutely unnecessary. Furthermore, the domain models used to query and process the information are often different because they are tailored to accomplish different goals.

Independent scaling

Today, it's common to hear developers, software architects, and technical people in general talking about creating separate services to solve different needs. Creating separate services supports the independent scaling approach because it makes it possible to scale the created services separately.

The main idea, in this case, is creating separate systems that can be built and deployed independently. The source of data for these different applications can either be the same or different, depending on what the requirements are. The most common scenario here is where the same data storage is used for both systems because the applied changes should be immediately reflected. Otherwise, delayed data could cause confusion or errors during the normal operation of an application.

Let's think about an online store. Imagine that you added many items to your shopping cart, and after checking out your order, you realize you paid a lower amount of money than required because not all items were considered during the check-out process. This is undesired behavior within an application.

On the other hand, in some cases, it is okay to use different data storage because retrieving data that is delayed by hours or days is enough to solve the business needs associated with an application. Imagine that you are tasked with creating a report showing the months when people tend to request vacations. Of course, a database that does not have the latest changes, and is a bit behind the current state of the application, will work perfectly. When we have this kind of requirement, we can use reporting databases (see `https://martinfowler.com/bliki/ReportingDatabase.html` for more details) to retrieve the information. This approach is often taken when an application is intended to provide executive reporting information for taking strategic decisions rather than getting a list of all the existing records in the database tables.

Having separate systems to query and process information gives us the benefit of independent scaling capabilities on both systems. This is useful when one of the systems requires many more resources for processing. Let's take the example of the online store mentioned previously—people are always looking for items to buy, making comparisons, checking sizes, prices, brands, and so on.

In the preceding example, the number of requests to check out orders is less than the number of requests to check for item information. So, in this case, having separate systems allows us to avoid unnecessarily wasting resources and allows us to only add more resources or instances of the service that has the highest volume of traffic.

Summary

In this chapter, we covered event-driven architectures and the four common patterns that are used to implement applications using this architectural style. We explained each of these patterns in detail, and wrote some code to understand how they can be implemented using Spring Framework. At the same time, we looked at some use cases where they can be utilized, and learned how they help us to reduce the complexity that is introduced as part of the system requirements that we would eventually have.

As part of these patterns, we talked about event sourcing, which is getting more and more popular within the microservices world, and which we will learn about later in Chapter 8, *Microservices*.

Pipe-and-Filter Architectures 7

In this chapter, we will review a useful paradigm architecture named Pipe-and-Filter, and you will learn how to implement an application using the Spring Framework.

We will also explain how to build a pipeline that encapsulates an independent chain of tasks aimed at filtering and processing large amounts of data, focusing on the use of Spring Batch.

The following topics will be covered in this chapter:

- An introduction to Pipe-and-Filter concepts
- Boarding Pipe-and-Filter architectures
- Use cases for Pipe-and-Filter architecture
- Spring Batch
- Implementing pipes with Spring Batch

We'll start by providing an introduction to Pipe-and-Filter architecture and the concepts associated with it.

Introducing Pipe-and-Filter concepts

Pipe-and-Filter architecture refers to a style of architecture that was introduced in the early 1970s. In this section, we will introduce Pipe-and-Filter architecture, along with concepts such as filters and pipes.

Doug McIlroy introduced Pipe-and-Filter architecture in Unix in 1972. The implementations are also known as pipelines, and they consist of a chain of processing elements, arranged so that the output of each element is the input of the next one, as illustrated in the following diagram:

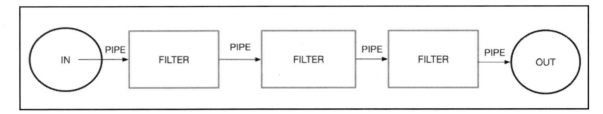

As shown in the preceding diagram, Pipe-and-Filter architecture consists of several components, named filters, that can transform (or filter) data across the process. The data is then passed to other components (filters) via pipes that are connected to each component.

Filters

Filters are components that serve to transform (or filter) data that is received as an input from a previous component via pipes (connectors). Each filter has an input pipe and an output pipe, as shown in the following diagram:

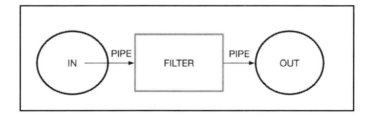

Another characteristic of this concept is that the filter can have several input pipes and several output pipes, as shown in the following diagram:

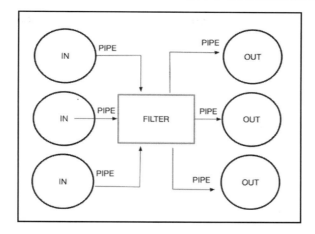

Pipes

Pipes are the connectors for filters. The role of a pipe is to pass messages, or information, between filters and components. What we must keep in mind is that the flow is unidirectional, and the data should be stored until the filter can process it. This is shown in the following image, where the connector can be seen between the filters:

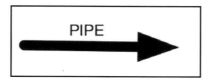

 The Pipe-and-Filter architectural style is used to divide a larger process, task, or data into a sequence of small and independent steps (or filters) that are connected by pipes.

Boarding Pipe-and-Filter architectures

Based on the concepts that we recently introduced about Pipe-and-Filter in the field of enterprise applications, we use this kind of architecture in several scenarios in order to process a large amount of data (or large files) that trigger several steps (or tasks) that need to be processed. This architecture is highly beneficial when we need to perform a lot of transformations in the data.

To understand how Pipe-and-Filter works, we are going to review a classic example of processing payroll records. In this example, a message is being sent through a sequence of filters, where each filter processes the message in different transactions.

When we apply a Pipe-and-Filter approach, we decompose the whole process into a series of separate tasks that can be reused. Using these tasks, we can change the format of the received message, and then we can split it to execute separate transactions. As a benefit of doing this, we improve the performance, scalability, and reusability of the process.

This architectural style makes it possible to create a recursive process. In this case, a filter can be contained by itself. Inside of the process, we can include another Pipe-and-Filter sequence, as illustrated in the following diagram:

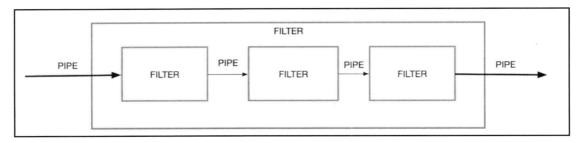

In this case, every filter receives an input message via a pipe. The filter then processes the message and publishes the result to the next pipe. This repeatable process continues as many times as we need it to. We can add filters, accept or omit the received input, and reorder or rearrange the tasks into a new sequence, based on our business requirements. In the following section, we will detail the most common use cases for applying a Pipe-and-Filter architectural style.

Use cases for Pipe-and-Filter architecture

The most common use cases for Pipe-and-Filter architecture are as follows:

- To break a large process into several small and independent steps (filters)
- To scale systems with processes that can be scaled independently with parallel processing, via several filters
- To transform input or messages received
- To apply filtering in **Enterprise Service Bus** (**ESB**) components as an integration pattern

Spring Batch

Spring Batch is a complete framework for creating a robust batch application (`https://projects.spring.io/spring-batch/`). We can create reusable functions to process large volumes of data or tasks, commonly known as bulk processing.

Spring Batch provides many useful features, such as the following:

- Logging and tracing
- Transaction management
- Job statistics
- Managing the process; for example, through restarting jobs, skipping steps, and resource management
- Administration Web Console

This framework is designed to manage a high volume of data and achieve high-performance batch processes by using partition features. We will start with a simple project, to explain each principal component of Spring Batch.

As mentioned in the Spring Batch documentation (`https://docs.spring.io/spring-batch/trunk/reference/html/spring-batch-intro.html`), the most common scenarios for using the framework are as follows:

- Committing batch processes periodically
- Concurrent batch processing for parallel processing a job
- Staged, enterprise message-driven processing
- Large parallel batch processing
- Manual or scheduled restart after failures
- Sequential processing of dependent steps (with extensions to workflow-driven batches)
- Partial processing: Skip records (for example, on rollback)
- Whole-batch transaction: For cases with a small batch size or existing stored procedures/scripts

In enterprise applications, the need to process millions of records (data) or read from a source is very common. This source may contain large files with several records (such as CSV or TXT files) or database tables. On each of these records, it is common to apply some business logic, execute validations or transformations, and finish the task, writing the result to another output format (for example, the database or file).

Spring Batch provides a complete framework to implement this kind of requirement, minimizing human interaction.

We are going to review the basic concepts of Spring batch, as follows:

- A job encapsulates the batch process, and must consist of one or more steps. Each step can run in sequence, run in parallel, or be partitioned.
- A step is the sequential phase of a job.
- JobLauncher is in charge of taking a JobExecution of a job that is running.
- JobRepository is the metadata repository of the JobExecution.

Let's create a simple example of a job using Spring Batch, in order to understand how it works. First, we will create a simple Java project and include the `spring-batch` dependency. For this, we will create a Spring Boot application using its initializer (`https://start.spring.io`), as shown in the following screenshot:

Note that we added the dependency for Spring Batch. You can do this by typing `Spring Batch` into the search bar within the dependencies box, and clicking *Enter*. A green box with the word **Batch** in it will appear on the selected dependencies section. When this has been done, we will click on the **Generate Project** button.

The structure of the project will be as follows:

```
→ simple-batch git:(master) × tree
.
├── mvnw
├── mvnw.cmd
├── pom.xml
└── src
    ├── main
    │   ├── java
    │   │   └── com
    │   │       └── packpub
    │   │           └── simplebatch
    │   │               └── SimpleBatchApplication.java
    │   └── resources
    │       └── application.properties
    └── test
        └── java
            └── com
                └── packpub
                    └── simplebatch
                        └── SimpleBatchApplicationTests.java
```

If we look at the dependencies section that was added by the initializer, we will see the spring-batch starter on the pom.xml file, as follows:

```xml
<dependency>
    <groupId>org.springframework.boot</groupId>
    <artifactId>spring-boot-starter-batch</artifactId>
</dependency>
<dependency>
    <groupId>org.springframework.boot</groupId>
    <artifactId>spring-boot-starter-test</artifactId>
    <scope>test</scope>
</dependency>
<dependency>
    <groupId>org.springframework.batch</groupId>
    <artifactId>spring-batch-test</artifactId>
    <scope>test</scope>
</dependency>
```

If we are not using Spring Boot, we can add `spring-batch-core` explicitly, as a project dependency. The following shows how it looks using Maven:

```
<dependencies>
  <dependency>
    <groupId>org.springframework.batch</groupId>
    <artifactId>spring-batch-core</artifactId>
    <version>4.0.1.RELEASE</version>
  </dependency>
</dependencies>
```

Alternatively, we can do this using Gradle, as follows:

```
dependencies
{
  compile 'org.springframework.batch:spring-batch-core:4.0.1.RELEASE'
}
```

The project will need a data source; if we try to run the application without one, we will get a message in the console showing an error, as follows:

```
***************************
APPLICATION FAILED TO START
***************************

Description:

Failed to auto-configure a DataSource: 'spring.datasource.url' is not specified and no embedded datasource could be auto-configured.

Reason: Failed to determine a suitable driver class


Action:

Consider the following:
        If you want an embedded database (H2, HSQL or Derby), please put it on the classpath.
        If you have database settings to be loaded from a particular profile you may need to activate it (no profiles are currently active).
```

To fix this issue, we are going to add a dependency as a part of the pom.xml file, to configure an embedded data source. For testing purposes, we are going to use HSQL (http://hsqldb.org/), as follows:

```
<dependency>
    <groupId>org.hsqldb</groupId>
    <artifactId>hsqldb</artifactId>
    <scope>runtime</scope>
</dependency>
```

Now, we need to add the @EnabledBatchProcessing and @Configuration annotations to the application:

```
@SpringBootApplication
@EnableBatchProcessing
@Configuration
public class SimpleBatchApplication {
```

Next, we will set up our first job by using the JobBuildFactory class with one task process, based on Spring Batch, using the StepBuilderFactory class:

```
@Autowired
private JobBuilderFactory jobBuilderFactory;

@Autowired
private StepBuilderFactory stepBuilderFactory;
```

The Job method will then show that it is starting, which will look as follows:

```
@Bean
public Job job(Step ourBatchStep) throws Exception {
    return jobBuilderFactory.get("jobPackPub1")
            .incrementer(new RunIdIncrementer())
            .start(ourBatchStep)
            .build();
}
```

Once the Job has been created, we will add a new task (Step) to the Job, as follows:

```
@Bean
public Step ourBatchStep() {
    return stepBuilderFactory.get("stepPackPub1")
            .tasklet(new Tasklet() {
                public RepeatStatus execute(StepContribution contribution,
                ChunkContext chunkContext) {
                    return null;
```

```
            }
        })
        .build();
    }
```

The following code shows what the application class looks like:

```
@EnableBatchProcessing
@SpringBootApplication
@Configuration
public class SimpleBatchApplication {

    public static void main(String[] args) {
        SpringApplication.run(SimpleBatchApplication.class, args);
    }

    @Autowired
    private JobBuilderFactory jobBuilderFactory;

    @Autowired
    private StepBuilderFactory stepBuilderFactory;

    @Bean
    public Step ourBatchStep() {
        return stepBuilderFactory.get("stepPackPub1")
            .tasklet(new Tasklet() {
                public RepeatStatus execute
                    (StepContribution contribution,
                        ChunkContext chunkContext) {
                    return null;
                }
            })
            .build();
    }

    @Bean
    public Job job(Step ourBatchStep) throws Exception {
        return jobBuilderFactory.get("jobPackPub1")
            .incrementer(new RunIdIncrementer())
            .start(ourBatchStep)
            .build();
    }
}
```

In order to check that everything is okay, we will run the application. To do this, we will execute the following on the command line:

```
$ mvn spring-boot:run
```

Alternatively, we could build the application by running maven, as follows:

```
$ mvn install
```

Next, we will run our recently built jar on the Terminal, as follows:

```
$ java -jar target/simple-batch-0.0.1-SNAPSHOT.jar
```

Don't forget that you will need to have installed Maven or Gradle before building or running the application and JDK 8.

Finally, we will see the following output in the console:

Pay attention to the console output. To do this, we run the job named `jobPackPub1` and execute the bean as `stepPackPub1`.

Now, we will look at the components behind the following steps in more detail:

- **ItemReader** represents the retrieval of the input for a step
- **ItemProcessor** represents the business processing of an item
- **ItemWriter** represents the output of a step

The following diagram shows the big picture of Spring Batch's main elements:

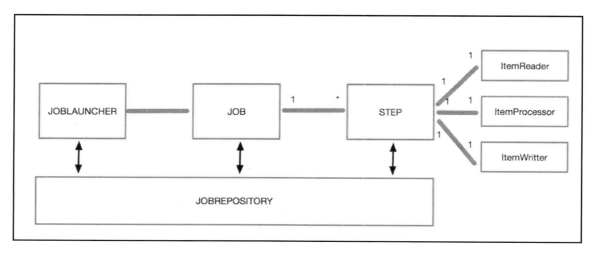

Now, we will complete our example by using an **ItemReader**, **ItemProcessor**, and an **ItemWriter.** By using and explaining these components, we will show you how Pipe-and-Filter architectures can be implemented using Spring Batch.

Implementing pipes with Spring Batch

Now that we have illustrated what Spring Batch is, we are going to implement the payroll file processing use case (as defined in the previous section) through the following steps:

- Coding a process that imports payroll data from a CSV spreadsheet
- Transforming the file tuples with a business class
- Storing the results in a database

The following diagram illustrates our implementation:

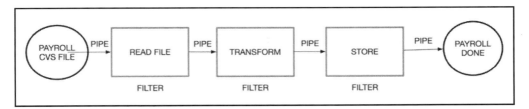

First, we are going to create a new, clean project, using the Spring initializer (`https://start.spring.io`), as we did in the previous section:

 Remember to add the `Batch` reference to our project, like we did in the previous example.

Don't forget to add a database driver as a dependency in the `pom.xml` file. For testing purposes, we are going to use HSQL (`http://hsqldb.org/`), as follows:

```
<dependency>
    <groupId>org.hsqldb</groupId>
    <artifactId>hsqldb</artifactId>
    <scope>runtime</scope>
</dependency>
```

If you want to use another database, you can refer to the detailed explanation available in the Spring Boot documentation (`https://docs.spring.io/spring-boot/docs/current/reference/html/boot-features-sql.html`).

Now, we will create input data as a file and the output structure as a database table, as you can see in the following diagram:

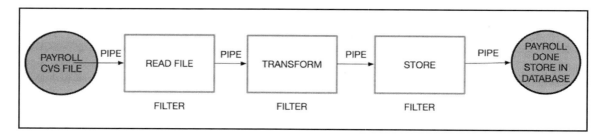

We are going to add a CSV file to our resource folder (`src/main/resources/payroll-data.csv`), with the following content:

```
0401343844,USD,1582.66,SAVING,3550891500,PAYROLL MARCH 2018,JAIME PRADO
1713430133,USD,941.21,SAVING,2200993002,PAYROLL MARCH 2018,CAROLINA SARANGO
1104447619,USD,725.20,SAVING,2203128508,PAYROLL MARCH 2018,MADALAINE
RODRIGUEZ
0805676117,USD,433.79,SAVING,5464013600,PAYROLL MARCH 2018,BELEN CALERO
1717654933,USD,1269.10,SAVING,5497217100,PAYROLL MARCH 2018,MARIA VALVERDE
1102362626,USD,1087.80,SAVING,2200376305,PAYROLL MARCH 2018,VANESSA ARMIJOS
1718735793,USD,906.50,SAVING,6048977500,PAYROLL MARCH 2018,IGNACIO
BERRAZUETA
1345644970,USD,494.90,SAVING,6099018000,PAYROLL MARCH 2018,ALBERTO SALAZAR
0604444602,USD,1676.40,SAVING,5524707700,PAYROLL MARCH 2018,XIMENA JARA
1577777593,USD,3229.75,SAVING,3033235300,PAYROLL MARCH 2018,HYUN WOO
1777705472,USD,2061.27,SAVING,3125662300,PAYROLL MARCH 2018,CARLOS QUIROLA
1999353121,USD,906.50,SAVING,2203118265,PAYROLL MARCH 2018,PAUL VARELA
1878363820,USD,1838.30,SAVING,4837838200,PAYROLL MARCH 2018,LEONARDO
VASQUEZ
```

The structure of our project will look as follows:

```
→  payroll-process git:(master) × tree
.
├── mvnw
├── mvnw.cmd
├── payroll-process.iml
├── pom.xml
└── src
    ├── main
    │   ├── java
    │   │   └── com
    │   │       └── packpub
    │   │           └── payrollprocess
    │   │               └── PayrollProcessApplication.java
    │   └── resources
    │       ├── application.properties
    │       └── payroll-data.csv
    └── test
        └── java
            └── com
                └── packpub
                    └── payrollprocess
                        └── PayrollProcessApplicationTests.java

12 directories, 8 files
```

 This spreadsheet contains the identification, currency, account number, account type, description of the transaction, beneficiary telephone, and beneficiary name. These are displayed on each row, separated by commas. This is a common pattern, which Spring handles out of the box.

We will now create the database structure where we will store the results processed by the payroll. We will add this to our resource folder (`src/main/resources/schema-all.sql`) with the following content:

```
DROP TABLE PAYROLL IF EXISTS;

CREATE TABLE PAYROLL  (
    transaction_id BIGINT IDENTITY NOT NULL PRIMARY KEY,
    person_identification VARCHAR(20),
    currency VARCHAR(20),
    tx_ammount DOUBLE,
    account_type VARCHAR(20),
```

```
    account_id VARCHAR(20),
    tx_description VARCHAR(20),
    first_last_name VARCHAR(20)
);
```

 The file that we will create will follow this pattern name: `schema-@@platform@@.sql`. Spring Boot will run the SQL script during startup; this is the default behavior for all platforms.

Up until this point, we have created the input data as a `.csv` file, as well as the output repository where it is going to store our complete payroll process. Consequently, we are now going to create the filters and use the default pipes that bring us Spring Batch.

First, we are going to create a class that represents our business data, with all of the fields that we are going to receive. We will name this `PayRollTo.java` (**Payroll Transfer Object**):

```java
package com.packpub.payrollprocess;

public class PayrollTo {

    private Integer identification;

    private String currency;

    private Double ammount;

    private String accountType;

    private String accountNumber;

    private String description;

    private String firstLastName;

    public PayrollTo() {
    }

    public PayrollTo(Integer identification, String currency, Double
ammount, String accountType, String accountNumber, String description,
String firstLastName) {
        this.identification = identification;
        this.currency = currency;
        this.ammount = ammount;
        this.accountType = accountType;
        this.accountNumber = accountNumber;
```

```
        this.description = description;
        this.firstLastName = firstLastName;
    }

    // getters and setters

    @Override
    public String toString() {
        return "PayrollTo{" +
                "identification=" + identification +
                ", currency='" + currency + '\'' +
                ", ammount=" + ammount +
                ", accountType='" + accountType + '\'' +
                ", accountNumber='" + accountNumber + '\'' +
                ", description='" + description + '\'' +
                ", firstLastName='" + firstLastName + '\'' +
                '}';
    }
}
```

Now, we will create our filters, which are represented as processors in Spring Batch. Similar to how the framework gives us out-of-the-box behavior, we are first going to concentrate on translating our business classes that are intended to transform the input data, as shown in the following diagram:

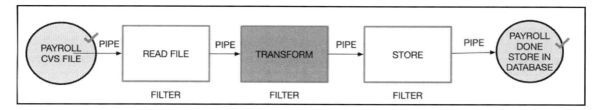

After including a representation of our file as a `PayrollTo` class on each row, we are going to need a filter that will transform each of our data files into uppercase. Using Spring Batch, we will create a processor that will transform the data files and then send the data to the following step. So, let's create a `PayRollItemProcessor.java` object that implements the `org.springframework.batch.item.ItemProcessor<InputObject, OutputObjet>` interface, as follows:

```
package com.packpub.payrollprocess;

import org.slf4j.Logger;
import org.slf4j.LoggerFactory;
import org.springframework.batch.item.ItemProcessor;
```

```
public class PayRollItemProcessor implements
                    ItemProcessor<PayrollTo, PayrollTo> {

    private static final Logger log = LoggerFactory
                    .getLogger(PayRollItemProcessor.class);

    @Override
    public PayrollTo process(PayrollTo payrollTo) throws Exception {

        final PayrollTo resultTransformation = new PayrollTo();
        resultTransformation.setFirstLastName
            (payrollTo.getFirstLastName().toUpperCase());
        resultTransformation.setDescription
            (payrollTo.getDescription().toUpperCase());
        resultTransformation.setAccountNumber
            (payrollTo.getAccountNumber());
        resultTransformation.setAccountType(payrollTo.getAccountType());
        resultTransformation.setCurrency(payrollTo.getCurrency());
        resultTransformation.setIdentification
            (payrollTo.getIdentification());

        // Data Type Transform
        final double ammountAsNumber = payrollTo.getAmmount()
                                            .doubleValue();
        resultTransformation.setAmmount(ammountAsNumber);

        log.info
            ("Transforming (" + payrollTo + ") into ("
                        + resultTransformation + ")");
        return resultTransformation;
    }
}
```

According to the API interface, we will receive an incoming `PayrollTo` object, after which we will transform it to an uppercase `PayrollTo` for the `firstLastName` and description properties.

It does not matter if the input object and the output object are different types. In many cases, a filter will receive one kind of message or data that needs a different kind of message or data for the next filter.

Now, we are going to create our Batch job and use some Spring Batch out-of-the-box features. For example, the **ItemReader** has a useful API to process files, and the **ItemWriter** can be used to specify how to store the produced data:

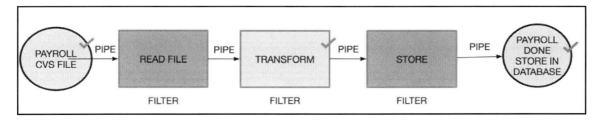

Finally, we are going to connect all of our flow data using a job.

Using Spring Batch, we need to concentrate on our business (like we did in the `PayRollItemProcessor.java` class), and then connect all of the pieces together, as follows:

```
@Configuration
@EnableBatchProcessing
public class BatchConfig {

    @Autowired
    public JobBuilderFactory jobBuilderFactory;

    @Autowired
    public StepBuilderFactory stepBuilderFactory;

    // READ THE INPUT DATA
    @Bean
    public FlatFileItemReader<PayrollTo> reader() {
        return new FlatFileItemReaderBuilder<PayrollTo>()
                .name("payrollItemReader")
                .resource(new ClassPathResource("payroll-data.csv"))
                .delimited()
                .names(
                    new String[]{
                        "identification", "currency", "ammount",
                        "accountType", "accountNumber", "description",
                        "firstLastName"})
                .fieldSetMapper(
                    new BeanWrapperFieldSetMapper<PayrollTo>() {{
                    setTargetType(PayrollTo.class);
                }})
                .build();
    }
```

```java
// PROCESS THE DATA
@Bean
public PayRollItemProcessor processor() {
    return new PayRollItemProcessor();
}

// WRITE THE PRODUCED DATA
@Bean
public JdbcBatchItemWriter<PayrollTo> writer(DataSource dataSource) {
    return new JdbcBatchItemWriterBuilder<PayrollTo>()
            .itemSqlParameterSourceProvider(
                new BeanPropertyItemSqlParameterSourceProvider<>())
            .sql(
                "INSERT INTO PAYROLL (PERSON_IDENTIFICATION,
                    CURRENCY, TX_AMMOUNT, ACCOUNT_TYPE, ACCOUNT_ID,
                    TX_DESCRIPTION, FIRST_LAST_NAME) VALUES
                    (:identification, :currenxcy, :ammount, :accountType,
                     :accountNumber, :description, :firstLastName)")
            .dataSource(dataSource)
            .build();
}

@Bean
public Job importPayRollJob(JobCompletionPayRollListener listener, Step
step1) {
    return jobBuilderFactory.get("importPayRollJob")
            .incrementer(new RunIdIncrementer())
            .listener(listener)
            .flow(step1)
            .end()
            .build();
}

@Bean
public Step step1(JdbcBatchItemWriter<PayrollTo> writer) {
    return stepBuilderFactory.get("step1")
            .<PayrollTo, PayrollTo> chunk(10)
            .reader(reader())
            .processor(processor())
            .writer(writer)
            .build();
}
}
```

 For a detailed explanation of what you can do with Spring
Batch ItemReaders and ItemWriters, go to https://docs.spring.io/
spring-batch/trunk/reference/html/readersAndWriters.html.

Let's review how the `Step` bean works, as follows:

```
@Bean
    public Step step1(JdbcBatchItemWriter<PayrollTo> writer)
    {
            return stepBuilderFactory.get("step1")
                    .<PayrollTo, PayrollTo> chunk(10)
                    .reader(reader())
                    .processor(processor())
                    .writer(writer)
                    .build();
    }
```

First, it configures the step to read the data in chunks of **10 records**, and after that, the step is configured with the corresponding `reader`, `processor`, and `writer` objects.

We have now implemented all of the pipes and filters that we planned, as shown in the following diagram:

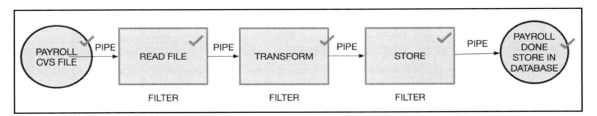

Finally, we are going to add a listener, in order to check our processed payroll data. To do this, we will create a `JobCompletionPayRollListener.java` class that extends the class `JobExecutionListenerSupport` and implement the `afterJob(JobExecution jobExecution)` method.

Now, we will review how many `insert` operations we process from our processed data:

```
@Component
public class JobCompletionPayRollListener
            extends JobExecutionListenerSupport {

    private static final Logger log =
        LoggerFactory.getLogger(JobCompletionPayRollListener.class);

    private final JdbcTemplate jdbcTemplate;

    @Autowired
    public JobCompletionPayRollListener(JdbcTemplate jdbcTemplate) {
        this.jdbcTemplate = jdbcTemplate;
```

```
        }

        @Override
        public void afterJob(JobExecution jobExecution) {
            if (jobExecution.getStatus() == BatchStatus.COMPLETED) {
                log.info(">>>>> PAY ROLL JOB FINISHED! ");

                jdbcTemplate
                .query(
                    "SELECT PERSON_IDENTIFICATION, CURRENCY, TX_AMMOUNT,
ACCOUNT_TYPE, ACCOUNT_ID, TX_DESCRIPTION,
                        FIRST_LAST_NAME FROM PAYROLL",
                    (rs, row) -> new PayrollTo(
                            rs.getInt(1),
                            rs.getString(2),
                            rs.getDouble(3),
                            rs.getString(4),
                            rs.getString(5),
                            rs.getString(6),
                            rs.getString(7))
                ).forEach(payroll ->
                    log.info("Found <" + payroll + "> in the database.")
                    );
            }
        }
    }
```

In order to check that everything is okay, we are going to execute the application, using the following command:

```
$ mvn spring-boot:run
```

Alternatively, we could build the application using maven, as follows:

```
$ mvn install
```

Next, we will run the recently built `jar` on the Terminal:

```
$ java -jar target/payroll-process-0.0.1-SNAPSHOT.jar
```

Finally, we will see the following output on our console. This output represents the filter that has been implemented as an ItemProcessor that transforms the data:

```
2018-05-16 12:08:08.511 INFO 44741 --- [           main] c.p.payrollprocess.PayRollItemProcessor  : Transforming (PayrollTo{identification=401343844, currency='USD', amount=1582.66, accountType='SAVING', accountNumber='3550891500', description='Payroll march 2018', firstLastName='John Smith'}) into (PayrollTo{identification=401343844, currency='USD', amount=1582.66, accountType='SAVING', accountNumber='3550891500', description='PAYROLL MARCH 2018', firstLastName='JOHN SMITH'})
2018-05-16 12:08:08.511 INFO 44741 --- [           main] c.p.payrollprocess.PayRollItemProcessor  : Transforming (PayrollTo{identification=1713430133, currency='USD', amount=941.21, accountType='SAVING', accountNumber='2200993002', description='Payroll march 2018', firstLastName='Caro Madame'}) into (PayrollTo{identification=1713430133, currency='USD', amount=941.21, accountType='SAVING', accountNumber='2200993002', description='PAYROLL MARCH 2018', firstLastName='CARO MADAME'})
2018-05-16 12:08:08.511 INFO 44741 --- [           main] c.p.payrollprocess.PayRollItemProcessor  : Transforming (PayrollTo{identification=1104447619, currency='USD', amount=725.2, accountType='SAVING', accountNumber='2203128508', description='Payroll march 2018', firstLastName='Madalaine Rodrigues'}) into (PayrollTo{identification=1104447619, currency='USD', amount=725.2, accountType='SAVING', accountNumber='2203128508', description='PAYROLL MARCH 2018', firstLastName='MADALAINE RODRIGUES'})
2018-05-16 12:08:08.511 INFO 44741 --- [           main] c.p.payrollprocess.PayRollItemProcessor  : Transforming (PayrollTo{identification=805676117, currency='USD', amount=433.79, accountType='SAVING', accountNumber='5464013600', description='Payroll march 2018', firstLastName='Belen Salas'}) into (PayrollTo{identification=805676117, currency='USD', amount=433.79, accountType='SAVING', accountNumber='5464013600', description='PAYROLL MARCH 2018', firstLastName='BELEN SALAS'})
2018-05-16 12:08:08.511 INFO 44741 --- [           main] c.p.payrollprocess.PayRollItemProcessor  : Transforming (PayrollTo{identification=1717654933, currency='USD', amount=1269.1, accountType='SAVING', accountNumber='5497217100', description='Payroll march 2018', firstLastName='Mariah Carrey'}) into (PayrollTo{identification=1717654933, currency='USD', amount=1269.1, accountType='SAVING', accountNumber='5497217100', description='PAYROLL MARCH 2018', firstLastName='MARIAH CARREY'})
2018-05-16 12:08:08.512 INFO 44741 --- [           main] c.p.payrollprocess.PayRollItemProcessor  : Transforming (PayrollTo{identification=1102362626, currency='USD', amount=1087.8, accountType='SAVING', accountNumber='2200376305', description='Payroll march 2018', firstLastName='Alicia Silverston'}) into (PayrollTo{identification=1102362626, currency='USD', amount=1087.8, accountType='SAVING', accountNumber='2200376305', description='PAYROLL MARCH 2018', firstLastName='ALICIA SILVERSTON'})
2018-05-16 12:08:08.512 INFO 44741 --- [           main] c.p.payrollprocess.PayRollItemProcessor  : Transforming (PayrollTo{identification=1718735793, currency='USD', amount=906.5, accountType='SAVING', accountNumber='6048977500', description='Payroll march 2018', firstLastName='Shakira Vizuete'}) into (PayrollTo{identification=1718735793, currency='USD', amount=906.5, accountType='SAVING', accountNumber='6048977500', description='PAYROLL MARCH 2018', firstLastName='SHAKIRA VIZUETE'})
2018-05-16 12:08:08.512 INFO 44741 --- [           main] c.p.payrollprocess.PayRollItemProcessor  : Transforming (PayrollTo{identification=1345644970, currency='USD', amount=494.9, accountType='SAVING', accountNumber='6099018000', description='Payroll march 2018', firstLastName='Alberto Salazar'}) into (PayrollTo{identification=1345644970, currency='USD', amount=494.9, accountType='SAVING', accountNumber='6099018000', description='PAYROLL MARCH 2018', firstLastName='ALBERTO SALAZAR'})
2018-05-16 12:08:08.512 INFO 44741 --- [           main] c.p.payrollprocess.PayRollItemProcessor  : Transforming (PayrollTo{identification=604444602, currency='USD', amount=1676.4, accountType='SAVING', accountNumber='5524707700', description='Payroll march 2018', firstLastName='Charles Darwin'}) into (PayrollTo{identification=604444602, currency='USD', amount=1676.4, accountType='SAVING', accountNumber='5524707700', description='PAYROLL MARCH 2018', firstLastName='CHARLES DARWIN'})
2018-05-16 12:08:08.512 INFO 44741 --- [           main] c.p.payrollprocess.PayRollItemProcessor  : Transforming (PayrollTo{identification=1577777593, currency='USD', amount=3229.75, accountType='SAVING', accountNumber='3033235300', description='Payroll march 2018', firstLastName='Rene Enriquez'}) into (PayrollTo{identification=1577777593, currency='USD', amount=3229.75, accountType='SAVING', accountNumber='3033235300', description='PAYROLL MARCH 2018', firstLastName='RENE ENRIQUEZ'})
2018-05-16 12:08:08.524 INFO 44741 --- [           main] c.p.payrollprocess.PayRollItemProcessor  : Transforming (PayrollTo{identification=1777705472, currency='USD', amount=2061.27, accountType='SAVING', accountNumber='3125662300', description='Payroll march 2018', firstLastName='Packpub Books'}) into (PayrollTo{identification=1777705472, currency='USD', amount=2061.27, accountType='SAVING', accountNumber='3125662300', description='PAYROLL MARCH 2018', firstLastName='PACKPUB BOOKS'})
2018-05-16 12:08:08.524 INFO 44741 --- [           main] c.p.payrollprocess.PayRollItemProcessor  : Transforming (PayrollTo{identification=1999353121, currency='USD', amount=906.5, accountType='SAVING', accountNumber='2203118265', description='Payroll march 2018', firstLastName='Paul Sam'}) into (PayrollTo{identification=1999353121, currency='USD', amount=906.5, accountType='SAVING', accountNumber='2203118265', description='PAYROLL MARCH 2018', firstLastName='PAUL SAM'})
```

We can also see the verification of our process via the listener, implemented as a `JobExecutionListenerSupport`, which prints the results stored in the database:

```
2018-05-16 12:08:08.524 INFO 44741 --- [           main] c.p.payrollprocess.PayRollItemProcessor  : Transforming (PayrollTo{identification=1878363820, currency='USD', amount=1838.3, accountType='SAVING', accountNumber='4837838200', description='Payroll march 2018', firstLastName='Luke SkyW'}) into (PayrollTo{identification=1878363820, currency='USD', amount=1838.3, accountType='SAVING', accountNumber='4837838200', description='PAYROLL MARCH 2018', firstLastName='LUKE SKYW'})
2018-05-16 12:08:08.533 INFO 44741 --- [           main] c.p.p.JobCompletionPayRollListener       : >>>>> PAY ROLL JOB FINISHED!
2018-05-16 12:08:08.537 INFO 44741 --- [           main] c.p.p.JobCompletionPayRollListener       : Found <PayrollTo{identification=401343844, currency='USD', amount=1582.66, accountType='SAVING', accountNumber='3550891500', description='PAYROLL MARCH 2018', firstLastName='JOHN SMITH'}> in the database.
2018-05-16 12:08:08.537 INFO 44741 --- [           main] c.p.p.JobCompletionPayRollListener       : Found <PayrollTo{identification=1713430133, currency='USD', amount=941.21, accountType='SAVING', accountNumber='2200993002', description='PAYROLL MARCH 2018', firstLastName='CARO MADAME'}> in the database.
2018-05-16 12:08:08.538 INFO 44741 --- [           main] c.p.p.JobCompletionPayRollListener       : Found <PayrollTo{identification=1104447619, currency='USD', amount=725.2, accountType='SAVING', accountNumber='2203128508', description='PAYROLL MARCH 2018', firstLastName='MADALAINE RODRIGUES'}> in the database.
2018-05-16 12:08:08.539 INFO 44741 --- [           main] c.p.p.JobCompletionPayRollListener       : Found <PayrollTo{identification=805676117, currency='USD', amount=433.79, accountType='SAVING', accountNumber='5464013600', description='PAYROLL MARCH 2018', firstLastName='BELEN SALAS'}> in the database.
2018-05-16 12:08:08.542 INFO 44741 --- [           main] c.p.p.JobCompletionPayRollListener       : Found <PayrollTo{identification=1717654933, currency='USD', amount=1269.1, accountType='SAVING', accountNumber='5497217100', description='PAYROLL MARCH 2018', firstLastName='MARIAH CARREY'}> in the database.
2018-05-16 12:08:08.542 INFO 44741 --- [           main] c.p.p.JobCompletionPayRollListener       : Found <PayrollTo{identification=1102362626, currency='USD', amount=1087.8, accountType='SAVING', accountNumber='2200376305', description='PAYROLL MARCH 2018', firstLastName='ALICIA SILVERSTON'}> in the database.
2018-05-16 12:08:08.542 INFO 44741 --- [           main] c.p.p.JobCompletionPayRollListener       : Found <PayrollTo{identification=1718735793, currency='USD', amount=906.5, accountType='SAVING', accountNumber='6048977500', description='PAYROLL MARCH 2018', firstLastName='SHAKIRA VIZUETE'}> in the database.
2018-05-16 12:08:08.543 INFO 44741 --- [           main] c.p.p.JobCompletionPayRollListener       : Found <PayrollTo{identification=1345644970, currency='USD', amount=494.9, accountType='SAVING', accountNumber='6099018000', description='PAYROLL MARCH 2018', firstLastName='ALBERTO SALAZAR'}> in the database.
2018-05-16 12:08:08.543 INFO 44741 --- [           main] c.p.p.JobCompletionPayRollListener       : Found <PayrollTo{identification=604444602, currency='USD', amount=1676.4, accountType='SAVING', accountNumber='5524707700', description='PAYROLL MARCH 2018', firstLastName='CHARLES DARWIN'}> in the database.
2018-05-16 12:08:08.543 INFO 44741 --- [           main] c.p.p.JobCompletionPayRollListener       : Found <PayrollTo{identification=1577777593, currency='USD', amount=3229.75, accountType='SAVING', accountNumber='3033235300', description='PAYROLL MARCH 2018', firstLastName='RENE ENRIQUEZ'}> in the database.
2018-05-16 12:08:08.543 INFO 44741 --- [           main] c.p.p.JobCompletionPayRollListener       : Found <PayrollTo{identification=1777705472, currency='USD', amount=2061.27, accountType='SAVING', accountNumber='3125662300', description='PAYROLL MARCH 2018', firstLastName='PACKPUB BOOKS'}> in the database.
2018-05-16 12:08:08.543 INFO 44741 --- [           main] c.p.p.JobCompletionPayRollListener       : Found <PayrollTo{identification=1999353121, currency='USD', amount=906.5, accountType='SAVING', accountNumber='2203118265', description='PAYROLL MARCH 2018', firstLastName='PAUL SAM'}> in the database.
2018-05-16 12:08:08.543 INFO 44741 --- [           main] c.p.p.JobCompletionPayRollListener       : Found <PayrollTo{identification=1878363820, currency='USD', amount=1838.3, accountType='SAVING', accountNumber='4837838200', description='PAYROLL MARCH 2018', firstLastName='LUKE SKYW'}> in the database.
2018-05-16 12:08:08.551 INFO 44741 --- [           main] o.s.b.c.l.support.SimpleJobLauncher      : Job: [FlowJob: [name=importPayRollJob]] completed with the following parameters: [{run.id=1}] and the following status: [COMPLETED]
```

We can package the Spring Batch application in a WAR file, and then run a servlet container (like Tomcat) or any JEE application server (like Glassfish or JBoss). To package the `.jar` file into a WAR file, use `spring-boot-gradle-plugin` or `spring-boot-maven-plugin`. For Maven, you can refer to the Spring Boot documentation (`https://docs.spring.io/spring-boot/docs/current/reference/htmlsingle/#build-tool-plugins-maven-packaging`). For Gradle, you can refer to `https://docs.spring.io/spring-boot/docs/current/gradle-plugin/reference/html/#packaging-executable-wars`.

Summary

In this chapter, we discussed the concept of Pipe-and-Filter architecture, the principal use cases of its implementation, and how to use it with enterprise applications. In addition, you learned how to implement the architecture using Spring Batch, along with how to manage different amounts of data and split the process into smaller tasks.

In the next chapter, we will review the importance of containerizing your applications.

8
Microservices

We are constantly looking for new ways to create software systems that cater for both happy customers who have applications that support their business needs and developers who are challenged by cutting-edge technologies. The balance of satisfying these two types of target user is important; it allows us to achieve our business goals and avoid losing skilled developers.

On the other hand, as developers, we are also trying to create modules and specialized libraries that address specific technical or business needs. Later, we will reuse these modules and libraries across different projects to comply with the **don't repeat yourself (DRY)** principle.

Using this introduction as a point of departure, we are going to review how microservices architectures can address these concerns and more. In this chapter, we are going to look at the following topics:

- Principles of microservices
- Modeling microservices

    - How to implement microservices using Spring Cloud:
        - Supporting dynamic configuration
        - Enabling service discovery and registration
    - Edge services
    - The circuit breaker pattern and Hystrix

Principles of microservices

There are a lot of definitions of microservices that are available on the web. One that comes up frequently is the following:

"Microservices are small and autonomous services that work well together."

Let's start looking at this definition and what it means in a little more detail.

Size

The fact that the word microservices contains the word *micro* leads us to think that the service's size must be really small. However, it's almost impossible to define what the right size of the services should be using metrics such as how many lines of code or files there are, or the size of a particular deployable artifact. Instead, it's much simpler to use the following idea:

"A service should be focused on doing one thing well."

- Sam Newman

That *one thing* can be thought of as one business domain. If you're building systems for an online store, for example, they might cover the following **business domains**:

- Customer management
- Product catalog
- Shopping cart
- Orders

The idea is to build one service that is able to address all the demands of a particular business domain. Eventually, you might also end up breaking a service into other microservices when the business domain becomes too big to be handled as just one microservice.

Autonomous

Autonomy is really important when we are talking about microservices. A microservice should have the ability to change and evolve independently to the rest of the services around it.

The best way to verify whether a microservice is autonomous enough is by applying a change to it and deploying the new version of the service. The deployment process should not require you to modify anything other than the service itself. If you need to restart other services or anything else during the deployment process, you should consider ways of removing those additional steps. On the other hand, the autonomy of a service is also related to the organization of the team that is building it. We will discuss this in detail later on in this chapter.

Working well together

It is not possible to build systems in isolation that don't interact with one another. Even though we are building separate services to address the requirements of different business domains, we eventually need to make them interact as a whole in order to meet the demands of the business. This interaction is carried out by using **application programming interfaces** (**API**).

> *"An API is a set of commands, functions, protocols, and objects that programmers can use to create software or interact with an external system. It provides developers with standard commands for performing common operations so they do not have to write the code from scratch."*
>
> *- API definition from https://techterms.com/definition/api*

Monolithic applications tend to carry out database integration. This is something that should be avoided at all costs; any required interaction between services should only be done using the provided service APIs.

Advantages

Microservices offer many advantages that are worth knowing to understand how a company might benefit. The most common advantages are as follows:

- Alignment to the single responsibility principle
- Continuous releases
- Independent scalability
- Increased adoption of new technology

Alignment to the single responsibility principle

Using microservices involves creating separate components. Every component is designed to address a specific business domain model. Consequently, this domain model defines the service's single responsibility. The service should not violate its limits and it should request any information that falls outside of them using the provided APIs of other microservices. Each microservice should expose an API with all the required functionality to allow other microservices to obtain information from it.

Continuous releases

Since large, monolithic applications handle many business domain models, they are comprised of a huge amount of source code and configuration files. This produces large artifacts that take a considerable amount of time to be deployed. Furthermore, large monolithic applications often involve large teams that are distributed around the world, which makes communication difficult. This becomes a problem when working on new features or fixing bugs in the application. Microservices are able to tackle this problem easily because one team will be in charge of one or more services, and a service is rarely written by more than one team. This means that new releases can be planned within the team, which allows them to roll out new versions faster and more frequently.

Additionally, even the smallest change in the code involves a new deployment of the large artifact, which makes the entire application unavailable during the deployment process. For microservices, however, only the service that has the patch for the bug or the new feature should be deployed. The deployment is fast and doesn't affect other services.

Independent scalability

If we need to scale a monolithic application, the entire system should be deployed on different servers. The servers should be really powerful to allow the application to perform well. Not all of the features have the same traffic, but since all the code is bundled as a single artifact, there is no way to scale only the desired features. With microservices, we have the freedom to scale only what we need. It's common to find cloud providers offering the chance to scale an application by provisioning more servers on demand or adding more resources automatically when they are needed.

Increased adoption of new technologies

Not all business domain models are equals, which is why different sets of technologies are needed. Since one microservice should only address the demands of one domain model, different services can adopt different technologies easily. It's common to find companies using different programming languages, frameworks, cloud providers, and databases to code their microservices. Furthermore, we have the ability to experiment with new technologies for small applications, which can then be used elsewhere. As a consequence of embracing new technologies, companies end up with heterogeneous applications, as shown in the following diagram:

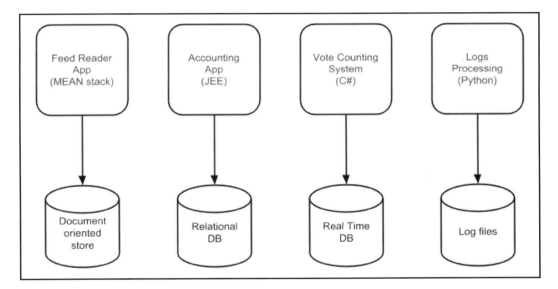

 Heterogeneous applications allow us to create specialized systems to solve specific business demands using the right set of technologies. As a result of this, we end up having small artifacts that are easy to deploy and scale in isolation.

Drawbacks

Even though microservices have all the benefits that we listed earlier, it's important to understand that they do have a few downsides as well. Let's review these and consider how they can be dealt with:

- Too many options
- Slow at the beginning
- Monitoring
- Transactions and eventual consistency

Too many options

Since you have the opportunity to choose which technology you want to build a microservice with, you might feel overwhelmed because of the wide variety of options available. This can be solved by using just a few new technologies instead of trying to fit them all in at once.

Slow at the beginning

When you're in the process of adopting microservices, you have to build the entire ecosystem in order to make them work. You need to look for new ways to connect the distributed systems, secure them, and make them work as a whole. Writing just one application to do all this is easier. However, after a few months, the other microservices will reuse all the work that you put in at the beginning, meaning the process speeds up significantly. To take full advantage of this way of creating systems, it is important to try out new ways of deploying applications, making them scale on demand, monitoring them, and logging them. It's also important to review the functionality of microservices that handle the core of the business. These systems sometimes end up being semi-monoliths that should be split up in order to make them easier to manage.

Monitoring

Monitoring a single application is easier than monitoring many instances of different services. It's important to create dashboards and automated tools that provide metrics in order to make this task easier to accomplish. When a new error occurs, it can be hard to figure out where the problem is. A good log-tracing mechanism should be used to identify which service of the application is not working as expected. This means that you don't have to analyze all the services.

Transactions and eventual consistency

While large monoliths have their transaction boundaries well-defined, and because we often use techniques such as two-phase commits when we are writing microservices, we have to approach these requirements in another way.

We should remember that each microservice is the owner of its own data storage, and we should access their data using only their APIs. It is important to keep your data up to date and use compensating transactions when an operation doesn't work as expected. When we write monolithic applications, many operations are executed as a single transaction. For microservices, we need to rethink the operations and transactions to make them fit within each microservice boundary.

Modeling microservices

As developers, we always try to create reusable components to interact with systems or services in order to avoid writing code more than once. Most monolithic applications that we have built so far have followed a three-tier architectural pattern, as shown in the following diagram:

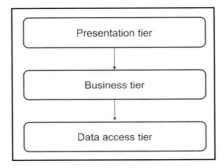

Three-tier architecture

When a change is required in an application that is built using this model, you often need to modify all three layers. Depending on how the application is created, you might need many deployments. Furthermore, since large monolithic applications share a lot of functionality, it's common to find more than one team working on them, which makes it even harder for them to evolve quickly. Sometimes, specialized teams work on particular layers because these layers are comprised of many components. In this way, changes are applied horizontally to make the application grow and evolve.

With microservices, applications evolve vertically because they are modeled around a specific business domain. The following diagram shows a few microservices for an online store application:

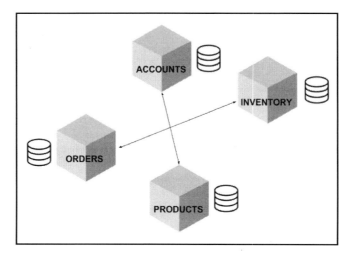

Microservices diagram

The names by themselves explain the intention and the collection of capabilities associated with the microservices. Just by reading the names, anyone can understand what they do; how the tasks are carried out and how they are implemented is irrelevant at this point. Since these services are built around a well-defined business domain, only one service should be modified when a new change is required. Since no more than one team should work on a microservice, making them evolve is easier in comparison to large monoliths. The team in charge of the service has a deep understanding of how that particular service works and how to make it evolve.

 The team in charge of a microservice is composed of experts in that service's business domain, but not in the technology of the other services around it. After all, technology choices consist of details; the principle motivation of the service is the business domain.

Speeding up

We mentioned earlier in this chapter that developing an application based on microservices is a time-consuming process at the beginning because you are literally starting from scratch. Whether you're starting a new project or splitting an existing legacy application into separate microservices, you have to work on all the necessary steps to bring an application from development to production.

Accelerating the development process

Let's start at the development stage. When you're working on old applications,
you usually have to go through the following steps before writing the first line of code:

1. Install the required tools in your local machine.
2. Set up all the required dependencies.
3. Create one or more configuration files.
4. Discover all the missing parts that were not listed as part of the documentation.
5. Load the test data.
6. Run the application.

Now, let's say you're working as part of a team that owns many microservices that are written in different programming languages and that use different database technologies. Can you imagine the effort required before writing your first line of code?

Using microservices is supposed to be able to provide you with faster solutions, but all the setup required makes it slower initially. For a large monolithic application, you only have to set up one environment, but for heterogeneous applications, you'll have to set up many different environments. In order to approach this problem effectively, you need to embrace a culture of automation. Instead of executing all the aforementioned steps manually, you can run a script to do that for you. In this way, every time you want to work on a different project, you only need to execute the script instead of repeating all the steps listed.

There are some really cool tools available on the market, such as Nanobox (`https://nanobox.io`), Docker Compose (`https://docs.docker.com/compose/`), and Vagrant (`https://www.vagrantup.com`). These can help you by providing an environment similar to the production environment by running a single command.

Adopting tools such as the ones mentioned in the preceding tip will have a great impact on the productivity of the development team. You don't want developers wasting their time by providing their own environments; instead, you want them writing code to add new features to your product.

Embracing tests

Let's talk about the code-writing process. When we are working on large monoliths, many people need to be notified every time that a new feature or bug fix is released. In extreme cases, the QA team needs to check the entire environment themselves to ensure that the new changes didn't affect the application's existing functionality. Imagine how time-consuming it would be to repeat this task for every release with multiple microservices. For this reason, you need to adopt testing as an essential part of your development process.

There are many different levels of testing. Let's take a look at the pyramid test introduced by Jason Huggins in 2005, which is shown in the following diagram:

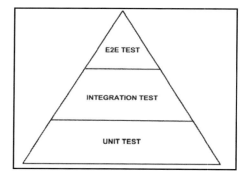

Pyramid test

The tests that are part of the pyramid's base are easy and quick to write and execute. Running unit tests only takes a few minutes, and is useful to validate that isolated pieces of code work as expected. Integration tests, on the other hand, are useful to validate that the code works when it's interacting with external services, such as databases, third-party applications, or other microservices. These tests will take a few tens of minutes to run. Finally, **end-to-end (e2e)** tests help you to validate that the code works as expected from an end user perspective. If you're writing a REST API, the e2e tests will validate the HTTP response codes from your API using different data. These tests are usually slow, and they change all the time.

Ideally, all of your new features should go through all of these tests to verify that your code is working as expected before going into production. The more tests you write, the more confidence you will gain. After all, if you've covered all the possible scenarios, what could go wrong? To add to this, Michael Bryzek introduced the idea of testing in production (see `https://www.infoq.com/podcasts/Michael-Bryzek-testing-in-production` for more information). This helps you to assess whether your services are working by executing automated tasks or bots regularly to exercise the key parts of your systems in production.

Going to production

You have to automate the production environment in the same way that you automate the development environment. Today, it is common to find companies using cloud providers to deploy their systems and API-driven tools to provide servers.

Installing an OS and adding the dependencies needed to make an application work is something that must be automated. If you want to provide many servers, you just have to execute the same script several times. Technologies such as Docker, Puppet, and Chef can help you to do this. An indirect benefit of using code to provide environments is that you'll have the perfect documentation for all the required dependencies to make an application work. Over time, these scripts can be improved. They are stored in version control systems, which makes it easy to track every single change made to them. We will look at this further in `Chapter 11`, *DevOps and Release Management*.

Implementing microservices

Now that we have a good understanding of what microservices are and what they are intended for, we are going to start looking at how to implement a microservice architecture using Spring Framework. Over the next few sections, we are going to look at some of the important concepts that we haven't covered so far. It's better to approach these from a practical viewpoint to make them easier to understand.

Dynamic configuration

We have all worked on applications that use different configuration files or associated metadata to allow you to specify configuration parameters that make an application work. When we are talking about microservices, we need to approach this configuration process in a different way. We should avoid configuration files and instead adopt the twelve-fact app configuration style (as outlined at `https://12factor.net`), proposed by Heroku. When we are using this configuration style, we want to externalize all the properties that are different in each environment and make them easy and convenient to create and change.

By default, Spring Boot applications can work using command-line arguments, JNDI names, or environment variables. Spring Boot also provides the ability to use a `.properties` or `.yaml` configuration file. In order to work with configuration variables in a safe way, Spring Boot has introduced the `@ConfigurationProperties` annotation, which allows you to map properties to **plain old Java objects** (**POJOs**). When the application is starting, it checks that all the configurations are provided, have the right format, and comply with the requirements demanded by the `@Valid` annotation. Let's take a look at how this mapping works.

Let's say that you have the following `application.yaml` file as part of your application:

```
middleware:
  apiKey: ABCD-1234
  port: 8081

event-bus:
  domain: event-bus.api.com
  protocol: http
```

Now, let's map these variables to two different POJOs using the `@ConfigurationProperties` annotation. Let's start with the middleware configuration that is given:

```
@Data
@Component
@ConfigurationProperties("middleware")
public class Middleware
{
  private String apiKey;
  private int port;
}
```

The following code snippet represents the class needed for the eventBus configuration section:

```
@Data
@Component
@ConfigurationProperties("event-bus")
public class EventBus
{
    private String domain;
    private String protocol;
}
```

The @Data annotation from lombok has been used to avoid writing standard accessors methods. You can now print the .toString() result of these classes, and you will see the following output in your console:

```
EventBus(domain=event-bus.api.com, protocol=http)
Middleware(apiKey=ABCD-1234, port=8081)
```

It can be useful to have all of these configuration variables hardcoded. This means that when you want to deploy the application in another environment, you can simply override them by providing additional parameters, as follows:

```
$ java -Dmiddleware.port=9091 -jar target/configuration-demo-0.0.1-
SNAPSHOT.jar
```

Here, we are overriding one of the configuration variables before running the .jar file, so the output that you will get is shown as follows:

```
EventBus(domain=event-bus.api.com, protocol=http)
Middleware(apiKey=ABCD-1234, port=9091)
```

Even though this configuration is easy to achieve, it is not good enough for microservices, or any modern application in general. First of all, after applying any change, you need to restart the application, which is not desirable. The worst part is that you can't keep track of the changes that you have applied. This means that if an environment variable is provided, there is no way to know who provided it. In order to tackle this problem, Spring provides a way to centralize all of the configurations using the Spring Cloud Configuration server.

The server provides a centralized, journaled, and secure way to store the configuration values. Since it stores all the configuration values in a Git repository that can be local or remote, you'll have all the benefits associated with a version-control system for free.

Implementing a configuration server

A Spring Cloud configuration server is built on the top of a regular Spring Boot application. All you need to do is add the following additional dependency:

```
compile('org.springframework.cloud:spring-cloud-config-server')
```

Once the dependency has been added, you need to activate the configuration server using an additional annotation in the application, as shown in the following code:

```
@SpringBootApplication
@EnableConfigServer
public class ConfigServerApplication
{
  public static void main(String[] args)
  {
    SpringApplication.run(ConfigServerApplication.class, args);
  }
}
```

Finally, you need to provide the Git repository URL, which stores the configuration for your microservices in the `application.yaml` file, as follows:

```
spring:
  cloud:
    config:
      server:
        git:
          uri:
https://github.com/enriquezrene/spring-architectures-config-server.git
```

The preceding Git repository has separate configuration files to manage the configuration for each microservice. For example, the `configuration-demo.properties` file is used to manage the configuration for the configuration demo microservice.

Implementing a configuration client

Configuration clients are regular Spring Boot applications. All you need to do is provide the server configuration URI to read the centralized configuration, as follows:

```
spring:
  application:
    name: configuration-demo
  cloud:
    config:
      uri: http://localhost:9000
```

The following code snippet shows a REST endpoint reading a centralized configuration and serving the read value as its own response:

```
@RestController
@RefreshScope
public class ConfigurationDemoController {

    @Value("${configuration.dynamicValue}")
    private String dynamicValue;

    @GetMapping(path = "/dynamic-value")
    public ResponseEntity<String> readDynamicValue() {
        return new ResponseEntity<>(this.dynamicValue, HttpStatus.OK);
    }
}
```

The following screenshot shows the configuration file stored in the Git repository:

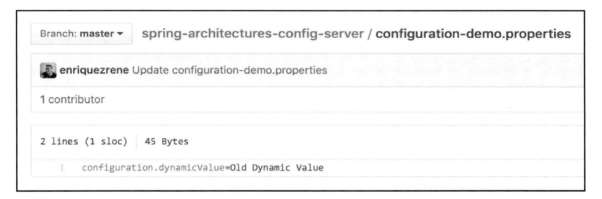

Configuration file stored in a Git repository

Once you execute a request against the preceding endpoint, it will produce the following output:

```
$ curl http://localhost:8080/dynamic-value
Old Dynamic Value
```

Change the value of the configuration variable in the file stored in Git, as shown in the following screenshot:

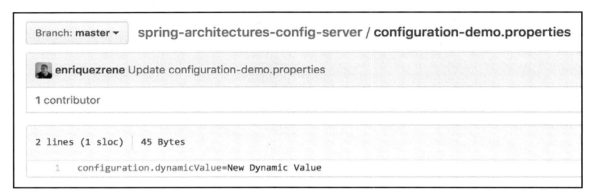

Branch: **master** ▾   spring-architectures-config-server / **configuration-demo.properties**

enriquezrene Update configuration-demo.properties

1 contributor

2 lines (1 sloc) | 45 Bytes

1   configuration.dynamicValue=New Dynamic Value

The configuration file with the change applied

If you hit the endpoint, you will retrieve the same output as before. In order to reload the configuration, you will need to reload the configuration variables by hitting the /refresh endpoint by using a POST request, as shown in the following code:

```
$ curl -X POST http://localhost:8080/actuator/refresh
["config.client.version","configuration.dynamicValue"]
```

After reloading the configuration, the endpoint will serve a response using the new provided value, as you can see in the following output:

```
$ curl http://localhost:8080/dynamic-value
New Dynamic Value
```

Service discovery and registration

In the past, our applications lived on a single physical server where we had a 1:1 relation between the application and the backend implementing it. In this case, looking for a service is really simple: you only need to know the server IP address or the associated DNS name.

Later on, applications were distributed, which means that they lived on many physical servers to provide high availability. In this case, we have a 1:N relationship between a service and the backend servers, where N can represent more than one. Incoming requests are managed using a load balancer to route the requests among the available servers.

The same approach is used when the physical servers are replaced by virtual machines. Load balancers need some configuration to register the new servers available and route the requests properly. This task used to be executed by the operations team.

Today, it's common to find applications deployed within containers, which we will discuss further in Chapter 10, *Containerizing your Applications*. Containers are constantly being provided and destroyed every millisecond, so registering new servers manually is an impossible task and must be automated. For this purpose, Netflix created a project named the Eureka project.

Introducing Eureka

Eureka is a tool that allows you to discover and register servers automatically. You can think about it as a phone directory where all the services are registered. It helps to avoid establishing direct communications among servers. For example, let's say you have three services and all of them are interacting with each other. The only way to make them work as a whole is by specifying the IP addresses and ports for the servers or their load balancers, as shown in the following diagram:

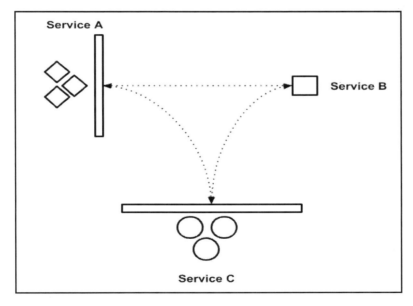

Services interacting with each other

As you can see in the preceding image, the interaction occurs directly between the servers or their load balancers. When a new server is added, it should be registered in the load balancer either manually or with an existing automated mechanism. Additionally, using Eureka, you can establish a communication using the service names registered on it. The following diagram shows how the same interactions would work with Eureka:

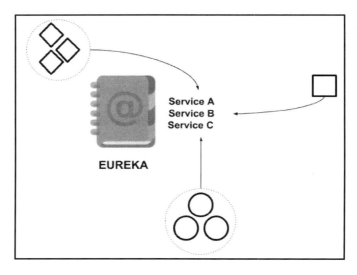

Services registered using Eureka

This means that when you need to establish a communication among services, you only need to provide the name instead of the IP address and port. Eureka will also work as a load balancer when more than one instance of a service is available.

Implementing a Netflix Eureka service registry

Since Eureka was created to allow a smooth integration with Spring Boot, a service registry can be implemented simply by adding the following dependency:

```
compile
    ('org.springframework.cloud:spring-cloud-starter-netflix-eureka-server')
```

The `application` class should be modified as well to indicate that the application will work as a Eureka server, as follows:

```
@EnableEurekaServer
@SpringBootApplication
public class ServiceRegistryApplication
```

```
{
  public static void main(String[] args)
  {
    SpringApplication.run(ServiceRegistryApplication.class, args);
  }
}
```

After running the application, you can see the web console at `http://localhost:8901/`, as shown in the following screenshot:

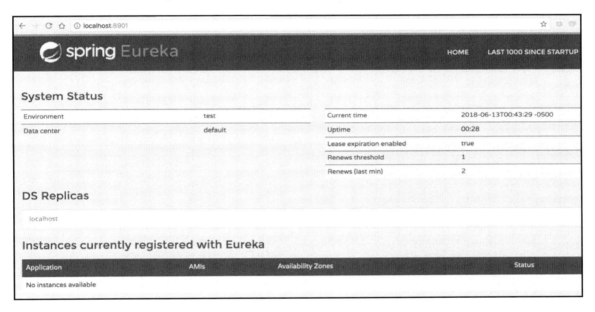

Eureka web console

Implementing a service registry client

Previously, we mentioned that a load balancer used to be used to offer high scalability by using more than one server as a backend. Eureka works in the same way, but the main benefit is that you won't need to add any configuration in the service registry when more instances of a server are provisioned. Instead, every instance should let Eureka know that it wants to be registered.

Registering a new service is quite simple. You just need to include the following dependency:

```
compile
  ('org.springframework.cloud:spring-cloud-starter-netflix-eureka-client')
```

The service application class should include an additional annotation that will be discovered, as follows:

```
@EnableDiscoveryClient
@SpringBootApplication
public class MoviesServiceApplication
{
  public static void main(String[] args)
  {
    SpringApplication.run(MoviesServiceApplication.class, args);
  }
}
```

To finish up, you will need to specify the Eureka server URI as part of the `application.properties` file, as shown in the following code:

```
# This name will appear in Eureka
spring.application.name=movies-service
eureka.client.serviceUrl.defaultZone=http://localhost:8901/eureka
```

After running this Spring Boot application, it will be automatically registered in Eureka. You can verify this by refreshing the Eureka web console. You will see that the service is registered, as shown in the following screenshot:

Instances currently registered with Eureka			
Application	AMIs	Availability Zones	Status
MOVIES-SERVICE	n/a (1)	(1)	UP (1) - 192.168.100.4:movies-service:8081

Registered instances in Eureka

Once the services are registered, you will want to consume them. One of the easiest ways to consume services is by using Netflix Ribbon.

Netflix Ribbon

Ribbon is a client-side, load balancing solution that has a smooth integration with the Spring Cloud ecosystem. It can consume a service that is exposed using Eureka simply by specifying the service name. Since all the server instances are registered in Eureka, it will choose one of them to execute the request.

Let's say we have another service named cinema-service. Say that this service has an endpoint that can be used to query a cinema by its ID. As part of the cinema payload, we want to include all the movies that are available in the movies-service.

First of all, we need to add the following dependency:

```
compile('org.springframework.cloud:spring-cloud-starter-netflix-ribbon')
```

Then, as part of the application class, we need to create a new RestTemplate bean that will be injected in order to consume the services available in Eureka:

```
@EnableDiscoveryClient
@SpringBootApplication
public class CinemaServiceApplication
{
  public static void main(String[] args)
  {
    SpringApplication.run(CinemaServiceApplication.class, args);
  }
  @LoadBalanced
  @Bean
  RestTemplate restTemplate()
  {
    return new RestTemplate();
  }
}
```

The RestTemplate phrase is a client that is used to consume RESTful web services. It can execute a request against the movies-service as follows:

```
@RestController
public class CinemasController
{
  private final CinemaRepository cinemaRepository;
  private final RestTemplate restTemplate;
  public CinemasController(CinemaRepository cinemaRepository,
  RestTemplate restTemplate)
  {
    this.cinemaRepository = cinemaRepository;
    this.restTemplate = restTemplate;
```

```
  }
  @GetMapping("/cinemas/{cinemaId}/movies")
  public ResponseEntity<Cinema> queryCinemaMovies
  (@PathVariable("cinemaId") Integer cinemaId)
  {
    Cinema cinema = cinemaRepository.findById(cinemaId).get();
    Movie[] movies = restTemplate
    .getForObject(
    "http://movies-service/movies", Movie[].class);
    cinema.setAvailableMovies(movies);
    return new ResponseEntity<>(cinema, HttpStatus.OK);
  }
}
```

Note how the service name is specified, and we don't have to provide any other information, such as the IP address or the port. This is good because it would be impossible to determine this information when new servers are being created and destroyed on demand.

Edge services

An edge service is an intermediary component that is exposed to both the outside world and the downstream services. It works as a gateway that allows for interaction between all the services around it. The following diagram shows how an edge service is used:

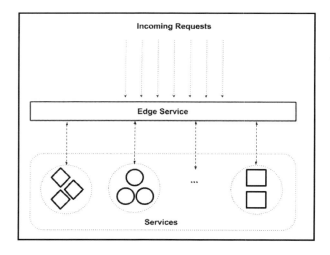

An edge service

Note that all the incoming requests are pointing directly to the edge service, which will later look for the right service to redirect the request properly.

Edge services are used in different ways to add additional behavior or functionalities according to the services around them. The most common example is a cross-origin resource sharing (CORS) (`https://developer.mozilla.org/en-US/docs/Web/HTTP/CORS`) filter. You can add a CORS filter to an edge service, and this would mean that the downstream services won't need to implement anything. Say that we only want to allow incoming requests from the domain **abc.com**. We can implement this logic as part of the edge service, as shown in the following diagram:

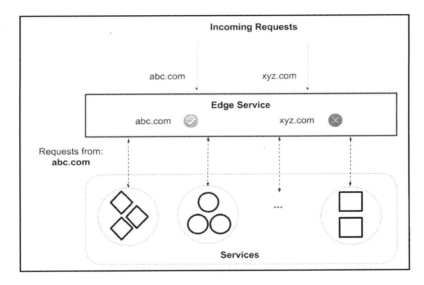

A CORS filter using an edge service

Here, we can see that all the logic is added in one place only, and that the downstream services don't have to implement anything to manage the required behavior.

Edge services are also used for many other requirements that we will discuss in the next section. Different implementations of edge services are available on the market. In the next section, we are going to talk about Netflix's Zuul, because it provides a smooth integration with Spring Cloud.

Introducing Zuul

Zuul is an edge service created by Netflix that bases its functionality around filters. Zuul filters follow the interceptor filter pattern (as described at `http://www.oracle.com/technetwork/java/interceptingfilter-142169.html`). Using filters, you can perform a set of actions on HTTP requests and responses during their routing.

 Zuul is the name of a gatekeeper that is taken from a movie (see `http://ghostbusters.wikia.com/wiki/Zuul` for more details), and represents exactly the functionality that this project has, namely that of a gatekeeper.

You can apply the filter during four phases, as shown in the following diagram:

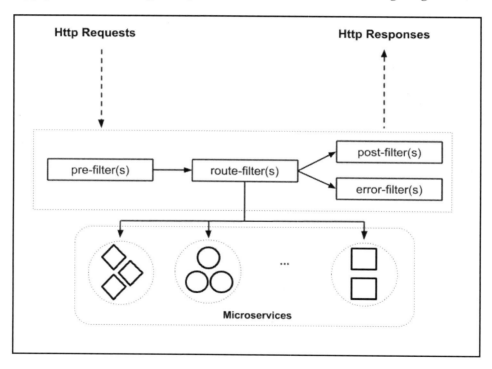

Zuul filters

Let's review each one of these phases:

- **pre**: Before the request is processed
- **route**: During the routing of the request to the service

- **post**: After the request has been processed
- **error**: When an error occurs during the request

Using these phases, you can write your own filter to handle different requirements. Some common uses for filters during the `pre` phase are as follows:

- Authentication
- Authorization
- Rate limits
- Translation and transformation operations in the request body
- Custom headers injection
- Adapters

Some common uses of filters in the `route` phase are as follows:

- Canary releases
- Proxying

Once a request has been processed by the microservice, you have two scenarios:

- Succesful processing
- Error during the processing of the request

If the request was successful, all the filters associated with the `post` phase will be executed. Some common uses of filters that are executed during this phase are as follows:

- Translation and transformation operations in the response payload
- Storing of metrics associated with the business itself

On the other hand, when errors occur during the processing of the requests, then all the `error` filters will be executed. Some common uses of filters in this phase are as follows:

- Saving the associated metadata of requests
- Removing technical details from the response for security reasons

 The preceding points are just a few common uses of filters during each phase. Think about your own business when writing filters that target your needs.

In order to write a Zuul filter, the `ZuulFilter` class should be extended. This class has the following four abstract methods that needed to be implemented:

```
public abstract class ZuulFilter
implements IZuulFilter, Comparable<ZuulFilter>
{
  public abstract String filterType();
  public abstract int filterOrder();
  public abstract boolean shouldFilter();
  public abstract Object run() throws ZuulException;
  ...
}
```

The two methods shown in bold are not directly declared in the `ZuulFilter` class, but are instead inherited from the `IZuulFilter` interface that is implemented by this class.

Let's review each one of these methods to understand how a Zuul filter works.

First, you have the `filterType` method, where you need to specify the phase in which you want to execute the current filter. The valid values of this method are as follows:

- pre
- post
- route
- error

You can write the preceding values by yourself, but it is better to use the `FilterConstant` class, as follows:

```
@Override
public String filterType()
{
  return FilterConstants.PRE_TYPE;
}
```

All the phases are listed in the class that we mentioned previously:

```
public class FilterConstants
{
  ...
  public static final String ERROR_TYPE = "error";
  public static final String POST_TYPE = "post";
  public static final String PRE_TYPE = "pre";
  public static final String ROUTE_TYPE = "route";
}
```

The `filterOrder` method is used to define the order in which the filter will be executed. It's common to have more than one filter in each phase, so by using this method, you can configure the desired order for each filter. The highest value represents a low order of execution.

It is easy to configure the execution order by using the `org.springframework.core.Ordered` interface, which has two values that can be used as references:

```
package org.springframework.core;
public interface Ordered
{
   int HIGHEST_PRECEDENCE = -2147483648;
   int LOWEST_PRECEDENCE = 2147483647;
   ...
}
```

The `shouldFilter` method is used to determine whether the filter logic should be executed or not. In this method, you can access the request information using the `RequestContext` class, as follows:

```
RequestContext ctx = RequestContext.getCurrentContext();
// do something with ctx
```

This method should return a boolean value that indicates whether the `run` method should be executed or not.

Finally, the `run` method contains the logic that's applied in the filter. In this method, you can also use the `RequestContext` class to perform the desired logic.

For example, let's use the endpoint implemented previously to query the movies screened by a cinema:

curl http://localhost:8701/cinemas-service/cinemas/1/movies

The following is a simple implementation to print the requested method and URL:

```
@Override
public Object run() throws ZuulException {
    RequestContext ctx = RequestContext.getCurrentContext();
    HttpServletRequest request = ctx.getRequest();
    log.info("Requested Method: {}", request.getMethod());
    log.info("Requested URL: {}", request.getRequestURL());
    return null;
}
```

Once the request has been processed, you will have the following output:

```
PRE FILTER
Requested Method: GET
Requested URL: http://localhost:8701/cinemas-service/cinemas/1/movies
```

CAP theorem

In 2000, during the **Symposium on Principles of Distributed Computing (SPDC)**, Eric Brewer presented the following theory:

"It is impossible for a shared-data system to simultaneously provide more than two of the three properties (consistency, high-availability and partition tolerance) at the same time."

- Eric Brewer

Let's review these three properties.

Consistency

A consistent system is able to report its current state in every subsequent operation until the state is explicitly changed by an external agent. In other words, every read operation should retrieve the data that was last written.

High availability

High availability refers to the system's ability to always provide a valid response when it retrieves any request from an external agent. In a perfect world, the system should always be able to handle incoming requests and never produce errors. It should at least handle them in a way that is not perceptible to the user.

Partition tolerance

A partition tolerant distributed system should always keep operating, even when communication with one of its nodes cannot be established.

Brewer's theory can be applied to any distributed system in general. Since microservices architectures are based on the concepts of distributed computing, this means that this theory applies to them as well.

Even though the theory states that a system won't be able to accomplish all three properties at the same time, we should build systems that are able to handle failures gracefully. This is where the circuit breaker pattern can be applied.

Circuit breaker

The circuit breaker pattern is intended to handle failures that are created when a system interacts with other systems that are running in different processes using remote calls. The main idea behind this pattern is to wrap the call with an object that is able to monitor failures and produce successful responses, as shown in the following diagram:

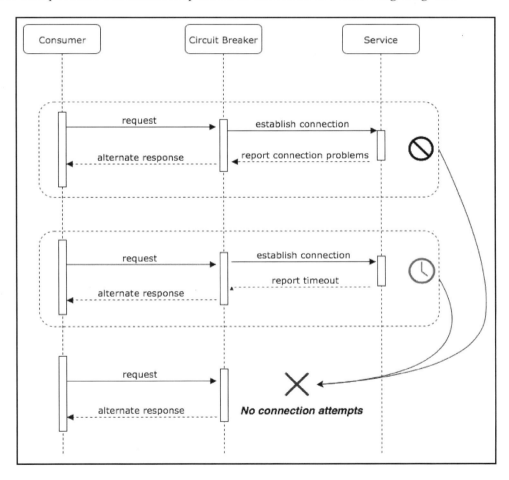

Circuit breaker pattern

Note that the circuit breaker pattern provides an alternate response once a connection can't be established with the targeted service. Let's look at how to implement this pattern and make it part of our application using Hystrix.

Hystrix

Hystrix is a library that was created by Netflix in 2011. It was created to deal with latency and connection problems when interactions with external services are executed. The main aim of Hystrix was to provide an alternate method to be executed when a communication problem occurs. It can be implemented as follows:

```
@Service
public class MoviesService {

    private final RestTemplate restTemplate;

    public MoviesService(RestTemplate restTemplate) {
        this.restTemplate = restTemplate;
    }

    @HystrixCommand(fallbackMethod = "emptyMoviesArray")
    public Movie[] getMovies(){
        return restTemplate.getForObject
            ("http://movies-service/movies", Movie[].class);
    }

    public Movie[] emptyMoviesArray(){
        Movie movie = new Movie();
        movie.setId(-1);
        movie.setName("Coming soon");
        return new Movie[]{movie};
    }
}
```

Note how the getMovies method tries to interact with another service to get a list of movies. The method is annotated with @HystrixCommand(fallbackMethod = "emptyMoviesArray"). The fallbackMethod value indicates the alternate method to be used as an alternative if an error occurs during communication with other services. In this case, the alternate method provides an array with a hard-coded movie. In this way, you can avoid cascade failures when interactions with external services are needed. This provides a better experience to end users by handling failures gracefully.

Summary

In this chapter, we looked at the principles of microservices and their advantages and drawbacks. After that, we learned how to model microservices and discussed some important concepts regarding distributed computing that are inherent to this architectural style. Finally, we reviewed the CAP theorem and how to handle failures gracefully during interaction with other services. In the next chapter, we are going to look at the serverless architectural style, which can also be integrated as part of your microservices environment.

9
Serverless Architectures

Serverless architectures are becoming a popular trend in IT system building. As a consequence, it's quite common to hear people discussing cloud providers such as **Amazon Web services** (**AWS**), Google Cloud, and Microsoft Azure, among others.

In this chapter, we will explore the meaning of serverless architecture and how this new way of building systems can help us to address business requirements in shorter amounts of time, thus reducing the effort required to build business solutions. We will also look at how this approach can be used to drastically reduce the time required to reach production by utilizing ready-to-use, third-party services and implementing custom functionalities, thereby creating stateless functions that can be deployed on the cloud.

In this chapter, we will cover the following topics:

- An introduction to serverless architecture
- Infrastructure and file storage
- Benefits and pitfalls
- Backend as a service
- Function as a service
- Concerns about serverless architectures:
    - Vendor lock-in concerns
    - Security concerns
    - Framework support
    - Troubleshooting
- Examples and commons uses of serverless architecture
- Implementing applications using serverless architecture:
    - How to write functions with Spring
    - Using adapters for AWS Lambda and Azure

An introduction to serverless architecture

Serverless architecture was born through the initiative of Amazon. The company was looking to promote an environment wherein a development team could be autonomous, small, and self-managed, allowing it to work on the whole software development cycle, from writing the code to shipping and delivering to production environments.

Serverless architecture is sometimes misunderstood as the concept of software systems that are deployed without the need for a physical server. To understand this idea, you can review the definition of serverless in Martin Fowler's blog:

> *"It's important to understand that a serverless architecture is the approach in which developers code business logic as functions, forgetting about the server's provisioning and scaling concerns where the logic will be executed."*

> - https://martinfowler.com/articles/serverless.html

Common examples of serverless and FaaS include:

- Authentication
- SMS notifications
- Email services

On the other hand, within a serverless world, it's common to create applications in which third-party services are adopted as a part of the system (rather than creating services from scratch). These services are commonly known as **backend as a service (BaaS)** or **mobile backend as a service (MBaaS)**.

Following the same approach, we can code our custom business logic in the form of functions that can be deployed on the cloud. These services are known as **function as a service (FaaS)**.

The following diagram illustrates how third-party services and custom functions are created, deployed, and consumed by different software systems:

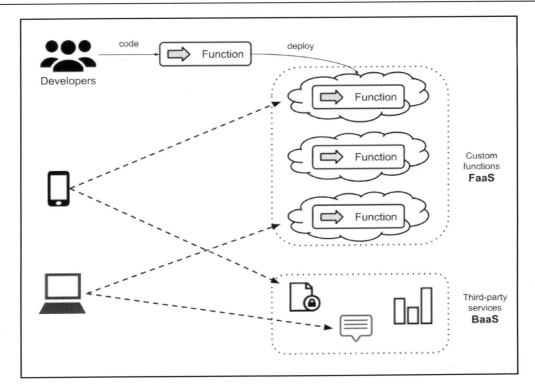

Third-party services and custom functions

Infrastructure and file storage

Infrastructure and file storage are also considered serverless, because the business (or person) that owns the system does not have to purchase, rent, or provision servers or virtual machines to use them.

As developers, if we take the old-fashioned approach (provisioning all of the infrastructure by using an on-premise environment), we have to set up all of the software and hardware requirements for every environment in which we want to deploy our software systems. This provisioning process has to be repeated for all of the environments, until we get into production, at which point we have to take care of other features, such as scaling and monitoring. In many cases, our infrastructure will be under-utilized, which is a waste of money, since we have purchased powerful servers to deploy applications that don't need many resources.

Benefits and pitfalls

Adopting a serverless architecture approach to creating applications provides us with many benefits, but there are also some pitfalls that we should address. Let's start by reviewing the benefits:

- Developers using a serverless architecture can focus primarily on the code, and can forget everything related to provisioning servers, which is a task handled by the cloud provider itself.
- The scaling of the code is ephemeral, meaning that it can be scaled and can spin up or down, based on the number of requests retrieved.
- By definition, all of the functions used to code the business logic must be stateless, and therefore, loosely coupled. In this way, the tasks are focused on well-defined responsibilities.
- Functions can be asynchronously triggered by events.
- We only have to pay for the compute time consumed.
- The functions base their functionality on an event-driven model.
- Infinite scaling can be achieved for developers in a transparent way.

On the other hand, there are also some pitfalls:

- A lack of documentation and showcases that can be used as references
- Latency issues that are introduced when many services have to be consumed at the same time
- Some features are only available from certain cloud providers.
- Vendor lock-in

In order to tackle the pitfall of vendor lock-in, it is highly recommended to use a **polycloud** approach as a part of a serverless architecture. A polycloud strategy involves using more than one cloud provider. This is important because, with it, we can take advantage of the strengths of different vendors and different products. For example, Google offers awesome services for machine learning, AWS provides a wide variety of standard services, and Microsoft Azure has awesome features for functions such as remote debugging. On the other hand, cloud-agnostic strategies recommend that we avoid sticking to a determined cloud provider as much as possible, in order to have the freedom to deploy systems whenever we want to. However, this would be difficult to achieve, because it would mean designing systems in a more generic way, ignoring specific vendor features that offer additional advantages.

Backend as a service

The simplest scenario for using a BaaS approach occurs when we create **single page applications (SPA)**, or mobile apps that interact with services available in the cloud.

It's common to find applications wherein the authentication process is delegated to third-party services, using standard protocols (such as OAuth), persisting information in cloud databases (such as Google Firebase), or sending notifications via SMS services (such as Twilio).

BaaS can help us with several concerns out of the box so that we can deploy into the production environment without having to worry about the server or virtual machine of the application. In addition, BaaS also provides us with a whole infrastructure and nodes, such as the following:

- Load Balancer
- Database to store our data (NoSQL or RDBMS)
- Filesystems
- Queue servers

BaaS also takes care of the following requirements:

- Backup
- Replication
- Patches
- Scale
- High availability

On the other hand, BaaS has increased the birth of new products as services, including the following:

- **Firebase**: This provides us with features such as analytics, databases, messaging, and crash reporting
- **Amazon DynamoDB**: This key-value of the store is a non-relational database
- **Azure Cosmos DB**: This is a globally distributed, multi-model database service

With all of these changes and new tools, we have to embrace a new way of thinking and break the paradigms of how we build our applications. As serverless is a new technology, it is recommended to experiment, starting with using a small piece of an application. Think of three examples from your current applications that would be interesting to refactor using a serverless approach. Now, confer with your team and organize an Architectural Clash (http://architecturalclash.org/) workshop to identify whether or not your ideas are feasible.

Function as a service

Since AWS Lambda gained popularity in 2014, the use of code implemented as functions has become increasingly popular. In some cases, there is even the option to build a whole application using a FaaS approach; in other cases, the approach is used to solve specific requirements.

Code deployed in the form of functions is executed when an event occurs. Once the event happens, the code is executed, and the function is then shut down. For that reason, functions are stateless by nature, since there is no state or context to share with other applications.

A FaaS is ephemeral, meaning that when a function needs to be executed, the cloud provider will automatically provision an environment using the metadata associated with the function. This will scale depending on the processing needs, and, once the processing has finished, the execution environment will be destroyed, as shown in the following diagram:

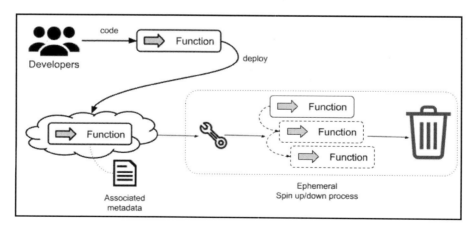

Ephemeral FaaS process

Implementing code using a FaaS approach will provide you with the following benefits:

- You won't have to worry about host configuration
- Transparent scale-up on demand
- Automatic spin up/down
- You will only pay for what you use

Concerns about serverless architectures

New technology trends sometimes create resilience and concerns, but they also provide the opportunity to experiment and gain benefits for applications and business.

The most common concerns involved in serverless architecture are as follows:

- Vendor lock-in
- Security
- Framework support
- Troubleshooting

Vendor lock-in

With vendor lock-in, the main concern is the impossibility of embracing new services as part of the vendors' serverless architecture. This concern comes down to a fear of being locked in with a cloud provider.

It is recommended to use as many features as you can of the cloud provider of your choosing. You can do so by starting a pilot and evaluating the cloud provider; be sure to create an assessment of pros and cons before moving more code onto the cloud.

Don't let this concern put you off of using serverless architecture. Instead, it is recommended to start a proof of concept and evaluate the cloud provider. Serverless is a new technology that will evolve with time, and there are ways to keep FaaS independent, such as by using Spring Cloud functionality. We will work on an example of this in a later section of this chapter.

Finally, you should understand that moving to another vendor (from cloud-to-cloud) is not as difficult as it was in the past (when we were moving our application or legacy code to on-premises environments).

Security

Security is a key concern, independent of the architecture of the application, and serverless is no exception. Since we are creating functions as services in the cloud, we need to take care in our authentication, authorization of execution, and the OWASP. However, in this context, the cloud provider—such as AWS or Azure—provides us with guides and practices out of the box, in order to minimize our concerns.

Another security concern to consider in serverless is the lack of a clearly shaped security perimeter. In other words, when the security perimeter of one of the functions ends and another starts, different cloud providers provide different ways to make those functions work as a whole; for example, AWS does this by using a service called an API Gateway. This API is used to orchestrate and compose the created FaaS. On the other hand, as is the case with everything that is ephemeral, many of these concerns may go away because the concept of ephemeral in FaaS is that the function will be created, run, and destroyed as many requests received on there are isolated each time that the FaaS is called.

To clarify any concerns, we will start to move some of our code to serverless/FaaS, creating an experimental development and incrementing when we feel more confident with the concept.

Framework support

There are several frameworks working to create environments that develop serverless architectures without being attached to the cloud provider. In my experience, it is preferable to create functions as services that exploit the cloud platform as much as possible. As a function is a small piece of code with a clear input or output, it is better to use the language and technology that you feel comfortable with, or even to try new technologies or programming languages, in order to determine how good they are.

At this stage, serverless supports several languages for building functions. Currently, the most common options to deploy FaaS are as follows:

- AWS Lamba
- Azure functions
- Google functions

One benefit for Java developers is that most cloud providers offer support for Java as a programming language to deploy functions. Moreover, Spring Framework has a project named Spring Functions that can be used to code functions; we will implement some functionality using this project later in this chapter.

A benefit of using Spring Functions is that we can develop and test our code in our local machine, and then wrap the code using an adaptor, in order to deploy it on a cloud provider.

Troubleshooting

Once an application (or function, in this case) is deployed into production, one of the key aspects to consider is how to trace, find, and fix bugs. With serverless, this can be tricky, because we are dealing with a more segregated scenario, and our system has small parts that are not divided into services and microservices. Several functions are smaller pieces of logic and code. To deal with this concern, each cloud provider has tools to monitor and trace functions, dealing with one error in an ephemeral environment. If we compose logic for several functions, we will have to apply techniques like aggregate logging and use tools to collect information associated with the executed code. We will review some techniques to deal with this concept in `Chapter 12`, *Monitoring*.

Examples and common use cases

Even when a serverless architecture provides us with a lot of benefits, those benefits cannot be applied to everything. It's quite common to find applications using hybrid models, when an application consumes a backend deployed on a traditional server (on-premise or cloud-based) and also using FaaS or third-party services for specific requirements.

Some common scenarios that serverless architectures can be applied to are as follows:

- Processing webhooks
- Tasks or jobs that should be scheduled or triggered under certain circumstances
- Data transformation, for example:
    - Image manipulation, compression, or conversion
    - Voice data transcribed into text, such as Alexa or Cortana
- A certain logic for mobile applications, based on the mobile backend as a service approach
- Single-page applications
- Chatbots

On the other hand, serverless architectures are not suitable for the following scenarios:

- Long-running processes where huge amounts of resources (such as CPU and memory) are required
- Any blocking processes

Adopting serverless architectures for SPA

Single-page applications (SPAs) provide one of the most suitable scenarios for adopting a serverless architecture approach. After all, they do not involve much-coded business logic, and they mainly serve and consume content provided by services deployed somewhere else.

For example, suppose that we need to build an application to send the World Cup results to users. In this example, we will need to address the following requirements:

- Authentication
- Data storage
- Notification mechanisms

Using a serverless architecture approach, these requirements can be addressed by the following service providers:

- **Authentication**: Google OAuth
- **Data storage**: Google Firebase
- **Notification mechanisms**:
    - SMS, using Twilio
    - Email, using SparkPost

The following diagram illustrates how to use the preceding services (Google OAuth, Firebase, Twilo, and SparkPost) as parts of an application:

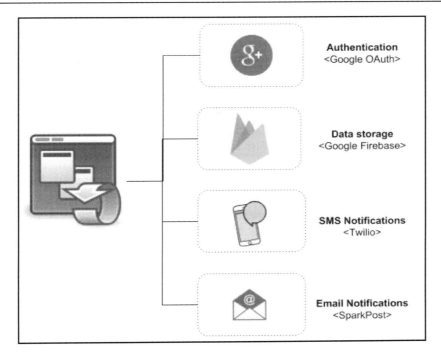

Integrating different third-party applications

The preceding diagram shows some of the most well-known service providers, but there are a lot of other options available on the internet.

One of the benefits of the preceding services is that all of them provide an SDK, or library, that can be used directly from an SPA, including common JavaScript libraries, such as Angular.

Implementing FaaS with Spring Cloud Functions

Under the umbrella of Spring projects, you will find the Spring Cloud Function project (`https://cloud.spring.io/spring-cloud-function/`), which is designed to implement applications using a serverless architecture model.

Using Spring Cloud Function, we can code functions that can be launched on different cloud providers that support FaaS. There's no need to learn something new from scratch, because all of the core concepts and main features of Spring Framework, such as autoconfiguration, dependency injection, and built-in metrics, are applied in the same way.

Once a function has been coded, it can be deployed as a web endpoint, a stream processor, or simple tasks that are triggered by certain events or via a scheduler.

Looking at an example of an SPA, we can implement an application using third-party services, the existing REST API, and custom functions. The following diagram illustrates how an application can be created by using all of the previously mentioned options:

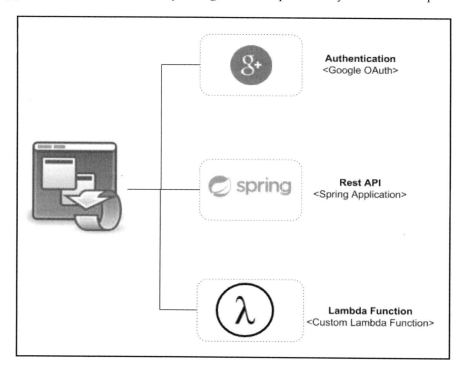

Integrating FaaS in applications

Let's review how the components in the preceding diagram work:

- Authentication is provided by a third-party service
- The application uses the business logic that resides in the REST API
- A custom function can be used as a part of the SPA

The following diagram illustrates how a function works:

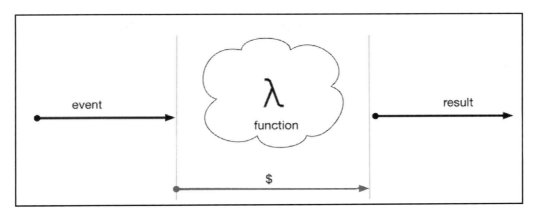

Function as a service

Let's review each part of the diagram:

- Functions provide a way to use an event-driven programming model.
- We can scale infinitely, in a way that is transparent to developers. This scale will be handled by the platform that we use to deploy the function.
- Finally, we only pay for the time and resources consumed by the functions during their execution.

Functions with Spring

Spring Cloud Function brings us four main features, described in detail in the official documentation (`https://github.com/spring-cloud/spring-cloud-function`), that are worth mentioning here:

- It provides the ability to wrap the `@Beans` type of function, consumer, and supplier. This makes it possible to expose functionalities as HTTP endpoints and stream messaging via listeners or publishers, with a message broker such as RabbitMQ, ActiveMQ, or Kafka.
- It provides compiled strings, which will be wrapped as function bodies.

- We can deploy a JAR file with our function, with an isolated classloader that will run on a single Java virtual machine.
- It provides adaptors for different cloud providers that support serverless architecture, such as the following:
  - AWS Lambda
  - Open Whisk
  - Azure

Coding the example

Now, we will create a function that masks bank account numbers. Let's start by creating a new Spring Boot application from scratch, using the Spring Initializr website (`https://start.spring.io`):

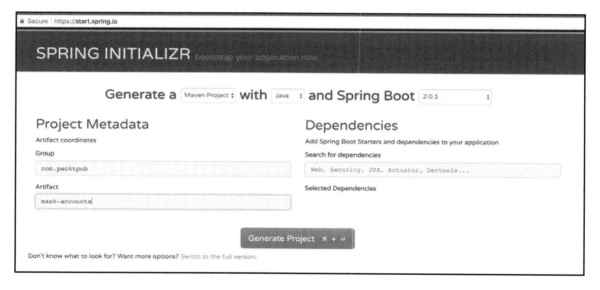

Spring Initializr website

At the moment, there's no need to include additional dependencies as a part of the project. The project structure is pretty simple, and it will look as follows:

```
[→ mask-accounts tree
.
├── mvnw
├── mvnw.cmd
├── pom.xml
└── src
    ├── main
    │   ├── java
    │   │   └── com
    │   │       └── packtpub
    │   │           └── maskaccounts
    │   │               └── MaskAccountsApplication.java
    │   └── resources
    │       └── application.properties
    └── test
        └── java
            └── com
                └── packtpub
                    └── maskaccounts
                        └── MaskAccountsApplicationTests.java
```

In order to write functions using Spring, we have to include the Spring Cloud Function project as a dependency; first, let's add some properties to specify the version that we are going to use, as follows:

```xml
<parent>
    <groupId>org.springframework.boot</groupId>
    <artifactId>spring-boot-starter-parent</artifactId>
    <version>1.5.11.RELEASE</version>
    <relativePath/>
</parent>

<properties>
    <project.build.sourceEncoding>UTF-
8</project.build.sourceEncoding>
    <project.reporting.outputEncoding>UTF-
8</project.reporting.outputEncoding>
    <java.version>1.8</java.version>
    <spring-cloud-function.version>
      1.0.0.BUILD-SNAPSHOT
    </spring-cloud-function.version>
    <reactor.version>3.1.2.RELEASE</reactor.version>
    <wrapper.version>1.0.9.RELEASE</wrapper.version>
</properties>
```

Note that we will downgrade the Spring version to 1.5.11 RELEASE, because Spring Cloud Function is not currently ready to be used in Spring Boot 2.

Now, we will add the dependency, as follows:

```xml
<dependency>
  <groupId>org.springframework.cloud</groupId>
  <artifactId>spring-cloud-starter-function-web</artifactId>
</dependency>
<dependency>
  <groupId>org.springframework.cloud</groupId>
  <artifactId>spring-cloud-function-compiler</artifactId>
</dependency>
```

Then, we have to add an entry as a part of the dependency management section, to allow Maven to automatically resolve all transitive dependencies:

```xml
<dependencyManagement>
  <dependencies>
    <dependency>
      <groupId>org.springframework.cloud</groupId>
      <artifactId>spring-cloud-function-dependencies</artifactId>
      <version>${spring-cloud-function.version}</version>
      <type>pom</type>
      <scope>import</scope>
    </dependency>
  </dependencies>
</dependencyManagement>
```

Finally, we will include some plugins that will allow us to wrap the coded functions, by adding the following entries as a part of the `pom.xml` file:

```xml
<build>
  <plugins>
    <plugin>
      <groupId>org.apache.maven.plugins</groupId>
      <artifactId>maven-deploy-plugin</artifactId>
      <configuration>
        <skip>true</skip>
      </configuration>
    </plugin>
    <plugin>
      <groupId>org.springframework.boot</groupId>
      <artifactId>spring-boot-maven-plugin</artifactId>
```

```
      <dependencies>
        <dependency>
          <groupId>org.springframework.boot.experimental</groupId>
          <artifactId>spring-boot-thin-layout</artifactId>
          <version>${wrapper.version}</version>
        </dependency>
      </dependencies>
    </plugin>
  </plugins>
</build>
```

We are now ready to implement a function to mask account numbers. Let's review the following code snippet:

```
package com.packtpub.maskaccounts;

import org.springframework.boot.SpringApplication;
import org.springframework.boot.autoconfigure.SpringBootApplication;
import org.springframework.cloud.function.context.FunctionScan;
import org.springframework.context.annotation.Bean;
import reactor.core.publisher.Flux;

import java.util.function.Function;

@FunctionScan
@SpringBootApplication
public class MaskAccountsApplication
{
  public static void main(String[] args) {
    SpringApplication.run(MaskAccountsApplication.class, args);
  }

  @Bean
  public Function<Flux<String>, Flux<String>> maskAccounts()
  {
    return flux ->
    {
      return flux
      .map(value ->
        value.replaceAll("\\w(?=\\w{4})", "*")
      );
    };
  }
}
```

The @FunctionScan annotation is used to allow the Spring Function adapter to find the beans that will be deployed as functions in the cloud provider.

Once the function has been coded, we will register it using the `application.properties` file, as follows:

```
spring.cloud.function.stream.default-route: maskAccounts
spring.cloud.function.scan.packages: com.packtpub.maskaccounts
```

Now, it's time to execute the function locally, using the following steps:

1. Generate the artifact:

```
$ mvn install
```

2. Execute the generated artifact:

```
$ java -jar target/mask-accounts-0.0.1-SNAPSHOT.jar
```

You should now see output similar to the following:

Console output

Let's try to execute the function using the following CURL command:

```
$ curl -H "Content-Type: text/plain" http://localhost:8080/maskAccounts -d
37567979
%****7979
```

As a result, we will get a masked account number: ****7979.

In the next section, we will review how to deploy the function using different cloud providers.

 In order to create an account on any cloud provider, such as AWS or Azure, you will need a credit or debit card, even if the provider offers free tiers.

Adapters

Spring Cloud Function provides adapters for different cloud providers, in order to deploy the coded business logic using functions. At the moment, there are adapters for use with the following cloud providers:

- AWS Lambda
- Azure
- Apache OpenWhisk

In the next section, we will cover how these adapters can be used.

AWS Lambda adapter

This project was designed to allow for deploying applications that use Spring Cloud Function to AWS Lambda (https://aws.amazon.com/lambda/).

This adapter is a layer over the Spring Cloud Function application that lets us deploy our functions into AWS.

You can find the sources of the project on GitHub, at the following link: https://github.com/spring-cloud/spring-cloud-function/tree/master/spring-cloud-function-adapters/spring-cloud-function-adapter-aws

Before using the AWS Lambda adaptor, we have to add it as a dependency of the project. Let's start by defining some properties inside of the pom.xml file:

```
<aws-lambda-events.version>
    2.0.2
</aws-lambda-events.version>
<spring-cloud-stream-servlet.version>
    1.0.0.BUILD-SNAPSHOT
</spring-cloud-stream-servlet.version>
<start-class>
    com.packtpub.maskaccounts.MaskAccountsApplication
</start-class>
```

Now, we have to add the required dependencies for AWS:

```
<dependency>
        <groupId>org.springframework.cloud</groupId>
        <artifactId>spring-cloud-function-adapter-aws</artifactId>
</dependency>
<dependency>
        <groupId>com.amazonaws</groupId>
        <artifactId>aws-lambda-java-events</artifactId>
        <version>${aws-lambda-events.version}</version>
        <scope>provided</scope>
    </dependency>
<dependency>
        <groupId>com.amazonaws</groupId>
        <artifactId>aws-lambda-java-core</artifactId>
        <version>1.1.0</version>
        <scope>provided</scope>
</dependency>
```

Now, add it to the dependency management section, as follows:

```
<dependency>
  <groupId>org.springframework.cloud</groupId>
  <artifactId>spring-cloud-stream-binder-servlet</artifactId>
  <version>${spring-cloud-stream-servlet.version}</version>
</dependency>
```

Finally, add it to the plugin section, as follows:

```
<plugin>
  <groupId>org.apache.maven.plugins</groupId>
  <artifactId>maven-shade-plugin</artifactId>
  <configuration>
    <createDependencyReducedPom>false</createDependencyReducedPom>
    <shadedArtifactAttached>true</shadedArtifactAttached>
```

```
    <shadedClassifierName>aws</shadedClassifierName>
  </configuration>
</plugin>
```

Next, we will write a class that will work as an adapter for AWS. This adaptor should extend the `SpringBootRequestHandler` class, as follows:

```
package com.packtpub.maskaccounts;

public class Handler
    extends SpringBootRequestHandler<Flux<String>, Flux<String>> {

}
```

Once the adapter has been written, we will need to modify the previously implemented function as a part of the `MaskAccountsApplication.java` file. Here, we are going to change the name of the method to `function`, and the input and output of the function will be **plain old Java objects (POJOs)** with setters and getters, as follows:

```
package com.packtpub.maskaccounts;

import org.springframework.boot.SpringApplication;
import org.springframework.boot.autoconfigure.SpringBootApplication;
import org.springframework.cloud.function.context.FunctionScan;
import org.springframework.context.annotation.Bean;

import java.util.function.Function;

@FunctionScan
@SpringBootApplication
public class MaskAccountsApplication {

    public static void main(String[] args) {
        SpringApplication.run(MaskAccountsApplication.class, args);
    }

    @Bean
    public Function<In, Out> function() {
            return value -> new Out(value.mask());
    }
}

class In {

    private String value;

    In() {
    }
```

```
    public In(String value) {
        this.value = value;
    }

    public String mask() {
        return value.replaceAll("\\w(?=\\w{4})", "*");
    }

    public String getValue() {
        return value;
    }

    public void setValue(String value) {
        this.value = value;
    }
}

class Out {

    private String value;

    Out() {
    }

    public Out(String value) {
        this.value = value;
    }

    public String getValue() {
        return value;
    }

    public void setValue(String value) {
        this.value = value;
    }
}
```

In order to wrap the coded function, we have to create a JAR file, using the following Maven goals:

```
$ mvn clean package
```

Once the JAR file has been created, we can use the **command-line interface (CLI)** provided by AWS (https://aws.amazon.com/cli/) to upload the generated JAR file, by running the following command:

```
$ aws lambda create-function --function-name maskAccounts --role
arn:aws:iam::[USERID]:role/service-role/[ROLE] --zip-file
fileb://target/mask-accounts-aws-0.0.1-SNAPSHOT-aws.jar --handler
org.springframework.cloud.function.adapter.aws.SpringBootStreamHandler --
description "Spring Cloud Function Adapter for packt Mastering Architecting
Spring 5" --runtime java8 --region us-east-1 --timeout 30 --memory-size
1024 --publish
```

The [USERID] quote is based on your AWS account and the [ROLE] quote. If you have any doubts about how to create an AWS account, go to https://aws.amazon.com/premiumsupport/knowledge-center/create-and-activate-aws-account/.

For more information about the AWS lambda create-function, refer to https://docs.aws.amazon.com/cli/latest/reference/lambda/create-function.html.

If you don't set the credentials of your AWS account, you will get an error message that states *unable to locate credentials.* You can configure credentials by running the aws configure command.

Don't forget that you will need to create an AWS user with a a role with permission to run AWS Lambda.

Once the function has been successfully deployed, you will see an output similar to the following in the Console:

```
{
    "TracingConfig": {
        "Mode": "PassThrough"
    },
    "CodeSha256": "Dir4akLNB972VmaUfrkhxqAiBJd3irv09CgeL4jC0VU=",
    "FunctionName": "maskAccounts",
    "CodeSize": 27300191,
    "RevisionId": "809471d7-0a07-4989-bea1-a44603dacec2",
    "MemorySize": 1024,
    "FunctionArn": "arn:aws:lambda:us-east-1:            :function:maskAccounts",
    "Version": "1",
    "Role": "arn:aws:iam::            :role/        ",
    "Timeout": 30,
    "LastModified": "2018-04-12T00:01:55.236+0000",
    "Handler": "org.springframework.cloud.function.adapter.aws.SpringBootStreamHandler",
    "Runtime": "java8",
    "Description": "Spring Cloud Function Adapter for packt Mastering Architecting Spring 5"
}
```

Output processing

The recently deployed function will now be listed in the AWS Lambda console, as follows:

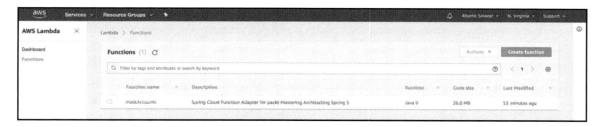

AWS Lambda console

If you don't see the recently deployed function in the web console, you must review the location where your function was created. In the example, we use the `us-east-1` region, which means that the function was deployed in North Virginia. You can check this value next to your name, at the top of the AWS Lambda console.

Finally, we are going to test our results in the AWS Lambda console. In the **Test** section, create some input with the value to mask, as follows:

```
{"value": "37567979"}
```

The expected result is as follows:

```
{"value": "****7979"}
```

In the AWS console, you will see the following results:

AWS console test result for the maskAccount function

Azure adapter

In this section, we will review how to deploy the previously coded function to Azure, which is a cloud provider supported by Microsoft. Azure supports functions by using Microsoft Azure Functions (https://azure.microsoft.com/en-us/services/functions/).

The Azure adapter is a layer coded over the Spring Cloud Function project. You can find the source of the project on GitHub (https://github.com/spring-cloud/spring-cloud-function/tree/master/spring-cloud-function-adapters/spring-cloud-function-adapter-azure).

Let's start by adding the following properties as a part of the `pom.xml` file, in the properties section:

```
<functionAppName>function-mask-account-
azure</functionAppName><functionAppRegion>westus</functionAppRegion>
<start-class>
    com.packtpub.maskaccounts.MaskAccountsApplication
</start-class>
```

Now, let's add the required dependencies for this adapter, as follows:

```
<dependency>
  <groupId>org.springframework.cloud</groupId>
  <artifactId>spring-cloud-function-adapter-azure</artifactId>
</dependency>
<dependency>
  <groupId>org.springframework.cloud</groupId>
  <artifactId>spring-cloud-starter-function-web</artifactId>
  <scope>provided</scope>
</dependency>
<dependency>
  <groupId>com.microsoft.azure</groupId>
  <artifactId>azure-functions-java-core</artifactId>
  <version>1.0.0-beta-2</version>
  <scope>provided</scope>
</dependency>
```

Then, we will add some plugins to allow the adapter to work, as follows:

```
<plugin>
  <groupId>com.microsoft.azure</groupId>
  <artifactId>azure-functions-maven-plugin</artifactId>
  <configuration>
    <resourceGroup>java-functions-group</resourceGroup>
    <appName>${functionAppName}</appName>
    <region>${functionAppRegion}</region>
    <appSettings>
      <property>
        <name>FUNCTIONS_EXTENSION_VERSION</name>
        <value>beta</value>
      </property>
    </appSettings>
  </configuration>
</plugin>
<plugin>
  <artifactId>maven-resources-plugin</artifactId>
  <executions>
    <execution>
```

```xml
      <id>copy-resources</id>
      <phase>package</phase>
      <goals>
        <goal>copy-resources</goal>
      </goals>
      <configuration>
        <overwrite>true</overwrite>
        <outputDirectory>${project.build.directory}/azure-
        functions/${functionAppName}
        </outputDirectory>
        <resources>
          <resource>
            <directory>${project.basedir}/src/main/azure</directory>
            <includes>
              <include>**</include>
            </includes>
          </resource>
        </resources>
      </configuration>
    </execution>
  </executions>
</plugin>
<plugin>
  <groupId>org.apache.maven.plugins</groupId>
  <artifactId>maven-shade-plugin</artifactId>
  <configuration>
    <createDependencyReducedPom>false</createDependencyReducedPom>
    <shadedArtifactAttached>true</shadedArtifactAttached>
    <shadedClassifierName>azure</shadedClassifierName>
    <outputDirectory>${project.build.directory}/azure-
    functions/${functionAppName}</outputDirectory>
  </configuration>
</plugin>
<plugin>
  <groupId>org.apache.maven.plugins</groupId>
  <artifactId>maven-assembly-plugin</artifactId>
  <executions>
    <execution>
      <id>azure</id>
      <phase>package</phase>
      <goals>
        <goal>single</goal>
      </goals>
      <inherited>false</inherited>
      <configuration>
        <attach>false</attach>
        <descriptor>${basedir}/src/assembly/azure.xml</descriptor>
        <outputDirectory>${project.build.directory}/azure-
```

```
            functions</outputDirectory>
            <appendAssemblyId>false</appendAssemblyId>
            <finalName>${functionAppName}</finalName>
        </configuration>
      </execution>
    </executions>
  </plugin>
```

Finally, we will create an adapter that should extend from the
AzureSpringBootRequestHandler class. The extended class will provide us with the
input and output types that enable Azure functions to inspect the class and perform any
JSON conversion to consume/produce data:

```
public class Handler
    extends AzureSpringBootRequestHandler<Flux<String>,Flux<String>> {
    public Flux<String> execute
                (Flux<String>in, ExecutionContext context) {
        return handleRequest(in, context);
    }
}
```

Now, we will modify the coded function that resides in the
MaskAccountsApplication.java file; we will change the input and output of the
function, in order to use a plain old Java object with setters and getters:

```
package com.packtpub.maskaccounts;

import org.springframework.boot.SpringApplication;
import org.springframework.boot.autoconfigure.SpringBootApplication;
import org.springframework.cloud.function.context.FunctionScan;
import org.springframework.context.annotation.Bean;

import java.util.function.Function;

@FunctionScan
@SpringBootApplication
public class MaskAccountsApplication {

    public static void main(String[] args) {
        SpringApplication.run(MaskAccountsApplication.class, args);
    }

    @Bean
    public Function<In, Out> maskAccount() {
            return value -> new Out(value.mask());
    }
}
```

```java
class In {

    private String value;

    In() {
    }

    public In(String value) {
        this.value = value;
    }

    public String mask() {
        return value.replaceAll("\\w(?=\\w{4})", "*");
    }

    public String getValue() {
        return value;
    }

    public void setValue(String value) {
        this.value = value;
    }
}

class Out {

    private String value;

    Out() {
    }

    public Out(String value) {
        this.value = value;
    }

    public String getValue() {
        return value;
    }

    public void setValue(String value) {
        this.value = value;
    }
}
```

Then we have to add a JSON configuration for Azure tooling, so we are going to create a JSON file named `function.json`, in a new folder behind the `src/main` folder, with the name of the function (`maskAccount`). This file will be used to let Azure know about the function that we want to deploy, by specifying the Java class that will be used as the entry point. The `src` folder should look as follows:

```
└── src
    ├── main
    │   ├── azure
    │   │   └── maskAccount
    │   │       └── function.json
    │   ├── java
    │   │   └── com
    │   │       └── packtpub
    │   │           └── maskaccounts
    │   │               ├── Handler.java
    │   │               └── MaskAccountsApplication.java
    │   └── resources
    │       └── application.properties
    └── test
        └── java
            └── com
                └── packtpub
                    └── maskaccounts
                        └── MaskAccountsApplicationTests.java
```

The content of the `function.json` file will be as follows:

```
{
    "scriptFile": "../mask-accounts-azure-1.0.0.BUILD-SNAPSHOT-azure.jar",
    "entryPoint": "com.packtpub.maskaccounts.Handler.execute",
"bindings": [
 {
 "type": "httpTrigger",
 "name": "in",
 "direction": "in",
 "authLevel": "anonymous",
 "methods": [
 "get",
 "post"
 ]
 },
 {
 "type": "http",
 "name": "$return",
 "direction": "out"
 }
 ],
```

```
"disabled": false
}
```

 The JSON files can be created with the Maven plugin for a non-Spring function, but the tooling doesn't work with the current version of the adapter.

Before generating the artifact that will be deployed, we have to create an `assembly` file, which is required by the Azure Maven plugin that we are using.

The `assembly` file should be placed in the `src/assembly` directory; the file will be named `azure.xml`, and will include the following content:

```
<assembly
xmlns="http://maven.apache.org/plugins/maven-assembly-plugin/assembly/1.1.3
"
    xmlns:xsi="http://www.w3.org/2001/XMLSchema-instance"
xsi:schemaLocation="http://maven.apache.org/plugins/maven-assembly-plugin/a
ssembly/1.1.3 http://maven.apache.org/xsd/assembly-1.1.3.xsd">
    <id>azure</id>
    <formats>
        <format>zip</format>
    </formats>
    <baseDirectory></baseDirectory>
    <fileSets>
        <fileSet>
            <directory>${project.build.directory}/azure-
functions/${functionAppName}</directory>
            <outputDirectory></outputDirectory>
            <includes>
                <include>*-azure.jar</include>
                <include>**/*.json</include>
            </includes>
        </fileSet>
    </fileSets>
</assembly>
```

Now, the JAR file can be created by using the following Maven goals:

```
$ mvn clean package
```

The function can be deployed locally for testing purposes, running the JAR file as a regular Java application by using the following command:

```
$ java -jar target/mask-accounts-azure-0.0.1-SNAPSHOT.jar
```

You will then see that the application is running, as follows:

The output of the Spring application, running locally

Let's try out the function using the following `curl` command:

```
$ curl -H "Content-Type: text/plain" localhost:8080/maskAccount -d
'{"value": "37567979"}'
```

You will see the following output:

Alternatively, we can deploy our function to Azure using Azure Functions Core Tools.

To do so, first, you have to install all of the required tools using the information provided at https://github.com/azure/azure-functions-core-tools#installing. Once the required tools have been installed, you can log in to Azure using the following command in your Terminal:

```
$ az login
```

After you have entered your credentials, you will see the following output on the console:

```
To sign in, use a web browser to open the page https://microsoft.com/devicelogin and enter the code FCJJ6BR47 to authenticate.
[
  {
    "cloudName": "AzureCloud",
    "id": "87487b30-19ef-4574-9177-3e24da9f5e70",
    "isDefault": true,
    "name": "Free Trial",
    "state": "Enabled",
    "tenantId": "b1ecec3c-c099-4a0f-9c20-6b2a0848c77e",
    "user": {
      "name": "asalazar@advlatam.com",
      "type": "user"
    }
  }
]
```

Deploying the coded function to Azure is pretty simple; you only have to execute the following Maven:

```
$ mvn azure-functions:deploy
```

Now, you can try out the deployed function using the following `curl` command:

```
$ curl https://<azure-function-url-from-the-log>/api/maskAccount -d
'{"value": "37567979"}'
```

The `<azure-function-url-from-the-log>` is the URL that you will get after running the `mvn azure-functions:deploy` command. For example, in the following screenshot, you can see the `https://function-mask-account-azure.azurewebsites.net/` URL:

```
[INFO] Step 4 of 4: Deleting deployment package from Azure Storage...
[INFO] Successfully deleted deployment package function-mask-account-azure.20180412191633550.zip
[INFO] Successfully deployed Function App at https://function-mask-account-azure.azurewebsites.net
[INFO] ------------------------------------------------------------------------
[INFO] BUILD SUCCESS
[INFO] ------------------------------------------------------------------------
[INFO] Total time: 12:59 min
[INFO] Finished at: 2018-04-12T19:17:31-05:00
[INFO] Final Memory: 47M/582M
[INFO] ------------------------------------------------------------------------
```

After executing the `curl` command, the output received will be as follows:

```
→  mask-accounts-azure git:(master) ✗ curl -H "Content-Type: text/plain" localhost:8080/maskAccount -d '{"value": "37567979"}'
{"value":"****7979"}
```

Output processing

We can also test the same function on the Azure Functions console, just as we did with AWS Lambda.

Summary

In this chapter, we discussed the concepts behind serverless architecture. You learned how functions can be implemented using Spring Cloud Functions, and we reviewed the adapters that can be used to deploy the functions in different cloud providers, such as AWS Lambda and Microsoft Azure Functions.

In the next chapter, we will describe what containers are, and how you can use them to containerize applications.

10
Containerizing Your Applications

Containers are becoming one of the key factors of software development, changing the way that developers are writing and deploying IT systems. These are mainly used to solve problems related to setup environments.

Working with containers can be overwhelming when you have to manage multiple containers and multi-instance environments. However, some really cool tools have been released that are designed to accomplish these container orchestration tasks. We are going to look at these tools throughout this chapter, along with the following topics:

- **Containers**:
    - Basic concepts
    - Basic commands
    - Building your own images
- **Containerizing Applications**: Docker Gradle plugin
- **Registries**: Publishing images
- **Provisioning multiple-container environments**: Docker Compose
- **Container orchestration with Kubernetes**:
    - Pods
    - Labels
    - Replication controllers
    - Services

Containers

Containers provide a lightweight approach to virtualization that consists of providing the bare minimum that an application requires in order to work. In the old days, VMs used to be the main choice for provisioning environments and running applications. However, they require a complete OS in order to work. Containers, on the other hand, reuse the host OS to run and provision the required environments. Let's learn more about this concept by looking at the following diagram:

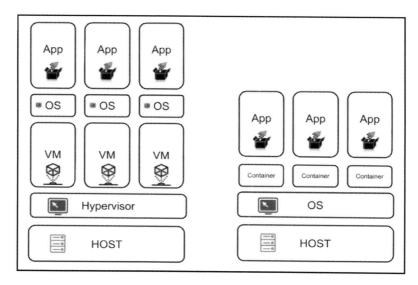

Virtual machines and containers

In the preceding diagram, we can see the **Virtual Machines** (**VMs**) on the left side and the **containers** on the right side. Let's start by learning how a Vm works.

VMs require their own OS using the hardware assigned to the VM, which is supported by the hypervisor. The preceding diagram shows three VMs, which means that we need to have installed three OSes, one per VM. When you're running applications within VMs, you have to consider the resources that will be consumed by the application and the OS.

On the other hand, containers use the kernel provided by the OS host, which also supplies the basic services for all containers using virtual-memory support for isolation. In this case, there is no need to install a whole OS for each container; this is an effective approach in terms of memory and storage usage. When you're running applications using containers, you only have to consider the resources consumed by the application.

Containers are small and can be measured in tens of megabytes, taking only a few seconds to be provisioned. In contrast, VMs are measured in tens of gigabytes, but they can take a few minutes to even start working. You should also consider OS licensing—when you're using VMs, you'll have to pay for the licenses of each installed OS. When using containers, you only need one OS that all the containers will use to function.

There are different containers currently available on the market, but Docker is the most popular implementation these days. For this reason, we are going to choose this option to explain all the concepts in this chapter.

Basic concepts

In this section, we are going to review some basic concepts and commands that you'll commonly use on a daily basis. This should help you to understand the rest of this chapter.

Containers and images

When talking about Docker, people often use the terms *containers* and *images*. The difference between these two terms is simple: a container is an instance of an image, while an image is an immutable file that's essentially a snapshot of a container. In terms of **object-oriented programming (OOP)**, we can say that images are like classes and containers are instances of these classes. For example, let's say you have a Docker image that is comprised of CentOS and Java 8. Using this image, you can create a container to run a Spring Boot application and another container to run a JEE application, as shown in the following diagram:

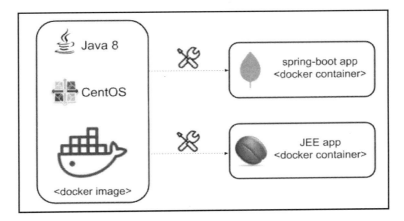

Docker images and containers

Basic commands

Docker has a large set of commands to execute different operations using containers and images. However, there is no need to be familiar with all of them. We will now review some of the most common commands that you need to know in order to work with Docker.

Running containers

We mentioned earlier that containers are instances of images. When you want to run a Docker container, you can use the following command:

```
docker run IMAGE_NAME
```

There are plenty of Docker images available on the internet. Before creating a custom image, you should first review the list of images available on Docker Hub (https://hub. docker.com/).

Docker Hub is a cloud-based registry service that allows you to link to code repositories, build your images, and test them. It also stores manually pushed images and links to Docker Cloud so that you can deploy images to your hosts. Docker Hub provides a centralized resource for container and image discovery, distribution, and change management; user and team collaboration; and workflow automation throughout the development pipeline.

Let's say that you want to run a container using nginx. In this case, all that you need to do is execute the following command in the Terminal:

```
docker run nginx
```

Once you run this command, Docker will try to find the image locally. If it's unable to find it there, it will look for the image using all the registries available (we will talk about registries later on). In our case, this is Docker Hub. The first thing you should see in the terminal is an output similar to the following:

```
⋊> ~ docker run nginx
 Unable to find image 'nginx:latest' locally
 latest: Pulling from library/nginx
 f2aa67a397c4: Downloading [===================================> ]
15.74MB/22.5MB
 3c091c23e29d: Downloading [======> ] 3.206MB/22.11MB
 4a99993b8636: Download complete
```

After executing this operation, you will get a string similar to
d38bbaffa51cdd360761d0f919f924be3568fd96d7c9a80e7122db637cb8f374 that
represents the image ID.

Some useful flags for running containers are as follows:

- The $-d$ flag runs the image as a daemon
- The $-p$ flag connects the image ports to the host

For example, the following command makes it possible to run nginx as a daemon and
maps port 80 from the container to port 32888 on the host:

```
docker run -p 32888:80 -d nginx
```

Now you will have control of the terminal again, and you can see the nginx homepage in
the http://localhost:32888/ URL, as shown in the following screenshot:

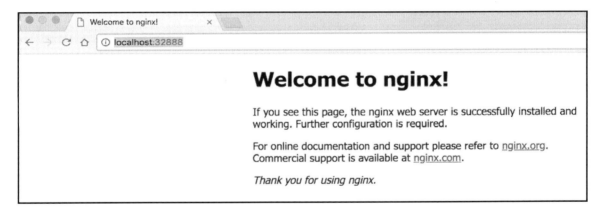

Nginx homepage

Containers only have the software and services that are strictly necessary for them to work,
which is why you'll find that they don't even include an SSH entry. If you want to get into a
container, you can use the $-it$ flag, which executes a command within the container as
follows:

```
>< ~ docker run -it nginx /bin/bash
# Now you're inside the container here
root@0c546aef5ad9:/#
```

Working with containers

If you are interested in checking all the containers running on your host, you can use the `ps` command as follows:

```
docker ps
```

The preceding command will list all the containers running on your host. If you also want to check the images that are not running, you can use the −a flag. After executing the preceding command, you'll have an output in your terminal similar to the following screenshot:

```
MacBook-Pro-de-Rene:~ moe$ docker ps
CONTAINER ID        IMAGE             COMMAND           CREATED          STATUS          PORTS        NAMES
d4ce9d0d6c83        nginx             "/bin/bash"       13 seconds ago   Up 12 seconds   80/tcp       sharp_ride
MacBook-Pro-de-Rene:~ moe$
```

The Docker ps command output

The first column of the preceding screenshot explains the information in the following list. The most useful part of this output is the **CONTAINER ID,** which can be used to perform the following operations:

- Restart the container:

  ```
  docker restart <CONTAINER ID>
  ```

- Stop the container:

  ```
  docker stop <CONTAINER ID>
  ```

- Start the container:

  ```
  docker start <CONTAINER ID>
  ```

- Remove the container:

  ```
  docker rm <CONTAINER ID>
  ```

These are the most common commands, and they provide all that you need in order to start working with Docker containers.

Working with images

Docker also has some commands that allow your system to work with images. The most commonly used commands are the following:

- Listing all the images available on the host:

```
⋊> ~ docker images
REPOSITORY TAG IMAGE ID CREATED SIZE
nginx latest ae513a47849c 4 weeks ago 109MB
```

- Removing images:

```
⋊> ~ docker rmi nginx
Untagged: nginx:latest
Untagged:
nginx@sha256:0fb320e2a1b1620b4905facb3447e3d84ad36da0b2c8aa8fe3a5a8
1d1187b884
Deleted:
sha256:ae513a47849c895a155ddfb868d6ba247f60240ec8495482eca74c4a2c13
a881
Deleted:
sha256:160a8bd939a9421818f499ba4fbfaca3dd5c86ad7a6b97b6889149fd39bd
91dd
Deleted:
sha256:f246685cc80c2faa655ba1ec9f0a35d44e52b6f83863dc16f46c5bca149b
fefc
Deleted:
sha256:d626a8ad97a1f9c1f2c4db3814751ada64f60aed927764a3f994fcd88363
b659
```

- Downloading images:

```
⋊> ~ docker pull <IMAGE NAME>
```

Building your own images

On the internet, we can find many Docker images that are ready to use. These images are created using a configuration file called the Dockerfile, which has all the instructions for provisioning the container.

The common commands that you will find as part of this file are as follows:

- FROM
- MAINTAINER
- RUN
- ENV
- EXPOSE
- CMD

Let's review all of these commands one by one in order to understand how they work.

FROM command

The FROM command is used to specify the base Docker image that will be used by the Dockerfile to build the new image. For example, if you want to create a custom image based on Debian, you should add the following line as part of your file:

```
FROM debian:stretch-slim
```

MAINTAINER command

The MAINTAINER command is used entirely for documentation purposes, and this has the Dockerfile's author name, as well as their email, as shown in the following code:

```
MAINTAINER  Your Name <your@email.com>
```

RUN command

A Dockerfile usually has more than one RUN command as part of it. These are intended to be executed as part of the system bash commands and are mainly used to install packages. For example, the following RUN command is used to install Java 8:

```
RUN \
    echo oracle-java8-installer shared/accepted-oracle-license-v1-1
    select true | debconf-set-selections && \
    add-apt-repository -y ppa:webupd8team/java && \
    apt-get update && \
    apt-get install -y oracle-java8-installer && \
    rm -rf /var/lib/apt/lists/* && \
    rm -rf /var/cache/oracle-jdk8-installer
```

The preceding command was taken from the Dockerfile provided by an image called `oracle-java8` (`https://github.com/dockerfile/java/blob/master/oracle-java8/Dockerfile`).

This command is easy to read, and each line describes how the installation process is done. The last two lines remove some directories from the container because they are no longer needed.

All installations are done as a single line because every `RUN` command generates a new layer. For example, in the `RUN` command, we can see that six instructions are executed at once. If we run those instructions one by one, we will end up having six images, each of which contains the base image plus the `RUN` command that was executed. We will not discuss layers in detail in this book, but if you feel curious, I highly encourage you to read about them at `https://docs.docker.com/storage/storagedriver/#images-and-layers`.

ENV command

The `ENV` command is used to create environmental variables in the system. The following `ENV` command is used as part of the previously mentioned Dockerfile in order to define the `JAVA_HOME` variable:

```
ENV JAVA_HOME /usr/lib/jvm/java-8-oracle
```

EXPOSE command

The `EXPOSE` command defines which ports we are going to expose from the container. For example, if you want to expose ports `80` and `32777`, you need to add the following line to your Dockerfile:

```
EXPOSE 80 32777
```

CMD command

The `CMD` command is used to specify which command should be executed once the container is started. For example, if you want to run a Java application using the standard `java -jar` command, you will need to add the following line to the file:

```
CMD java - jar your-application.jar
```

Once you have completed your Dockerfile, you should run the `build` command to create the image locally, as shown in the following code:

```
docker build -t <docker-image-name>
```

Containerizing applications

A dockerized application is a basic deployable unit that can be integrated later as part of your whole ecosystem of applications. When you're dockerizing your application, you'll have to create your own Dockerfile with all the required instructions to make your application work.

As we mentioned in the last section, we can create a container using an existing base image with the FROM command. You can also copy the Dockerfile content of the base image, but this practice is highly discouraged because it does not make sense to duplicate the code that was already written when the image was created.

It is strongly recommended that you find official images in DockerHub. Since the Dockerfile is available, you should always read it in order to avoid security issues and fully understand how the image works.

Before dockerizing an application, it is important that you make your system use environmental variables instead of configuration files. In this way, you can create images that can be reused by other applications. One of the biggest advantages of using Spring Framework is the ability to use different approaches to configure your applications. This is something that we did in Chapter 8, *Microservices*, when we used a configuration server to centralize all the application configurations. Spring makes it possible for us to use a local configuration file as part of our application, and we can override those configuration values using environment variables later.

Now let's look at how to dockerize a Spring Boot application.

In the first step, we will create the Dockerfile to run our application. The content of this file is shown in the following code:

```
FROM java:8
WORKDIR /
ARG JAR_FILE
COPY ${JAR_FILE} app.jar
EXPOSE 8080
ENTRYPOINT ["java","-jar","app.jar"]
```

Let's briefly review the commands listed in the Dockerfile:

Command	Description
FROM java:8	The base java:8 image is used
WORKDIR	Default directory within the image filesystem
ARG	We are going to use an argument for the JAR file
COPY	The provided file will be copied inside the container as app.jar
EXPOSE	Port 8080 of the container is exposed
ENTRYPOINT	Run the Java application inside the container

This Dockerfile should be located in the root of the project. The following screenshot shows the project layout:

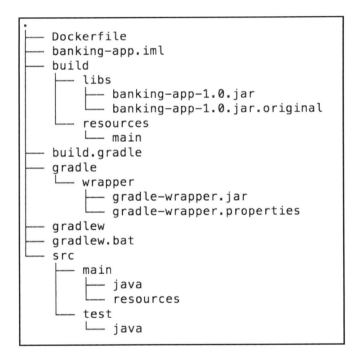

Project layout

The application JAR is located under the PROJECT/build/libs directory. This artifact is generated by running the bootRepackage task using the Gradle wrapper, as follows:

```
./gradlew clean bootRepackage
```

Once the artifact has been created, it's time to create the Docker image by running the following command:

```
$ docker build -t spring-boot:1.0 . --build-arg
JAR_FILE=build/libs/banking-app-1.0.jar
```

Once the command has finished, the image should exist locally. You can check this by running the `docker images` command:

```
$ docker images
REPOSITORY          TAG          IMAGE ID        CREATED           SIZE
spring-boot         1.0          32897af137ff    39 seconds ago    643MB
java                8            d23bdf5b1b1b    19 months ago     643MB
```

Docker images console output

Note that the `java` image is also present. This was downloaded during the `spring-boot` image build process. We can then create a container using the recently created image by running the following command:

```
$ docker run -p 8081:8080 -d --name banking-app spring-boot:1.0
```

You can now visit the application deployed in the container in the `http://localhost:8081/index` URL. The following screenshot shows this application:

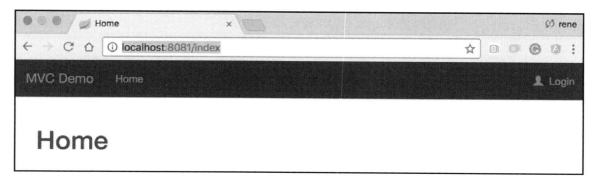

Application deployed in the container

The build process for the image can and should be automated using your preferred build tool. There are plugins for Gradle and Maven that can be integrated as part of your application. Let's look at how to integrate a Gradle plugin for this task.

Docker Gradle plugin

Even when generating a Docker image, using Docker commands is not hard or complex; it's always a good idea to automate all of these steps as much as we can. The Docker Gradle plugin is pretty useful for accomplishing this task. Let's learn how to make this part of our application.

First of all, we need to include the repository that contains the plugin and the plugin itself as a dependency within the buildscript section, as shown in the following code:

```
buildscript
{
  ...
  repositories
  {
    ...
    maven
    {
      url "https://plugins.gradle.org/m2/"
    }
  }
  dependencies
  {
    ...
    classpath('gradle.plugin.com.palantir.gradle.docker:gradledocker:
    0.13.0')
  }
}
```

Later, the plugin should be applied to the project in the same way as any other plugin—using its ID. This is shown in the following code:

```
apply plugin: 'com.palantir.docker'
```

The image build process can be customized using the parameters described in the official documentation at https://github.com/palantir/gradle-docker. To keep things simple, we are only going to indicate the image name that is required within a docker block, as shown in the following code:

```
docker
{
  name "enriquezrene/spring-boot-${jar.baseName}:${version}"
  files jar.archivePath
  buildArgs(['JAR_FILE': "${jar.archiveName}"])
}
```

As you may have noticed, we are now using the variables that are available in the `build.gradle` file, such as the generated JAR name and its version.

Now that the plugin has been fully integrated within the project, you can build the image by running the following Gradle task:

```
$ ./gradlew build docker
```

You can also check the recently created image, as shown in the following screenshot:

```
$ docker images
REPOSITORY                 TAG        IMAGE ID        CREATED          SIZE
spring-boot-banking-app    1.0        32897af137ff    24 seconds ago   680MB
java                       8          d23bdf5b1b1b    19 months ago    643MB
```

The docker images console output

It is a good idea to have all of these steps automated as this provides free documentation that can be improved in the future if needed.

Registries

As we have seen, Docker helps us to reproduce the setup used to deploy an application, but it also helps us to distribute the application to be used in different environments. This task can be performed using registries.

A registry is a service that is responsible for hosting and distributing Docker images. The default registry used by Docker is Docker Hub. There are other options available on the market that can be used as Docker registries, including the following:

- Quay
- Google Container Registry
- AWS Container Registry

Docker Hub is really popular because it works in ways that you do not even notice. For instance, if you're creating a container and the image doesn't exist in your local repository, it will automatically download the image from Docker Hub. All the existing images are created by someone else and published in these registries. In the same way, we can publish our own images in order to make them available to other people within an organization by using private repositories. Alternatively, you can publish them in public repositories. You can also self-host a Docker registry on your own hardware using solutions such as Nexus, JFrog, and so on.

Docker Hub has a free plan that allows you to create an unlimited number of public repositories and one private repository. It also offers another plan that enables you to have more private repositories, if necessary. We use Docker Hub for Docker in the same way that we use GitHub for Git repositories.

Publishing images

In order to publish a Docker image in Docker Hub, you will need to create an account and then log into Docker Hub using the terminal with the `docker login` command. After entering your credentials, you should see an output similar to the following code in the terminal:

```
$ docker login
Login with your Docker ID to push and pull images from Docker Hub. If you
don't have a Docker ID, head over to https://hub.docker.com to create one.
Username: enriquezrene
Password:
Login Succeeded
```

Now that you're logged in, you can push the image into the registry using the `docker push` command, as shown in the following code:

```
$ docker push <docker-hub-username/docker-image:tag-version>
```

When the tag version is not specified, the `latest` value is used by default. In our case, a pretty small change should be applied to the `build.gradle` file to append the `docker-hub-username` prefix required by Docker Hub, as shown in the following code:

```
docker
{
  name "enriquezrene/spring-boot-${jar.baseName}:${version}"
  files jar.archivePath
  buildArgs(['JAR_FILE': "${jar.archiveName}"])
}
```

After generating the image again, you should log into Docker Hub from the terminal using the `docker login` command, and the image can be pushed later, as shown in the following code:

```
# Login into Docker Hub
$ docker login
Login with your Docker ID to push and pull images from Docker Hub. If you
don't have a Docker ID, head over to https://hub.docker.com to create one.
Username: <username>
Password: <password>
Login Succeeded
# Push the image
$ docker push enriquezrene/spring-boot-banking-app:1.0
```

Once the image has been pushed, you can pull it and run a container in any other computer by typing the following command:

```
$ docker run enriquezrene/spring-boot:1.0
```

This will download the image from Docker Hub and run the application locally. In the same way, we can repeat this process to deploy an application in any environment.

The following screenshot shows how the pushed image looks on Docker Hub:

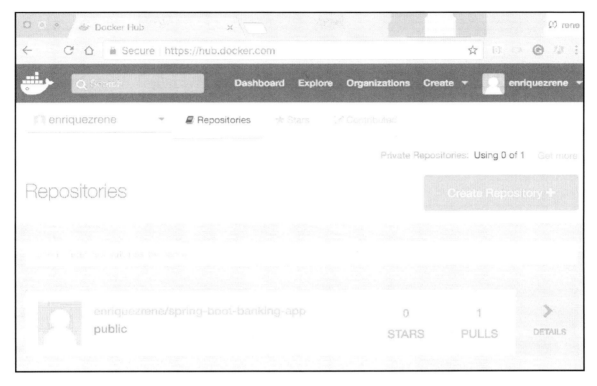

Docker image pushed into Docker Hub

The `push` command should be automated using continuous integration servers. A good idea is to execute this command once a branch is merged into a `master` tag or a new tag is created in the version control system. You should always avoid using the default `latest` tag value. Instead, you should create version numbers by yourself using an automatic process, as we did using the Gradle plugin in the previous section.

The integrated plugin also has the ability to push images using the `dockerPush` Gradle task.

Provisioning multiple-container environments

One of the biggest problems that we have when we are working with distributed applications is the difficulty of provisioning all the dependencies that an application needs in order to work. For example, let's say that you're working on an application that is persisting information in a MySQL database and using RabbitMQ for sending messages, as shown in the following diagram:

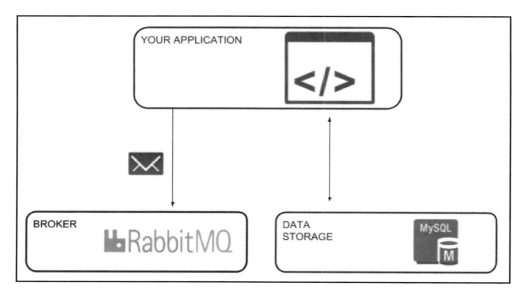

Application with RabbitMQ and MySQL dependencies

In this case, all the developers on the team will need to install MySQL and RabbitMQ on their computers if they want to have the whole environment working locally.

Installing a couple of tools is not so difficult, but as soon as your application begins to have more and more dependencies, this task becomes a nightmare. This is the exact problem that Docker Compose addresses.

Docker Compose

Docker Compose is a tool which lets you define and execute multiple-container Docker environments. This means that every dependency in your application will be containerized and managed by this tool. Docker Compose was born as an independent open source project called **FIG** that was later integrated as part of the Docker family. At present, the latest Compose version is 2.4.

In the preceding example, you need a couple of extra services running: MySQL and RabbitMQ.

When using Docker Compose, instead of installing the aforementioned services one by one, you'll able to build your application services in a `docker-compose.yaml` file, and then start and stop all of these services using this configuration file. This configuration file uses a YAML syntax that makes it easy to understand.

The content of the required configuration file to get RabbitMQ and MySQL services up and running locally is as follows:

```
mysql:
  image: mysql
  ports:
  - "3306:3306"
  environment:
  - MYSQL_ROOT_PASSWORD=my-password

rabbitmq:
  image: rabbitmq:management
  ports:
  - "5672:5672"
  - "15672:15672"
```

In the same way, we can keep adding as many services as we want within the configuration file. The use case of the `docker-compose.yaml` file is self-explanatory, and it's worth mentioning that this file has specific configurations that are not defined within the Dockerfile, such as port mapping. Running this file is not difficult at all: you only have to use the `up` command from Docker Compose, as shown in the following code:

```
$ docker-compose up
```

As a good practice, it is recommended that you provide a `docker-compose.yaml` file as part of your project. In this way, the provisioning process can be done easily by the team members.

Linking containers

When you're running distributed applications, you have to connect different services in order to make them work together. To achieve this requirement, you need to know the hostnames or IP addresses of the services, among other configuration variables. The order in which the services are made available is also important. Let's consider the following simple application:

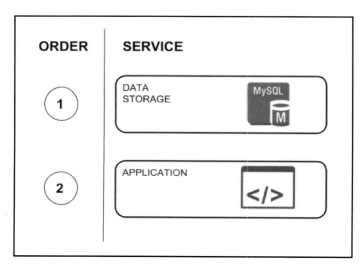

Services dependencies

The preceding diagram represents the most simple application; it has only one dependency on a database server. In this example, the application needs some database configuration parameters, such as the IP address, port, and so on. And of course, the database service should be available before starting the application; otherwise, the application won't be able to start.

In order to solve this simple requirement, you can use the following two options as part of your `docker-compose.yaml` file:

- `links`
- `depends_on`

links

The links option can be used to connect various containers by their names. This way, you won't need to know their hostnames or IP addresses at all.

depends_on

Using the depends_on option, you can specify the order in which the service should start. One service can have dependencies on more than one service, if that's needed.

Let's review the following docker-compose.yaml file, which uses both of these options:

```yaml
version: '3.1'
services:
    database:
        image: mysql:5
        ports:
            - "3306:3306"
        volumes:
            # Use this option to persist the MySQL data in a shared
            volume.
            - db-data:/host/absolute/path/.mysql
        environment:
            - MYSQL_ROOT_PASSWORD=example
            - MYSQL_DATABASE=demo
    application:
        image: enriquezrene/docker-compose-banking-app:1.0
        ports:
            - "8081:8080"
        depends_on:
            - database
        environment:
            - spring.datasource.url=jdbc:mysql://database:3306/demo
            - spring.datasource.password=example
        links:
            - database

volumes:
  db-data:
```

The `depends_on` and `links` options in the preceding code are highlighted in bold. It's pretty easy to understand from this that the application connects to the database server once the database is up.

The `enriquezrene/docker-compose-banking-app: 1.0` image has a Spring Boot application running inside of it. As part of this application, we have the configuration file named `application.properties` with the following content:

```
spring.thymeleaf.cache=false
spring.jpa.hibernate.ddl-auto=create-drop
spring.datasource.username=root
spring.datasource.url=jdbc:mysql://localhost:3306/demo
spring.datasource.password=root
```

You may notice that the password and data source URL parameters are already provided. However, Spring offers the ability to override these configurations by using environment variables, as we did in the `docker-compose.yaml` file.

Docker Compose is easy to use, and it has the same options as Docker. Let's quickly review some commands that will allow us to start using it.

This command allows us to start all the containers listed in the configuration file:

```
docker-compose up
```

The `up` command also allows the `-d` flag to run all processes as a daemon. If you want to, you can start only one service from the `docker-compose.yaml` file specifying the service name. Let's say we only want to run the database server. The command that allows you to perform this action is the following:

```
$ docker-compose up database
```

In this way, you can specify the service name for the other commands available in Docker Compose.

Once the services are up, you can list all the containers that are running using the following command:

```
$ docker-compose ps
```

If you want to stop all the commands that were started, you will need to use the following command:

```
$ docker-compose stop
```

Docker Compose is comprised of a large set of commands. For a complete reference, you can visit https://docs.docker.com/compose/reference/.

Container orchestration with Kubernetes

Kubernetes introduces a new set of concepts for an environment working with Docker containers. We could say that Kubernetes does in production what Docker Compose does in development, but there is much more to it than that. Kubernetes is an open source system originally created for Google Cloud Engine, but you can use it with AWS or any other cloud provider. It is intended for remotely managing Docker clusters in different environments.

Kubernetes introduces the following main concepts:

- Pods
- Replication controllers
- Services
- Labels

Pod

The pod is a new concept introduced by Kubernetes. A pod is comprised of a group of related containers that represent a specific application. This is the most basic unit within Kubernetes; you don't have to keep thinking about containers because pods are what you should focus on here.

Let's consider an application called XYZ that stores its information in a database that exposes a REST API that is consumed by its UI, as shown in the following diagram:

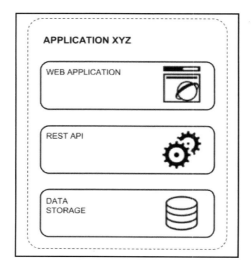

The XYZ application with its dependencies

It's obvious that we need three separate services to make this application work. If we were dealing with Docker, we would say that we need three different containers, but from a Kubernetes perspective, all these three containers represent a single pod. This abstraction allows us to manage distributed applications more easily. In order to create a pod definition, you should create a `.yaml` file describing all the containers that are part of the pod. An example of the XYZ application that we mentioned earlier is described in the following code:

```
apiVersion: v1
kind: Pod
metadata:
    name: application-xyz
spec:
    containers:
        - name: nginx
          image: nginx
          ports:
            - containerPort: 80

        - name: database
          image: mysql
          volumeMounts:
            - name: mysql-data
```

```
        mountPath: /path

    - name: api
      image: <your-api-image>
```

Once the file is created, you can execute the pod using the following Kubernetes command:

```
kubectl create -f <file-name.yaml>
```

Labels

As soon as the number of applications grows within an organization, managing all of them tends to be a nightmare. Imagine that you only have fifteen microservices and two environments: one for staging and the other for production. In this case, identifying all of the running pods would be really hard to do, and you would need to remember all of the pod names in order to query their statuses.

Labels are intended to make this task easier. You can use them to tag pods with label names that are easy to remember and which make sense to you. Since a label is a key–value pair, you have the chance to use whatever you want, including environment:<environment-name>, for instance. Let's review the following application-xyz-pod.yaml example file:

```
apiVersion: v1
kind: Pod
metadata:
    name: application-xyz
    labels:
        environment:production
        otherLabelName: otherLabelValue
spec:
    containers:
        - name: nginx
          image: nginx
          ports:
            - containerPort: 80

        - name: database
          image: mysql
          volumeMounts:
            - name: mysql-data
              mountPath: /path

        - name: api
          image: <your-api-image>
```

The code in bold shows how the label can be created. Here, you can add as many labels as you want. Let's create this pod with the following command:

```
kubectl create -f application-xyz-pod.yaml
```

Once the pod has been created, you can look for it using the labels with the following command:

```
kubectl get pod -l environment=production
```

Replication controllers

At first sight, one may think that we should care about pods, but Kubernetes recommends using another abstraction called replication controllers.

You will never run one pod instance in production. Instead, you will run many of them to offer high availability and to support all the traffic. Replication controllers are intended to ensure that a specified number of pods are up and running. It's common to have issues with services running in the wild, and sometimes a host crashes, making one or more pods unavailable. Replication controllers are constantly monitoring the system for such problems, and when a pod crashes, it automatically creates a new replica for this pod, as shown in the following diagram:

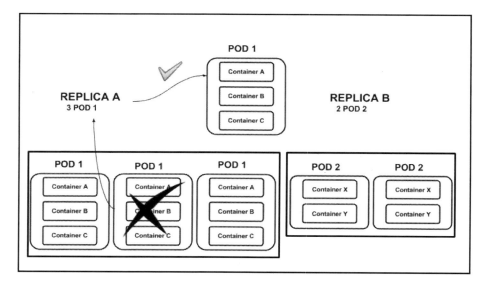

Replica services and pods

Replica controllers are also useful for rolling out new application versions. You can easily turn off all the pods associated with a specific replica and then turn the new one on.

Let's review the following file, which shows an example of a replication controller:

```
apiVersion: v1
kind: ReplicationController
metadata:
    name: application-xyz-rc
spec:
    replicas: 3
    selector:
        tier:front-end
    template:
        metadata:
            label:
                env:production
        spec:
            containers:
                ...
```

The content of this file is pretty similar for pods; the main difference is the kind of Docker Service that is specified. In this case, it uses the `ReplicaController` value. Later, we will define the desired number of replicas and the selector section can be used to specify labels.

Using this file, the replica can be created by running the `kubectl create` command, as follows:

```
kubectl create -f application-xyz-rc.yaml
```

You can verify how pods are being created when required. You can delete a pod with the following command:

```
kubectl delete pod <pod-name>
```

You can then query the available pods with the following command:

```
kubectl get pod
```

Services

It's common to have many replica services serving applications in production in order to offer a good user experience. However, no matter how many hosts or images are involved in this process, we need to offer a unique entry point for all this functionality: this is what Kubernetes services are intended for.

A Kubernetes service acts as both an endpoint and load balancer for a specific application. Since a service is located in front of a group of replicated pods, it will distribute the traffic across all the available instances.

 Remember, pods and Docker containers are ephemeral, and we can't rely on their IP addresses. This is why Kubernetes services are important for continuously providing a service.

Let's look at an example of a configuration file for a Kubernetes service:

```
apiVersion: v1
kind: Service
metadata:
    name: application-xyz-service
spec:
    ports:
        port:80
        targetPort: 80
        protocol: TCP
    selector:
        tier:front-end
```

The `kind` configuration entry in line 2 has a new value—in this case, the value is `Service`. The selector indicates the replica container associated with this service, and the rest of the configuration parameters are self-explanatory. Using this file, you can use the `kubectl create` command as follows:

```
kubectl create -f application-xyz-service.yaml
```

Furthermore, if you don't want to create a file for a service, you can directly expose an existing replica controller using the following command:

```
kubectl expose rc application-xyz-rc
```

Summary

In this chapter, we started reviewing the basic concepts of containers and how they are applied to Docker, one of the most popular products used for containerizing applications.

We then learned how to automate this process and made it part of the build process for a Java application, using Gradle as a build tool. The main intention behind automation is to be aligned to DevOps principles; we are going to talk about DevOps in detail in the following chapter. At the end of this chapter, we looked at other Docker tools that automate the provisioning process in development environments, and we also learned about Kubernetes and how it can be used for production environments. In the next chapter, we will review DevOps and release management concepts.

11
DevOps and Release Management

DevOps is an important technique that helps teams to prevent their work from becoming isolated. It also helps remove boring processes and unnecessary bureaucracy throughout the whole software development cycle. This technique is used throughout the whole software development process, from writing code to deploying applications to production.

This chapter will demonstrate how to achieve these goals by embracing automation in order to reduce the number of manual tasks and deploy applications using automated pipelines in charge of validating written code, provisioning infrastructure, and deploying the required artifacts into a production environment. In this chapter, we will review the following topics:

- Silos
- DevOps culture motivations
- DevOps adoption
- Embracing automation
- Infrastructure as code
- Applying DevOps practices using Spring Framework
- Release management pipelines
- Continuous delivery

Silos

Some years ago, the software industry used the waterfall model to manage the **systems development lifecycle (SDLC)**. The waterfall model includes many phases, such as gathering requirements, designing a solution, writing the code, verifying that the code meets the user requirements, and finally, delivering the product. In order to work on each of these phases, different teams and roles were created, including analysts, developers, software architects, QA teams, operations people, project managers, and so on. Each one of these roles were responsible for producing output and delivering it to the next team.

The steps needed to create a software system using the waterfall model are as follows:

1. Analysts gather the software requirements
2. Software architects review the requirements carefully and expand the documents with information about the tools and technologies that will be used, modules that have to be written to create the system, diagrams showing how the components are going to be connected in order to work as a whole, and so on
3. Developers follow the directions issued by the architects and code the application
4. QAs have to validate if the created software works as expected
5. The operations team deploys the software

As you might notice from these steps, at each stage, a different team is producing a well-defined output that is delivered to the next team creating a chain. This process perfectly describes how teams work using a silo mentality.

This software production process seems good at first glance. However, this approach has several disadvantages. Firstly, it is impossible to produce perfect output in each phase, and incomplete artifacts are often produced. As a result, teams and departments that are concentrated on their own processes begin to pay less attention to what everyone else in the organization does. If a member of a team feels less responsible for the problems that occur within another team, a wall of conflict arises in this area because each team works separately with several barriers between them, causing issues such as communication breakdowns, thereby disrupting the free and fluent flow of information.

How to break silos

In the previous section, we looked at how teams are organized to produce output. It's pretty self-evident that each team member by and large has the same skills as their fellow team members. As a consequence, it's impossible to ask a team of analysts to write code for a certain functionality or provision the infrastructure to deploy the application into production.

The first step to breaking silos is creating multidisciplinary teams. This means that a team should have members with different skills that will help the team approach different problems and needs.

 Ideally, each team member should have all the necessary skills to approach any kind of need. However, this goal is almost impossible to achieve.

Once you have a multidisciplinary team, you can easily end up having people working using a silo style within the same team. In order to solve this problem, you need to define a plan to make each member incorporate more skills as part of their portfolio. For example, you can make a developer work with a QA expert using the pair programming technique. In this way, the developer will learn how the QA expert thinks, and the QA will acquire development skills.

Multidisciplinary teams create an environment of collaboration across all stages of the SDLC.

DevOps culture

There a lot of definitions for DevOps. We are going to use the following:

> *"DevOps is a culture that encourages operation and development teams to work together without taking away from the specific skills and responsibilities that each team has."*

This means that the software development team takes the responsibility and ownership of the code they produce. DevOps changes the way that people are organized and the processes they follow across the SDLC.

This culture removes silos because it requires all roles to become involved in the SDLC and to work together, as shown in the following diagram:

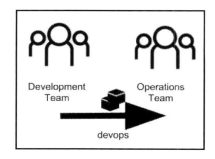

Breaking the silos in an organization

Motivations

To understand the motivation for adopting DevOps, let's look at a common real-life scenario that is often encountered in companies and organizations that develop software.

Suppose we are working at a company that hasn't yet adopted DevOps or practices for **continuous integration** (**CI**) and **continuous deployment** (**CD**) in the software development process. Let's imagine that this company has the following teams that are responsible for releasing a feature or a new piece of software:

- **Development team:** This team writes and commits code to a source version control system using branches that represent new features or bug fixes
- **Operations team:** This team installs the artifacts in the different environments—for example, through testing and production
- **QA team:** This team validates that the produced artifact works as expected from an end-user and technical perspective, and it approves or rejects the produced code

This process is repeated each time that features and bug fixes are released by developers. When first going through this common process, we realize that there are several problems, including the following:

- **Different environments:** The environment in which the code is developed often has a different environment and configuration to the staging and production environments.

- **Communication:** Forming a multidisciplinary team based on DevOps practices is going to help us break silos in organizations. Otherwise, lack of communication between teams is solved via meetings, conference calls, and/or emails.
- **Different behavior:** The number of bugs produced in a production environment varies in comparison to those produced in a development environment. There are also cases where bugs can't be reproduced at all.

As we can see, there are several problems that we need to solve here. Let's look at how to approach each one of the aforementioned problems:

- **Different environments**: With infrastructure-as-code practices, we can create files that are going to enable each environment to work with immutable servers, which is a concept that we are going to look at in a future section about infrastructure as code.
- **Communication**: Forming a multidisciplinary team based on DevOps practices is going to help us to break up silos in the organization in question.
- **Different behavior**: Using an infrastructure as code approach, we will be able to create immutable servers, guaranteeing the same behavior in different environments (such as development, test, and production).
- **Time to market**: Applying **continuous delivery** (**CD**), allows us to deploy new features to production as quickly as possible.

Most of these are common problems in real-life scenarios, which is why several organizations are adopting DevOps. This starts by breaking the silos, which has several advantages to development teams. For example, it allows them to deploy as soon as possible with fewer errors. It also allows them to react quickly to change, making the process more productive. As a result of this, I encourage your organization to break silos and become agile in order to produce higher quality applications fast.

DevOps adoption

The adoption of DevOps suits organizations' need to release applications faster, minimizing the bugs and risks associated with delivering software to production. As part of this process, we need to increase the number of automated processes for testing an application, and it's highly recommended that we remove manual processes to avoid human interaction, which can lead us to create errors.

A couple of such processes that could be automated are the environment configuration and deployment processes. Let's look at the improvements to the SDLC:

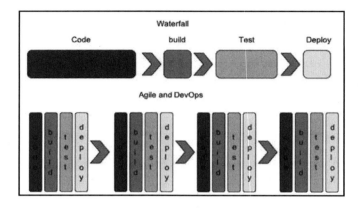

Waterfall method versus agile method and DevOps

However, there are several problems that we must handle in order to deliver software faster. First of all, we need to embrace a culture of automation. A culture of automation forces us to use many tools that we are going to introduce in the next section, and we need to understand that DevOps has become an essential part of our process because of the rise of microservices with more complex and distributed systems. However, don't forget that the *main goal of DevOps is collaboration, not just automation*.

Embracing automation

Embracing automation is one of the key factors in the adoption of DevOps. There are several tools that will help us with this process.

We need to find tools that help us to automate the process in all stages throughout the SDLC. These phases are shown in the following diagram:

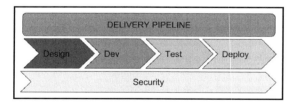

Pipeline in the organization

Within an organization, a pipeline is designed to keep the software delivery process simple. The first step is to identify the different stages, as we did in the preceding diagram, and then we should choose the right tools that will allow us to automate each stage. Let's review the stages and tools/software associated with each stage:

- Code (Git, SVN, and so on).
- Build (Maven, Gradle, npm, and so on).
- Test automation. This could also include integration testing (JUnit, Postman, Newman, JFrog, Selenium, Cucumber, Gherkin, and so on).
- Deployment (Ansible, Vagrant, Docker, Chef, Puppet, and so on).
- Monitoring (we are going to talk in depth about monitoring in `Chapter 12`, *Monitoring*).
- Continuous integration and continuous deployment (Jenkins, Hudson, and so on).
- Code analysis (Sonatype, Jacoco, PMD, FindBugs, and so on).

As we learned in `Chapter 10`, *Containerizing Your Applications*, we know how to provide environments based on containers, and we need to understand that the examples that we created can also be applied to the concept of infrastructure as code, which we are going to look at in the next section.

Infrastructure as code

Infrastructure as code refers to the process of creating files along with environment definitions and procedures that are going to be used to provision an environment. The DevOps concept started to use these scripts or files in a repository together with the code so that we can determine what code is going to be deployed in which environment. Using these practices, we can be sure that all servers and environments are consistent.

A typical organization or team will deploy their application in more than one environment, mainly for testing purposes. When we have environments for development, staging, and production, the biggest problem developers face is that each environment is different and requires different properties.

These properties may include the following configurations, among others:

- Server names
- IP addresses and port numbers
- Server queue connection
- Database connection
- Credentials

The modern era of software development suddenly brought us testability, repeatability, and transparency in building infrastructures. One of the key goals nowadays is to recreate or build complete software environments with nothing other than physical server resources within an on-premise or cloud environment.

As a consequence of this, we should be able to create database instances, populate them with initial data from scripts or backup files, and rebuild our source code to create artifacts that can be deployed whenever we want.

There are many tools that we can use to apply the concept of infrastructure as code:

- For configuration synchronization, we can use Chef, Puppet, or Ansible
- For containerized servers, we can use Docker to deploy new application versions

Some of the key benefits that we are going to embrace are as follows:

- *Immutable servers*, which apply changes by rebuilding servers in our infrastructure instead of modifying the existing servers
- *The testing of* changes to the infrastructure, which involves reproducing the environment with files that we can test in different stages of our application and infrastructure

The following diagram shows the main idea behind these two key benefits to recreate environments at each stage:

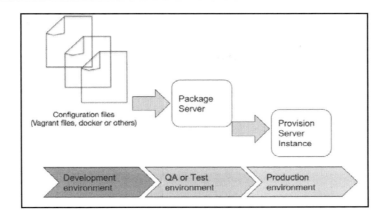

Immutable infrastructure

An automated process to provision servers gives, us the following benefits:

- It is possible to recreate any environment or server automatically
- Configuration files can store credentials or custom configurations that can be different for each environment
- The environment will always be the same at different stages

In the following section, we are going to create some examples of infrastructure as code.

Spring application and DevOps practices

Spring provides out-of-the-box features aligned to DevOps principles. Let's look at some of these.

First of all, we are going to create a new Spring Boot application using the Spring Initializr available at `https://start.spring.io.`

Supporting different environments

A common scenario in the delivery of an application is that we code the application on a development environment (almost always our own computer) and then the application is deployed in different test and production environments. Spring configuration files allow us to use different configurations on each environment. We can use a local configuration file as part of an application and then later, we can override those configuration values using environment variables. This is commonly needed because we use different credentials and configurations for each environment of our deployment configuration.

Before creating different Spring configuration files for each of the different environments that we need to deploy our application on, we are going to add an `index.html` static page behind the `/main/resources/static` folder with the following label:

```
<!DOCTYPE html>
<html lang="en">
<head>
    <meta charset="UTF-8">
    <title>Welcome devops</title>
</head>
```

For the next steps, we are going to show some features that Spring offers in favor of DevOps. We are also going to complete an exercise in which we provide Docker containers with layers that will be configured to support different environments, such as development, testing, and production environments.

First, we are going to create a different profile for our application. For example, we can create different configuration files for development, testing, and production, using three files named `application-dev.properties`, `application-test.properties` and `application-production.properties` in the `/infra-as-code/src/main/resources` folder:

```
→    resources git:(master) x  tree
.
├── application-dev.properties
├── application-production.properties
├── application-test.properties
├── application.properties
└── static
    └── index.html

1 directory, 5 files
```

In order to see how Spring Profiles work, we are going to change the port that our application is using. The property that is used to configure the port is `server.port`. Let's change this value for each one of the different files we have, as follows:

`application-dev.properties`:

```
server.port = 8090
```

`application-test.properties`:

```
server.port = 8091
```

`application-production.properties`:

```
            server.port = 8092
```

Selecting profiles

Before running an application supporting different profiles, you will need to select the desired profile to use the configuration needed. A profile can be selected using the `spring.profiles.active` flag using the JVM parameter, as follows:

```
$ java -Dspring.profiles.active=dev -jar target/infra-as-code-0.0.1-
SNAPSHOT.jar
```

Finally, you can check the application in the browser using the port associated with the profile provided. Valid values for the `spring.profiles.active` flag are as follows:

- `dev`
- `production`
- `test`

If you don't provide any value for the flag, then the configurations from `application.properties` will be used.

This is a simple example of exploring profiles in Spring. Remember that with profiles, we can also configure datasources, queues, beans, and anything you need. You can always override any of the provided configuration variables using environment variables.

Additionally, as we saw in `Chapter 10`, *Containerizing Your Applications*, we are able to dockerize a Spring Boot application, and with this knowledge, we can learn about immutable servers and how to test infrastructure changes.

In this section, we are going to learn a similar way to recreate the infrastructure using Vagrant (`https://www.vagrantup.com/`) version 1.7.0 or later. This may require virtualization software (for example, VirtualBox: `https://www.virtualbox.org/`).

Another tool that can perform the same task is Ansible (`http://ansible.com/`), which is not covered in this chapter.

Vagrant

Vagrant is a tool that is designed to recreate virtual environments that are primarily intended for development. The functionality is based on VirtualBox, and it can use provisioning tools such as Chef, Salt, or Puppet.

It also makes it possible to work with different providers, such as Amazon EC2, DigitalOcean, VMware, and others.

Vagrant uses a configuration file named `Vagrantfile`, which contains all the configurations needed to provision the desired environment. Once the aforementioned configuration file is created, the `vagrant up` command is used to install and configure the environment using the provided instructions.

Vagrant has to be installed on the machine before we continue. To do this, follow the tool's documentation available at `https://www.vagrantup.com/intro/getting-started/install.html`.

Working with Vagrant

Now, we are going to create a `Vagrantfile` configuration file in the root of our application to create a simple environment. We will provide a Linux distribution environment, which will be Ubuntu. The content of the `Vagrantfile` is as follows:

```
# Vagrantfile API/syntax version. Don't touch unless you know what you're
doing!
VAGRANTFILE_API_VERSION = "2"

Vagrant.configure(VAGRANTFILE_API_VERSION) do |config|

  config.vm.box = "hashicorp/precise32"
```

```
config.vm.network :forwarded_port, guest: 8090, host: 8090
config.vm.network "public_network", ip: "192.168.1.121"
#config.vm.synced_folder "target","/opt"

config.vm.provider "virtualbox" do |vb|
  vb.customize ["modifyvm", :id, "--memory", "2048"]
end

# provision
config.vm.provision "shell", path:"entrypoint.sh"

end
```

Pay attention to line 6 of Vagrantfile:

```
config.vm.box = "hashicorp/precise32"
```

We are creating our Linux environment from an already built VM box from hashicorp/precise32.

Before continuing with the provision of the environment using Vagrant, we are going to create an ssh file that will install JDK 8 for us. At the root of the project, create an entrypoint.sh file with the following content:

```
#!/usr/bin/env bash
sudo apt-get update

echo "Install Java 8.."
sudo apt-get install -y software-properties-common python-software-properties

echo oracle-java8-installer shared/accepted-oracle-license-v1-1 select true | sudo /usr/bin/debconf-set-selections
sudo add-apt-repository ppa:webupd8team/java -y

sudo apt-get update

sudo apt-get install oracle-java8-installer
echo "Set env variables for Java 8.."
sudo apt-get install -y oracle-java8-set-default

# Start our simple web application with specific JVM_ARGS and SPRING_PROFILE
echo "Run our springboot application."
java -Dspring.profiles.active=dev -jar /vagrant/target/infra-as-code-0.0.1-SNAPSHOT.jar
```

Then, to create the box and provision the VM, we are going to run the following on the Console:

```
vagrant up
```

On the first attempt, it will take some minutes to download the box and provision the server. Between these processes, you will be asked which network interface you will use to provision your server with the question *Which interface should the network bridge to?*. You can then choose what is more convenient for your machine.

At the end of the whole output of our execution, we will see our Spring application running on the provisioned server, as shown in the following screenshot:

Now we can check our application is running on port 8090 (http://localhost:8090/) in the browser. You can check the Java process running inside Vagrant by accessing ssh with the following command:

```
vagrant ssh
```

This will open an ssh session on our provision server, allowing us to see the process already created in the console:

```
vagrant@precise32:~$ ps aux | grep java
```

The output of the result will be our running Java process, as shown in the following screenshot:

```
0:07 java –Dspring.profiles.active=dev –jar /vagrant/target/infra-as-code-0.0.1-SNAPSHOT.jar
```

To stop the VM, we can use the vagrant halt command in the console:

```
vagrant halt
```

To destroy the created VM you can enter the following:

```
vagrant destroy
```

We just learned to express our infrastructure as code using Vagrant. We can create an environment or server needed for the different stages using different tools; we can review this in the previous chapter. In the next section, we are going to create an example of the process of release management.

Release management

To bring your code to production, the process must be planned out.

This process of planning is called **release management**. Throughout this process, we need to take care of the integrity and consistency of the existing services, guaranteeing the operation of our systems.

To understand the steps involved in the release management process, we are going to look at the following concepts:

- pipelines
- Continuous integration
- Continuous delivery and continuous deployment

pipelines

A pipeline is a sequence of steps that we must go through to accomplish a goal. We looked at this concept in `Chapter 7`, *Pipe-and-Filter Architectures*. The same concept in this context is used to execute a sequence of steps in our release management process. A pipeline will assist us during the software delivery process in different environments. We are going to create a simple pipeline that consists of five stages:

- Automatically building our projects
- Running tests (such as unit and integration)
- Deploying to staging
- Running an acceptance test
- Deploying to production (this includes deploying our application in a cloud or on-premise server)

The following diagram shows how the pipeline will look:

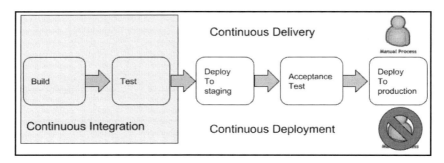

Pipeline CI/CD

Each stage could have one or more tasks or jobs, such as creating a database schema, provisioning a box with Vagrant, cloning a Docker container, and so on.

The previous diagram is divided into two parts:

- Continuous integration
- Continuous deployment

In the next few sections, we are going to briefly look at these two concepts.

Continuous integration

Continuous integration (CI) refers to the practice in which developers merge their produced code into the main branch as often as possible. The merged code should work without bugs and it should also provide value for the business.

Using CI, we can automatically validate the committed code by running a set of automated tests. When we are using this practice, we are working on a CI codebase, avoiding the problems that arose in the past when scheduling a specific date and time to release a build.

With the CI approach, the most important goal is to automate the test to guarantee that the application is not broken any time the new commits are pushed into the main source code branch.

Continuous delivery and continuous deployment

CD is a process based on CI. As part of the CD process, we need other steps that are required to deploy the application to a production environment including tasks such as configuring and provisioning servers (infrastructure as code), acceptance testing, and preparing the build for a production environment.

 A continuous deployment process differs from a continuous delivery process when deploying in a production environment without *human* intervention.

We are now going to create an example based on our simple pipeline. To focus on the processes of CI and CD, we are going to use the project that we created in the last chapter's *Docker Compose* section that showed you how to containerize your application. This project includes a complete environment that is ready to use, and which already includes an automated test.

Automating pipelines

As previously explained, we are going to need several tools to automate our pipeline for our example. For this, we are going to use the following:

- A GitHub repository for our code: We can push our code to a repository and create a merge that automatically launches the build and test
- Gradle or Maven to build our project
- Junit, Postman, and Newman to test the automation
- Docker to deploy into containersJenkins to act as our automation server for CI and CD

First, we are going to push our code to a repository. To do this, we are going to use GitHub. Create an account if you haven't already.

Open a terminal and go to the root folder of our application. For our convenience, we are going to push the repository from our machine, so we are going to initialize our project as a repository. In the command line, execute the following:

```
$ git init
```

The output of the command will look as follows:

```
Initialized empty Git repository in
/Users/alberto/TRABAJO/REPOSITORIES/banking-app/.git/
```

Then we are going to add all our files to a new local repository, as shown in the following code:

```
$ git add –A
```

Now we are going to commit our code locally, as shown in the following code:

```
$ git commit –m initial
```

The output of our local commit will print the following initial lines:

```
[master (root-commit) 5cc5f44] initial  40 files changed, 1221
insertions(+)
```

To push our code, we then need to create a repository in our GitHub account. We can create a new repository by going to the **Repositories** section, clicking on the green **Create Repository** button, and filling in the name and description of the repository, as shown in the following screenshot:

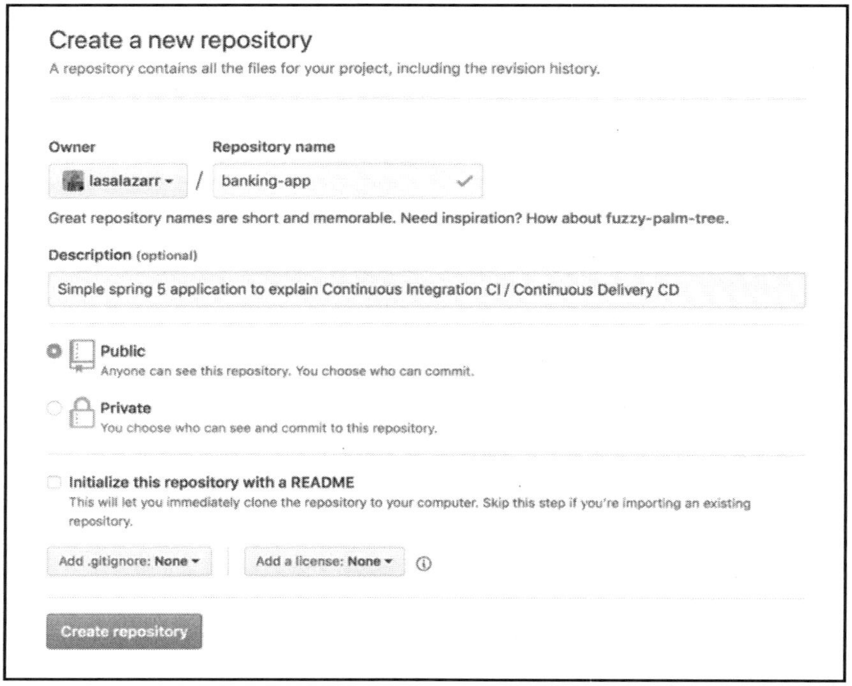

Creating a GitHub repository

We now have the URL of our repository—for
example, `https://github.com/$YOUR_GITHUB_USER/bank-app`. The result of the
repository that we created will look like the following screenshot:

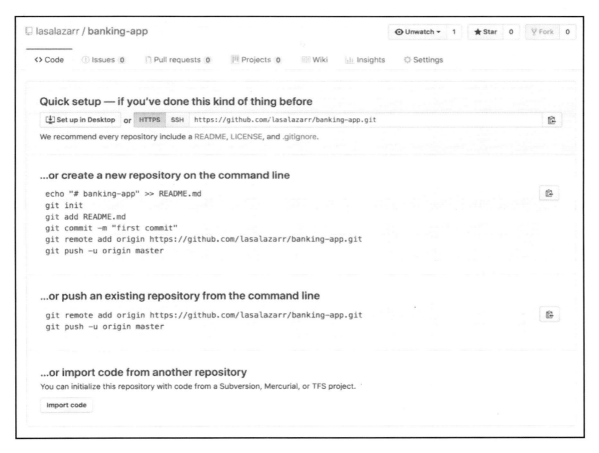

GitHub repository

As per the instructions given in GitHub, we now need to push our code to the repository
using the command line:

```
$ git remote add origin https://github.com/lasalazarr/banking-app.git
```

Then, we will push our changes from the local repository to our GitHub repository, as shown in the following code:

```
$ git push -u origin master
```

Now we can review our code on our GitHub account repository and, as recommended, add a README file to explain the purpose of the application.

In the next section, we are going to look at the concept of a CI server before continuing with our exercise.

Jenkins

Jenkins is a continuous integration server that is in charge of automating our pipeline. Before integrating with our Git repository to build our application automatically, let's review the key concepts behind the CI server:

- **Pipeline**: A pipeline consist of a set of sequential steps that will occur in the order in which they are arranged. The pipeline is also where we can parallelize tasks.
- **Job**: This is a small unit of work, such as *run test* or *pull our code*.
- **Queue**: This represents all queuing jobs that the CI server will run when there is the capacity to do so.
- **Plugin**: These are the features that we can add to our CI server. For example, we can use one plugin to connect to our Git repository.
- **Master/slave**: The master is the host that can delegate work to a slave client machine to scale our CI.

Jenkins has different methods of distribution. We can see more details about this project at https://jenkins.io/download/. For our example, we are going to use a Docker image that is ready to use.

As we already have Docker installed, we can pull the Jenkins image in the command line by running the following:

```
$ docker pull jenkins/jenkins
```

Now we can see our image by running the following:

```
$ docker images
```

Now we are going to run our Jenkins master from our container by running the following in the command line:

```
$ docker run -p 8080:8080 -p 50000:50000 -v jenkins_home:/var/jenkins_home
jenkins/jenkins:lts
```

Pay attention to the output of the console with the generated administrator password, as shown in the following screenshot:

****
****
****

Jenkins initial setup is required. An admin user has been created and a password generated.
Please use the following password to proceed to installation:

081b79835bbb400a833b7963b31afdf0

This may also be found at: /var/jenkins_home/secrets/initialAdminPassword

****
****

Generating the Jenkins password

We can now see our Jenkins server is running using `http://localhost:8080/`.

The first step is to paste the administrator password that we have just seen on the console, as shown in the following screenshot:

Unlocking Jenkins

We are now going to install the suggested plugins, which is going to take a while. Then we will continue the process by creating an admin user and URL.

We are going to enable build triggering, so we are going to configure our Jenkins instance for receiving push notifications from GitHub. To do this, go through the following steps:

1. Go to the Jenkins home page (`http://localhost:8080`) and then click on the **New item** icon in the left menu.
2. Enter the name of the project and select **Freestyle project**. After doing this, click on the **OK** button, as shown in the following screenshot:

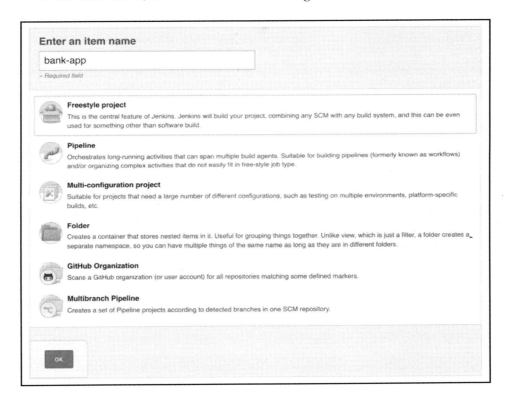

3. Jenkins will show a page where the job steps should be configured. First, enter a description for the project and GitHub URL repository created as shown in the following screenshot:

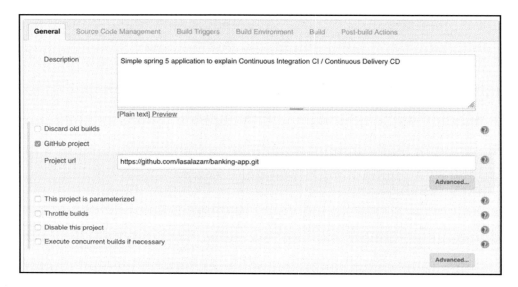

4. Enter the credentials of your user account for GitHub, as is shown in the following screenshot:

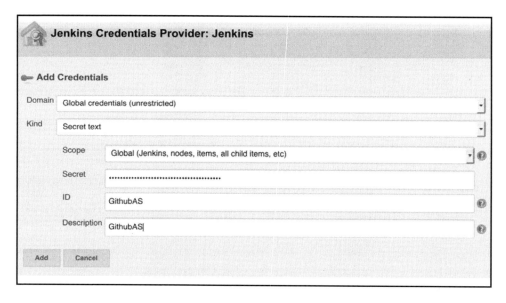

5. Finally, at the end of the page select Gradle as the build tool for the project:

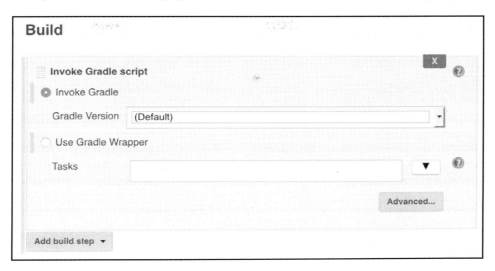

The job created can be configured to be triggered every time we commit code to GitHub. The job will download the code, run tests, and generate the deployable artifact (JAR file) using Gradle. You can add additional steps in this job to build, tag, and push Docker images in Docker Hub and later deploy it automatically on an on-premise or cloud-based server.

Summary

In this chapter, we have familiarized ourselves with the meaning of a DevOps culture and how it affects the processes of an organization. We also looked at how to automate the instrumentation process of servers, using techniques such as infrastructure as code to embrace automation. Furthermore, we learned how to build pipelines that are capable of getting the latest implemented features from a repository, validating the code, running tests on different levels, and bringing the application to production. In the next chapter, we will look at the concerns surrounding the monitoring of applications, looking at why it is so important to care for them.

12
Monitoring

Once an application is deployed to a production environment, monitoring is one of the key aspects that comes into play. Here, we need to take control of uncommon and unexpected behaviors; it's essential to be aware of how the application is working so we can take action as soon as possible in order to solve any undesired behavior.

This chapter gives some recommendations with regards to the techniques and tools that can be used to monitor the performance of an application, bearing in mind technical and business metrics.

Throughout this chapter, we will cover the following topics:

- Monitoring
  - Application Monitoring
  - Business Monitoring
- Monitoring Spring applications
- APM application monitoring tools
  - Response time
  - Database metrics
  - JVM metrics
  - Web transactions

Monitoring

Every single application is created to solve specific business requirements and accomplish certain business goals, so it is essential to assess on a regular basis an application to verify whether these goals are being accomplished. As part of this verification process, we want to measure the health and performance of our application using metrics that can give us insights into the following factors:

- **Application Monitoring**: When we are talking about the health of an application, it is important to know the amount of resources that are being used, such as CPU, memory consumption, threads, or I/O processes. Recognizing potential errors and bottlenecks is important to know whether or not we need to scale, tune, or refactor our code.
- **Business Monitoring**: These metrics are helpful to understand key business indicators about the business itself. For example, if we have an online store, we want to know whether or not we are accomplishing the established sales goals, or in a banking application, we would like to know how many transactions and customers we receive in a certain branch office, channel, and so on.

We are going to use the banking application created in `Chapter 5`, *Model-View-Controller Architectures,* as an example to list a number of monitoring concepts that can apply to it. Let's start showing how we can monitor the aforementioned application using the tooling that Spring Framework brings out-of-the-box.

Monitoring Spring applications

Spring Framework has some built-in features for monitoring and providing metrics to know the health of applications. We have multiple ways to do this, so let's review some of them:

- We can use an old-fashioned approach that implies creating interceptors around methods to log everything we want around them.
- Spring Actuator can be used along side Spring Boot applications. Using this library, we can review the health of an application; it provides an easy way to monitor applications via HTTP requests or JMX. Additionally, we can use tools to index the data produced and to create graphs that are helpful to understand the metrics. There are plenty of options to create graphs, including:
  - ELK Stack (ElasticSearch, Logstash, and Kibana)
  - Spring-boot-admin
  - Prometheus

- Telegraph
- Influx, and
- Graphana, among others

Spring Actuator can be integrated as part of an existing Spring Boot application adding the following dependency as part of the `build.gradle` file:

```
compile('org.springframework.boot:spring-boot-starter-actuator')
```

If we are using **Maven**, we would add the following dependency as part of the `pom.xml` file:

```
<dependency>
    <groupId>org.springframework.boot</groupId>
    <artifactId>spring-boot-starter-actuator</artifactId>
</dependency>
```

Actuator supports many configurations that must be provided in the `application.properties` file. We are going to add some properties to this file to provide metadata, such as the name, description, and version of our application. Also, we are going to run the Actuator endpoints in another port with the security model disabled:

```
info.app.name=Banking Application Packt
info.app.description=Spring boot banking application
info.app.version=1.0.0
management.port=8091
management.address=127.0.0.1
management.security.enabled=false
```

Then, after running the application, some endpoints provided by Actuator will be available. Let's review some of them:

- **Health**: This endpoint provides some information in general about the application health in the `http://localhost:8091/health` URL:

```
{
    "status": "UP",
    "diskSpace": {
        "status": "UP",
        "total": 499963170816,
        "free": 118312316928,
        "threshold": 10485760
    },
    "db": {
        "status": "UP",
        "database": "MySQL",
        "hello": 1
    }
}
```

Health endpoint result

- **Info**: This endpoint provides information about the metadata of the application, which was previously configured in the `application.properties` file. The information is available at `http://localhost:8080/info`:

```json
{
    "app": {
        "version": "1.0.0",
        "description": "Spring boot banking application",
        "name": "Banking Application Packt"
    }
}
```

Info endpoint result

- **Metrics**: This provides information about the OS, JVM, threads, classes loaded, and memory. We can view this information at `http://localhost:8080/metrics`:

```json
{
    "mem": 617992,
    "mem.free": 422793,
    "processors": 8,
    "instance.uptime": 80540,
    "uptime": 89247,
    "systemload.average": 2.8125,
    "heap.committed": 537600,
    "heap.init": 262144,
    "heap.used": 114806,
    "heap": 3728384,
    "nonheap.committed": 82368,
    "nonheap.init": 2496,
    "nonheap.used": 80393,
    "nonheap": 0,
    "threads.peak": 44,
    "threads.daemon": 37,
    "threads.totalStarted": 47,
    "threads": 40,
    "classes": 10676,
    "classes.loaded": 10676,
    "classes.unloaded": 0,
    "gc.ps_scavenge.count": 10,
    "gc.ps_scavenge.time": 122,
    "gc.ps_marksweep.count": 2,
    "gc.ps_marksweep.time": 131,
    "httpsessions.max": -1,
    "httpsessions.active": 0,
    "datasource.primary.active": 0,
    "datasource.primary.usage": 0
}
```

Metrics endpoint result

- **Trace**: This provides information about the most recent requests made to our application. We can view this information at `http://localhost:8080/trace`:

```
[
  {
    "timestamp": 1534129545525,
    "info": {
      "method": "GET",
      "path": "/notifications",
      "headers": {
        "request": {
          "host": "localhost:8080",
          "connection": "keep-alive",
          "upgrade-insecure-requests": "1",
          "user-agent": "Mozilla/5.0 (Macintosh; Intel Mac OS X 10_13_5) AppleWebKit/537.36 (KHTML, like Gecko) Chrome/66.0.3359.181 Safari/537.36",
          "accept": "text/html,application/xhtml+xml,application/xml;q=0.9,image/webp,image/apng,*/*;q=0.8",
          "referer": "http://localhost:8080/home",
          "accept-encoding": "gzip, deflate, br",
          "accept-language": "es-US,es-419;q=0.9,es;q=0.8",
          "cookie": "Idea-ad36c147=0f414a92-008d-4e96-b64d-d96429bf4bdb; Idea-ad36c507=28f5587a-daed-4174-a538-fec2b8102dbf; Idea-ad36c508=c40a7ec8
            -331c-4ba9-8c72-13f26fcbc953; LFR_SESSION_STATE_20120=1528146813351; GUEST_LANGUAGE_ID=es_ES; LFR_SESSION_STATE_30742=1528147037724;
            screenResolution=1680x1050; JSESSIONID.dcb1239b=node0mcuofpehqrxhfhlc0ym37mar22.node0; JSESSIONID.9b15404c
            =node9z8dj0syta0g23pawjcb58q623.node0; iconSize=32x32; JSESSIONID.38b4114e=node0cm5zokux6euv18shfm4zd2wfp2.node0; JSESSIONID.21fa506c
            =node0afuzhiiqe4shy4a45xlc1jko5.node0; hudson_auto_refresh=false; JSESSIONID.c8c39d61=node0aj7c35gorejwxi4lazhmpq630.node0; JSESSIONID
            .aaec70b6=node07xeuepc4rjk31qyukg4puic8p1.node0; JSESSIONID.16bb3ae9=node01vfct5k885ol119dne3gzrihZa1.node0; JSESSIONID
            =9353F6BE8D8BAD8A223CAB7983EA4AA1",
          "x-hola-urblocker-bext": "reqid 6783458: before request, vpn is not allowed, send headers",
          "x-hola-request-id": "6783458"
        },
        "response": {
          "X-Content-Type-Options": "nosniff",
          "X-XSS-Protection": "1; mode=block",
          "Cache-Control": "no-cache, no-store, max-age=0, must-revalidate",
          "Pragma": "no-cache",
          "Expires": "0",
          "X-Frame-Options": "DENY",
          "X-Application-Context": "application",
          "Content-Type": "text/html;charset=UTF-8",
          "Content-Language": "es-US",
          "Transfer-Encoding": "chunked",
          "Date": "Mon, 13 Aug 2018 03:05:45 GMT",
```

Trace endpoint result

If we want to review all endpoints, we can find these in the official documentation of spring: `https://docs.spring.io/spring-boot/docs/current/reference/htmlsingle/#production-ready-endpoints`.

As we have seen in the Actuator library, we are getting snapshots of our application at a certain time, knowing the status and health of the application, or even tracing the most commonly used endpoints.

Sometimes, the information provided is enough. If you are looking to have graphics and inspect historical data, you should integrate the tools we mentioned earlier.

Spring Actuator also offers the ability to collect custom metrics about the application; this is helpful for gathering business metrics. For example, if we are working with an application to create savings accounts, we can collect metrics to know how many accounts are being created. Then, after opening more branch offices, we can see how many more accounts are created and figure out the impact it has on the business itself.

The key factor when we are collecting business metrics is to understand what is important for the business. To achieve this task, it is important to work together with business people.

Business metrics are also helpful for understanding the impact we generate after releasing new features. It also facilitates an understanding of unexpected behaviors or bugs. Imagine that you roll out a new application version using a different email provider; you should compare the number of emails that are being delivered after the change with the number of emails delivered before changing the email provider. If you find a big difference in these numbers, you will need to check what is happening because the difference should not be too much. If you want to learn how to create custom metrics, I encourage you to visit this link: `https://docs.spring.io/spring-boot/docs/current/reference/html/production-ready-metrics.html`.

There are many tools available on the market that allow us to monitor applications without changing the code, and these tools are referred to as **Application Performance Management** tools (**APM**). We are going to review how these work in the next section.

Application Performance Management (APM) tools

A huge evolution has emerged in monitoring and tools since the rise of the cloud; there are tools and companies that just work on APM tools entirely. Several of them are based on the JVM and bytecode instrumentation, and today these tools have evolved to even measure user experiences of our applications. The most popular at the moment are the following:

- New Relic (`https://newrelic.com/`)
- App Dynamics (`https://www.appdynamics.com/`)
- Dynatrace (`https://www.dynatrace.com/technologies/java-monitoring/spring/`)
- DataDog (`https://www.datadoghq.com/`)

All of these tools give us the ability to monitor our application layers, health (CPU, memory, threads, I/O), databases, and top SQL queries. They also allow us to detect bottlenecks, business indicators, and responses time. For example, we are going to monitor our application using New Relic.

New Relic

New Relic is a tool that provides instrumentation for our entire environment, not just our application. Consequently, we can monitor the entire environment of our applications, including factors such as databases, application servers, load balancers.

For example, we are going to create a trial account at the following link (`https://newrelic.com/signup`). After you have signed up for a **New Relic** account, you will be directed to the control panel, as shown in the following screenshot:

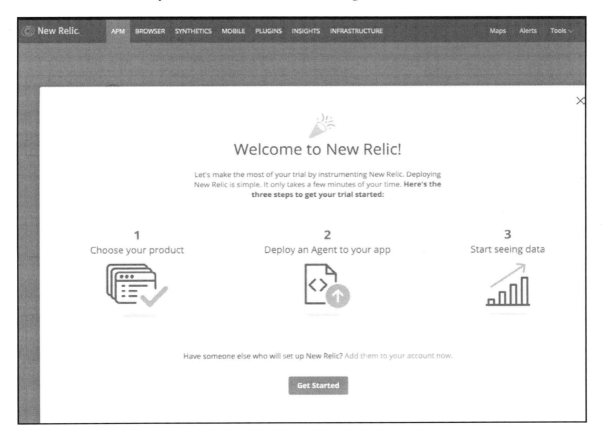

We are going to continue this process with the following steps:

1. Choose to monitor applications and accept a 14-day free trial:

2. Select the Java application option:

3. Generate a license key and download and install the agent. Here, we are going to create a folder name `newrelic` in the root of our application, and copy the content of the ZIP that was recently downloaded:

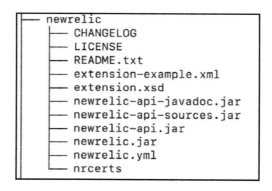

4. We are now going to replace `newrelic.yml` with our key license and application name, as in the following screenshot:

```
license_key: '835d673f2362c13ff336904c9461c82c5781652d'

# Agent Enabled
# Use this setting to disable the agent instead of removing it from the startup command.
# Default is true.
agent_enabled: true

# Set the name of your application as you'd like it show up in New Relic.
# If enable_auto_app_naming is false, the agent reports all data to this application.
# Otherwise, the agent reports only background tasks (transactions for non-web applications)
# to this application. To report data to more than one application
# (useful for rollup reporting), separate the application names with ";".
# For example, to report data to "My Application" and "My Application 2" use this:
# app_name: My Application;My Application 2
# This setting is required. Up to 3 different application names can be specified.
# The first application name must be unique.
app_name: Banking App Monitoring Packt
```

5. Restart your application, including the `javaagent` parameter, as shown in the following:

```
-javaagent:/full/path/to/newrelic.jar
```

6. In our case, to run the application with the agent would appear as follows:

```
java -javaagent:newrelic/newrelic.jar -jar build/libs/banking-
app-1.0.jar
```

Finally, we can see our new relic dashboard with the same name (**Banking App Monitoring Packt**), which we define in our `newrelic.yaml` file. This will contain all the information on our application:

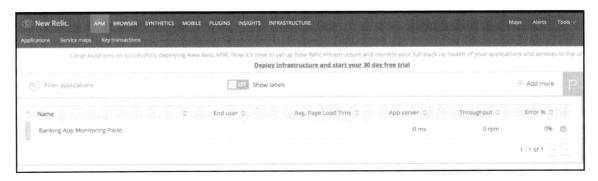

You can also navigate to the application several times to see more data provided to the APM.

We can then drill down on the information provided, including the following:

- The response time:

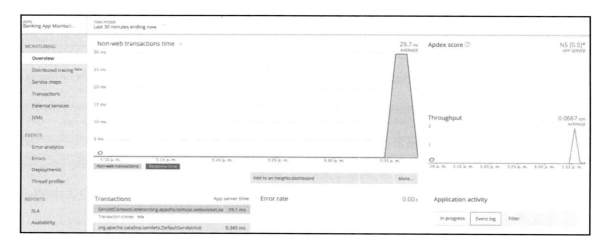

- Database metrics:

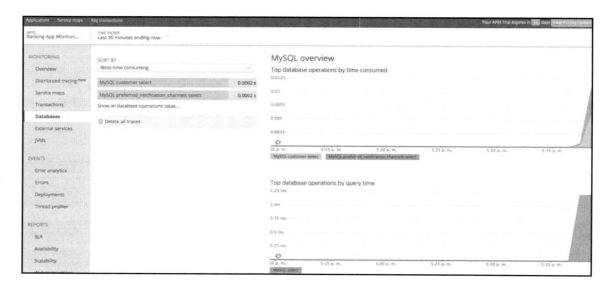

- JVM metrics:

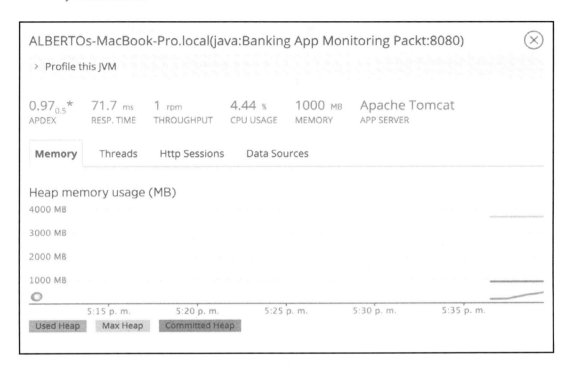

- Web transactions:

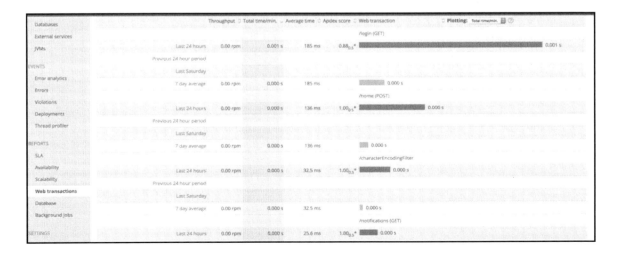

You can explore all the tabs from the left-hand menu to see more metrics of our applications. As we have learned, with all these tools, we can ensure the health of our applications and review whether we are free from problems and bottlenecks. You can then continue exploring the APMs.

Summary

Throughout this chapter, we have learned how to collect useful metrics regarding indicators both from a technical and business perspective. We have also learned how to use APMs to monitor our environment and get the information that we need in order to understand the health, status, and statistics of most-used transactions, including the response time of our applications. All this information will help us to maintain our applications in production, and to respond quickly to any possible performance issues.

In the next chapter, we are going to review security practices and how to write them using Spring.

13
Security

Security is a field that teams often do not pay close attention to when developing their products. There are a few key considerations that developers should keep in mind when writing code. Most of the considerations listed in this chapter are obvious, but others aren't, so we will discuss all of them.

We will cover, the following topics in this chapter:

- Why security is important as part of an application's architecture
- Key recommendations for keeping your software secure:
    - Authentication and authorization
    - Cryptographic
    - Data input validation
    - Sensitive data
    - Social engineering
    - Penetration testing
- Authentication as a service

We will start by introducing the importance of security as part of an application's architecture.

Why security is important as a part of an application's architecture

Over the past few years, I have seen many cases of organizations or companies reviewing their software security concerns after having already gone into production. This usually happens when their systems face security issues or their businesses lose money due to downtime or compromised data.

It is widely known that security concerns and processes should be included as a part of the **Software Development Life Cycle (SDLC)**. Since security is an aspect that should be considered as part of every single application, it is imperative to ensure that our applications and code have security constraints that allow us to feel confident about our software at all stages (design, development, testing, and deployment):

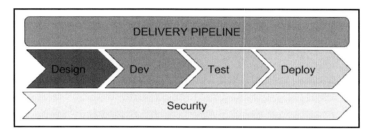

Security as a part of the SDLC

Our main goal should be to prevent our application from being compromised before we deliver it to a production environment. This avoids exposing sensitive data and to ensures that the application was designed while keeping possible vulnerabilities in mind. Ideally, we should address all of our security concerns before our systems are used by customers. As developers, we mostly only receive functional requirements. However, sometimes we don't receive a security requirement. When developing our code and applications, we must care about security as much as we care about performance, scalability, and other non-functional requirements.

Some key aspects to keep in mind when writing software that is designed to avoid security threats are as follows:

- Systems are hard to decrypt
- The system security should be tested in every stage of the SDLC
- Penetration tests should be executed against the application
- A secure end-to-end communication should be ensured in the system
- Anti-phishing practices should be applied in the application code

In the next section, we will provide a set of recommendations that should be followed to address security concerns during the SDLC process.

Key security recommendations

There are several types of attacks that can be directed at a system or network and can be used to establish communications. Common examples include viruses, malware, phishing, spear phishing, **Denial-of-Service (DoS)**, and so on. Every year, even more sophisticated attacks are discovered, with many different targets. In this section—which will be about key security recommendations—we will focus on securing the code and environment for web and mobile applications.

There are several processes and models that can be used to ensure security in web and mobile applications. In the upcoming sections, we will explore the main recommendations for keeping your software safe from common security threats.

Authentication and authorization

The simplest definition of authentication is the process of verifying the identity of a user; authorization is the process of verifying what an authenticated user can do. For example, when we log in as a user on our computer, we are granted access, allowing us to execute actions with the available resources (this includes files, applications, and so on).

In the applications that we create, authentication is the process of validating access to the application, and authorization is the process of protecting our resources, like pages, web services, databases, files, queues, and so on. During the authentication process, we validate the identities of those using the application. Authentication includes processes such as preventing to our application before providing valid credentials, multi-factor authentication (such as a secure image), **one-time password (OTP)**, tokens, and more.

With regards to implementation, we already created a few application examples in previous chapters using Spring Security, which is an extensible framework that can be used to secure Java applications. Spring Security can be used to handle authentication and authorization, as well, using a declarative style that is not intrusive to our existing code.

Today, there are several identity industry standards, open specifications, and protocols that specify how to design an authentication and authorization mechanism, including the following:

- **Basic authentication**: This is the most common method, involving sending usernames and passwords with every request. We already implemented this method with Spring Security in our banking app example, which we used in Chapter 10, *Containerizing Your Applications*, Chapter 11, *DevOps and Release Management*, and Chapter 12, *Monitoring*.

- **JSON Web Tokens (JWT)**: This is an open standard that defines how to establish a secure mechanism to securely exchange messages (information) between two parties. There are several well-tested libraries to use here, and we created an example of this in `Chapter 4`, *Client-Server Architectures*. The sequence can be illustrated as follows:

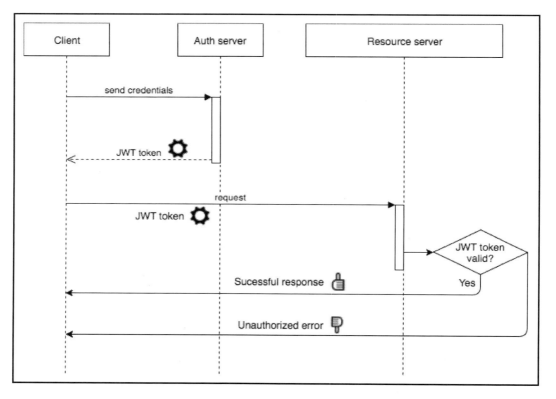

JWT authentication flow

As explained previously, the preceding sequence diagram can help us to understand the process of token validation. For authentication, the clients should send their credentials to the server, which will respond with a token in the form of a string. This token should be used for the subsequent requests. When they are executed, if the provided token is invalid or expired, we will receive a **401 UNAUTHORIZED** status code from the server. Otherwise, the request will be successful. The authentication mechanisms that we mentioned earlier follow the basic authentication model, which is preferred for web applications. However, when you're writing APIs, you will need other approaches, in order to deal with security based on the use of tokens (such as JWT). If you are not writing APIs, your application can be secured using the JSON Web Tokens RFC (`https://tools.ietf.org/html/rfc7519`).

Today, this is the most common method for authenticating mobile applications, modern single-page applications (SPA), and REST APIs.

Let's review some standards created around authentication mechanisms using tokens:

- **OAuth (Open Authorization)**: This is an open standard for authentication and authorization based on tokens that enable the use of a third-party actor to delegate the authentication process. You should only use this standard when you have three parties: yourself, your users, and third-party app developers that need your user data.
- **OAuth 2**: This is a more developed version of the OAuth standard, which allows the user to grant limited access to transfer resources from one application to another, without giving their credentials. You should use this standard whenever you log in to the site using your Google or GitHub account. When doing so, you will be asked whether or not you agree with sharing your email address or account.
- **Full request signature**: This was popularized by AWS authentication, and was explored in `Chapter 9`, *Serverless Architectures*, when we illustrated deploying our **functions as services (FaaS)** to AWS. We use this concept by sharing a secret between the server and the client. The client signs the completed request using the shared secret, and the server verifies it. For more detailed information, go to `http://docs.aws.amazon. com/general/latest/gr/sigv4_si gning.html`.

Cryptography

Cryptography is the process of changing text information to unintelligible text, and vice-versa: from crypto-text into intelligible text. In our application, we use cryptography in the process of creating data confidentiality and protecting it from unauthorized modification.

We use cryptography to encrypt communication between the client and the server. This is done through public key encryption using HTTPS, which uses the **Transport Layer Security (TLS)** protocol. The TLS protocol is the successor of the **Secure Sockets Layer (SSL)** protocol.

Data input validation

Data input validation refers to the process of controlling the data received in each integration, or layer, of our application. We need to validate the data input, in order to avoid creating any inconsistencies in our system. In other words, we should validate that the data in our application is consistent, and doesn't encounter any problems associated with SQL injection, the resource's control of the application, or servers, for example. More advanced techniques include whitelist validation and input type validation.

Sensitive data

This practice involves protecting sensitive data and determining how to do so in the right way. Data sensitivity involves the use of cryptography to preserve data confidentiality or integrity and redundancy.

For example, it is a common practice to use nonsense text in the passwords that our application uses to connect to a database, so we make this recommendation accurate by keeping credentials encrypted. Another case might involve working on a banking application and needing to present a credit card number. In this case, we would encrypt the number, and might even mask the number, to make it illegible to humans.

Social engineering

To help you understand what social engineering is, we are going to provide a simple definition; that is, the psychological manipulation of a person so that the person provides confidential information.

Taking this definition as a starting point, social engineering has become a security problem that is difficult for applications to control. That's because the point of failure is in the fact that the user is a human, capable of being analyzed and manipulated into handing over secret information or credentials that make it possible to access a system.

OWASP Top 10

The **Open Web Application Security Project (OWASP)** Top 10 lists the ten most important security risks in web applications, and is published and updated every three years by the OWASP organization. We need to follow the OWASP checklist in order to ensure that our web applications aren't leaving security holes. The list can be found at `https://www.owasp.org/images/7/72/OWASP_Top_10-2017_%28en%29.pdf.pdf`.

The latest checklist published in 2017 includes the following aspects:

- A1: Injection
- A2: Broken authentication and session management
- A3: **Cross-site scripting (XSS)**
- A4: Insecure direct object references
- A5: Security misconfiguration
- A6: Sensitive data exposure
- A7: Missing function level access control
- A8: **Cross-site request forgery (CSRF)**
- A9: Using components with known vulnerabilities
- A10: Unvalidated redirects and forwards

To test and verify several of these vulnerabilities, we can use the Burp suite (`https://portswigger.net/burp`). The process is easy to understand, and will check the application for most known security holes. As a tool, Burp comes with Kali Linux distributions, which we will explain in the following section.

Penetration testing

A **penetration test (pen test)** is a simulated attack on a system that evaluates its security. For this test, we can use tools like Kali Linux (`https://www.kali.org/`), which is a Debian-based Linux distribution, with a penetration testing platform that has several tools available for verifying the OWASP Top 10, and more.

Kali has an extensive list of tools that can be used for several purposes such as wireless attacks, information gathering, exploiting and verifying web applications, and so on. If you'd like to see a detailed list of tools, go to the following link: `https://tools.kali.org/tools-listing`. Teams should provide a pen test before delivering an application to a production environment.

In the next section, we will create a Java application based on Spring Security. We will use Auth0 as the authentication and authorization as a service platform, which is a third-party authorization based on the OAuth2 standard and JWTs.

Authentication and authorization as a service

We will be using Auth0 as the provider of a platform for authentication and authorization as a service. We will create an example of this to secure our application; you don't have to be a security guru to achieve this.The following screenshot was borrowed from the Auth0 getting started guide:

Auth0 authentication and identity validation process

After we plug in or connect to Auth0, this will be the authentication and authorization server used to verify their identity and send the required information back to the application each time a user tries to authenticate.

> We are not limited to Java; Auth0 provides several SDKs and APIs for different technologies and languages.

The steps to create an example of authentication and authorization as a service using Auth0 are as follows:

1. Create your free developer account in Auth0 at `https://auth0.com/`.
2. Log in to the **Auth0** portal and create an application:

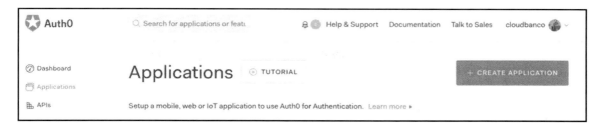

Auth0 create application

3. Give a name to the application, and then select the **Regular Web Application** option, which includes Java applications (you can also create native mobile applications, single-page applications, and **Internet of Things (IoTs)**):

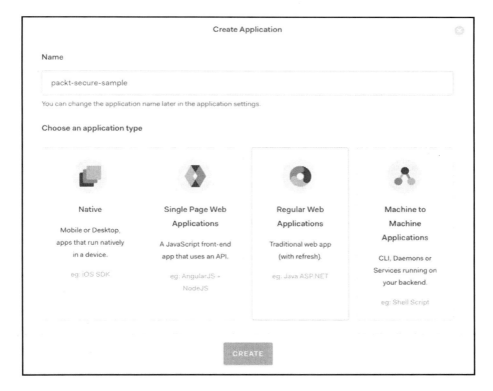

5. Select an example application that uses Spring Security.
6. Click on **Download the application** and change the folder name of the project to packt-secure-sample.

To run the example, we need to set the **callback URL**
(`http://localhost:3000/callback`) in the **Settings** tab of the application that we
created.

To run this on the console, execute the following commands in the sample's directory:

```
# In Linux / macOS./gradlew clean bootRun
# In Windowsgradlew clean bootRun
```

You can see the application at the URL, `http://localhost:3000/`, as follows:

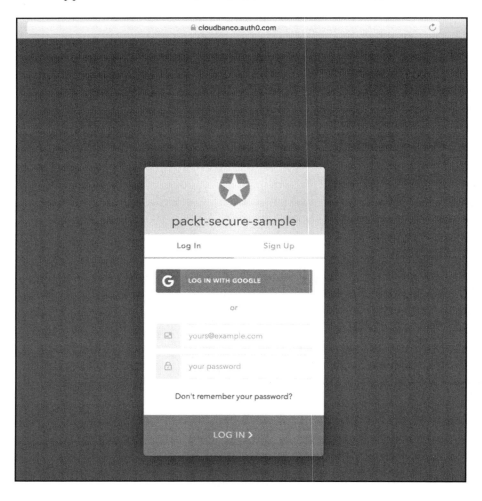

Note that the application login page redirects to Auth0. After we log in via a third-party application, through our Google account or with the credentials provided by Auth0, we will see the following result, which shows the token that was generated:

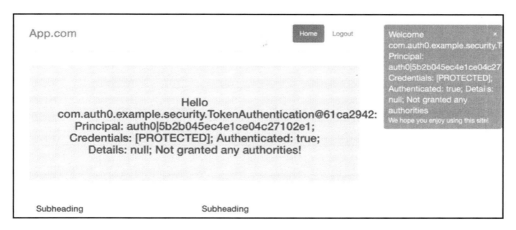

You have now learned how to use Auth0 as a platform for authentication and authorization as a service, using standards such as OAuth2 and JWT.

Summary

In this chapter, we explained how to apply security guidelines and practices to cover the most common security issues that you may encounter with your applications. Here, we covered authentication and authorization, cryptography, data input validation, sensitive data, the OWASP Top 10, social engineering, and penetration testing. These concepts and methodologies will strengthen the security of your applications.

In the next chapter, we will review high-performance techniques and recommendations in order to complete our journey of creating applications using Spring 5.

14
High Performance

Nothing is more disappointing than having to deal with issues in production when an application is behaving in an unexpected way. In this chapter, we are going to discuss some simple techniques that can be applied in order to get rid of these annoying problems, applying simple recommendations to your daily routine to take care of the performance of your applications. Throughout this chapter, we are going to review the following topics:

- Why performance matters
    - Scalability
    - Availability
    - Performance
- Key recommendations to keep your software away from performance issues
    - Profiling applications
    - SQL query optimizations
    - Load testing

Let's start by introducing the importance of performance.

Why performance matters

Over the last two decades as a consultant, I visited several government institutions, banks, and financial institutions, establishing a common factor for a lack of performance in applications that are working in production, and I found common issues that can be avoided if you use a set of good practices as part of your SDLC.

It's important to pay close attention to performance, because it brings huge trouble to companies, project sponsors, and customers since an application that faces this problem brings dissatisfaction on several levels.

Before giving recommendations, we are going to review and understand the non-functional requirements of scalability, availability, and performance.

Scalability

This describes the capacity of a system to deal with to a high workload and to increase its capacity in order to resolve more requests based on the demand for work.

Horizontal scalability

This is resolved by adding additional nodes with all the functionality of your system, redistributing the requests, as demonstrated in the following diagram:

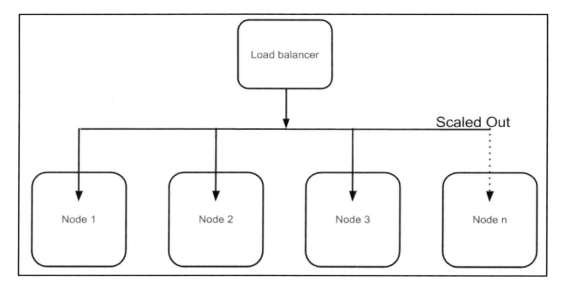

Horizontal scalability

Vertical scalability

We use vertical scaling by adding resources (such as the RAM, CPU, or hard disk) to the node or server, and so on, to process more requests for our system. One common practice that I saw is that it adds more hardware to the database server to better perform the multiple connections that are using it; we can only scale a service by adding more resources, as the following diagram shows:

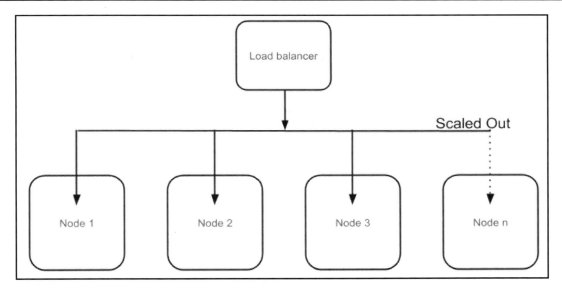

Vertical scalability

High availability

This refers to the capacity to guarantee that a system provides a service or resource continuously. This capacity is directly associated to the **Service Level Agreement (SLA)**.

An SLA is calculated based on the maintenance window of the system, and SLAs define whether a system should scale up or out.

Performance

This is the capacity of the responsiveness of a system to execute any action within a given time interval. As part of software systems, we need to start defining measurable performance goals such as the following:

- The minimum or average response time
- The average amount of concurrent users
- The number of requests per second during high load or concurrency

The principal challenge that we have today as developers is the number of customers and devices that our application must handle, and, even more, whether our application is going to run on the internet or within an intranet only. The following diagram shows the topology of how an application is usually deployed and consumed:

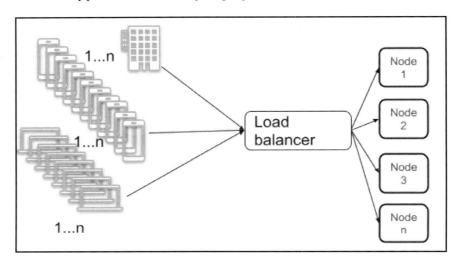

High-load requests to a system

After understanding the principal concepts behind performance, scalability, and availability, let's review some key recommendations to increase the performance of applications.

The key recommendation to avoid performance issues

It's common to use load testing tools, **Application Performance Monitors** (APMs), and profiling tools to find and fix performance issues in software systems. To simulate the number of users in production, we need to run load test-creating scenarios for the most commonly used functionalities of our system, and, at the same time, track and monitor the application health-measuring resources such as CPU, RAM, IO, heap usage, threads, and database access. At the output of these process, we can give some key recommendations to keep your software away from performance issues.

In the following section, we are going to explain the most common bottlenecks that we can find, and how to avoid them.

Identifying bottlenecks

Enterprise applications become more complex every day. When the business succeeds, the application supporting that business will have more users, which means a bigger load received every day, so we need to take care of the performance bottlenecks that could appear.

To understand the term **bottleneck**, we are going to give a simple definition. In software systems, a bottleneck happens when the function of an application or a system is starting to be limited for a single component, and it is like comparing the neck of a bottle slowing down overall water flow.

In other words, we can see a bottleneck if our application starts to perform slowly or starts to exceed the anticipated response time . This can happen for different kinds of bottlenecks, such as the following:

- **CPU**: This happens when this resource is busy and cannot respond to the system properly. It is common to start having this bottleneck when we start to see CPU at utilization exceed 80% for extended periods of time.
- **Memory**: This happens when the system doesn't have enough RAM or fast RAM. Sometimes the application logs show out-of-memory exceptions or leak-of-memory problems.
- **Network**: Associated with a lack of necessary bandwidth
- The application itself, code problems, too many exceptions not being controlled, poor use of resources, and so on

Using APMs to identify bottlenecks is a good approach because an APM can collect runtime information without slowing down application performance.

To identify bottlenecks, we can use a couple of practices; load testing and monitor tools, or profiling tools. The following section explains profiling tools.

Profiling applications

We can look at our code and start to profile the parts of the system we suspect have performance issues, or we can use a profiler and obtain information about the entire system as a whole. These tools gather runtime data and monitor resource consumption in terms of CPU, memory, threads, classes, and I/O.

There are several tools available for profiling Java applications, including the following:

- Tools that come with the JVM, such as VisualVM, JStat, JMap, and more
- Specialized tools, such as JProfiler, Java Mision Control, and Yourkit
- Lightweight profilers that come with APMs, like those we saw in Chapter 12, *Monitoring*, using New Relic

Visual VM

This is a visual tool integrated as part of the JDK, which has the capability to profile applications. Let's run our banking app from the previous chapters, and review which information we can gather using it.

 To run our previous banking application, go to the project folder and run the following via the command line: `java -jar build/libs/banking-app-1.0.jar`.

Now, we are going to use the VisualVM to gather some metrics about the JVM. We can run this tool from the console using the following command:

```
$ cd JAVA_HOME/bin
$ jvisualvm
```

We should see a screen similar to the following screenshot:

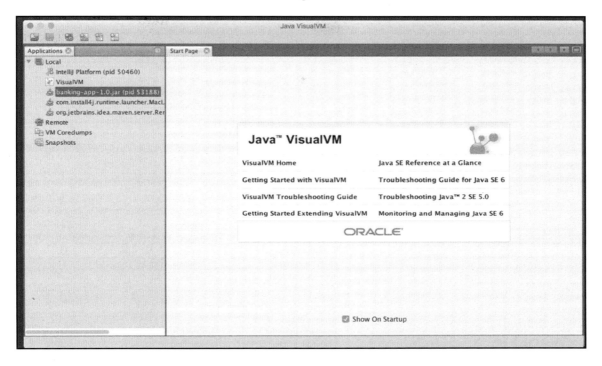

Java VisualVM

Using the **Locals** menu option, you have to attach the Java process that is going to be monitored. In this case, we are going to select **banking-app-1.0.jar**. Then, we should see a resume of the resources used for the application:

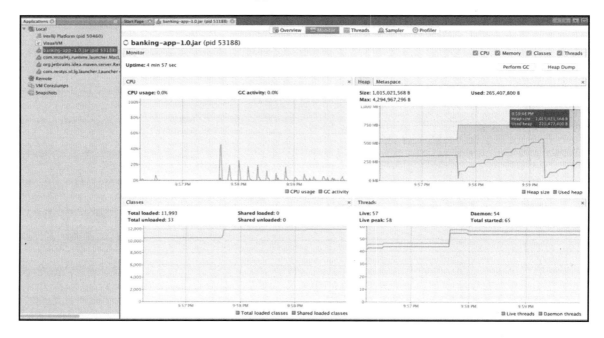

VisualVM CPU, RAM, classes, and threads

There is also a tab that provides information about **Threads**, which is shown in the

following screenshot:

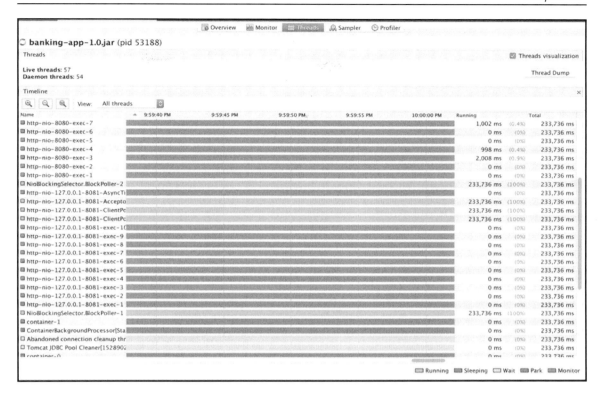

VisualVM threads

We can use any tool that we feel comfortable with; a great place to start, and a tool that is easy to use is Jprofiler, but all the tools give us similar information. We need to understand and follow the possible problems generated by any bottleneck that we find in our application.

Debugging performance issues in production can be a difficult task, and, in some cases hard to find and fix. We need a tool that we can feel confident about to understand the bottlenecks, so we need to try different tools and experiment load tests to find the right one for us.

Don't optimize before you know it's necessary; first, run the application and run a load test to see whether we can approach the non-functional requirements defined for performance.

SQL query optimizations

Optimizing queries and the data access layer of your enterprise application is key to avoiding bottlenecks and performance issues. We can use New Relic as an APM, and this will help us to detect bottlenecks and performance problems using database access graphics. With these graphics, we can find the SQL sentences used by your application, finding delay transactions or blocked tables if we continue to drilldown the information until we can also find the most SQL sentences used and the number of connections managed, as in the following screenshot:

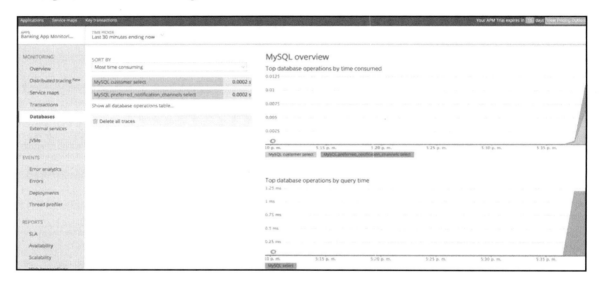

Database metrics from New Relic

From the app, we can identify the queries most used and check for opportunities to optimize them. We would need indexes or to refactor our code to get better performance. On the other hand, without using an APM or a profiling tool, we can use a number of techniques to improve our SQL and data access layers, such as the following:

- **Review SQL sentences**: This reviews the SQL sentences executed and optimized one by one via the profiler or the APM, applying indexes, choosing the right column types, and optimizing relationships using native queries when necessary.
- **JDBC batch**: This uses `prepared` statements for batching, and some databases such as Oracle support batching for `prepared` statements.
- **Connection managing**: This reviews the use of the connection pool, and measure and set the correct pool size.

- **Scale up and scale out**: This is explained in the *Scalability* section.

- **Caching**: This uses in-memory buffer structures to avoid disk access.

- **Avoid ORM**: **Object Relational Mapping (ORM)** tools are used to treat database tables as Java Objects to persist information. However, in some cases, it is better to use plain SQL statements to avoid unnecessary joins, which lead us to improve the performance of applications and databases at the same time.

In the next section, we will look at how to simulate virtual users in order to create a load test for your applications.

A load test example

Load tests are used to check how an application will behave once it is used for a determined number of concurrent users; the number of concurrent users is given for the number of users that the application will have in production. You should always define a performance test suite that tests the whole application with tools such as the following:

- Neoload
- Apache JMeter
- Load Runner
- Load UI
- Rational Performance Tester

We need to define a load test and profile as part of a pipeline of our applications, and run it before and after we work on performance improvement. We are going to create an example using Neoload to review these key recommendations in our application example.

First, we need to define a scenario to run a load test; in our case, we are going to take the banking application from `Chapter 12`, *Monitoring*, that is ready to use, and define a functional common scenario such as the following:

1. The user is going to log in using the credentials: `rene/rene`.
2. Then, the user will click on the menu notifications.
3. And finally, the user is going to click on the logout link.

First, we are going to download Neoload from the following URL: `https://www.neotys.com/download`.

> Neoload gives us a trial version where we can simulate up to 50 virtual concurrent users.

After installing Neoload, we are going to open the application and create a project:

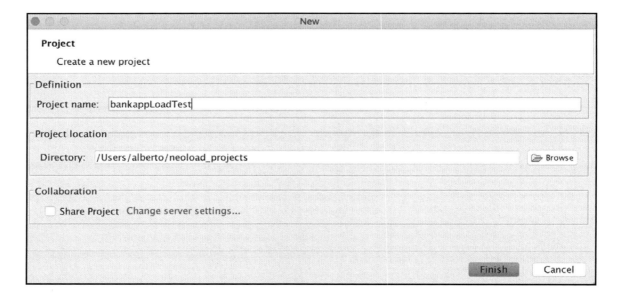

Then, we are going to click on **Start Recording**, and choose the browser that we are going to use to record our application:

Then, in the browser, we are going to enter the URL of our application:
http://localhost:8080/login, and navigate as a user to list the notification set of our customer. So the process is as follows:

1. Log in
2. Click on the menu notifications
3. Click on logout

Select the host that we are recording, which in our case is localhost, and follow the next instructions until the end. Finally, we are going click on the **Stop recording** button and we should see in the left-hand menu that our actions are recorded:

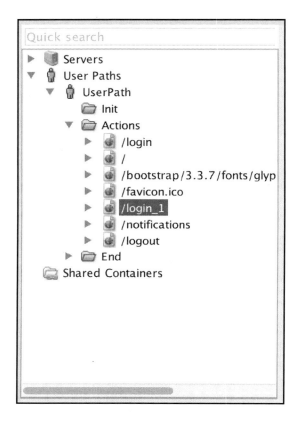

We are then going to run the recorded scenario by clicking on the check icon that can be seen hovering over the user icon:

We should see that our scenario runs without errors, simulating one concurrent user, as in

the following screenshot:

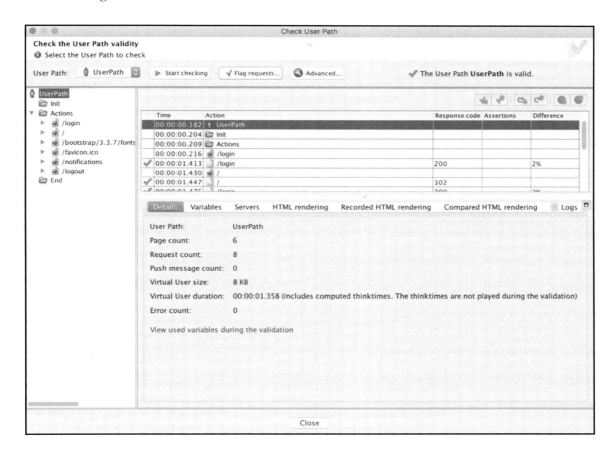

Now, let's generate load testing, creating a population (casual user simulated scenario):

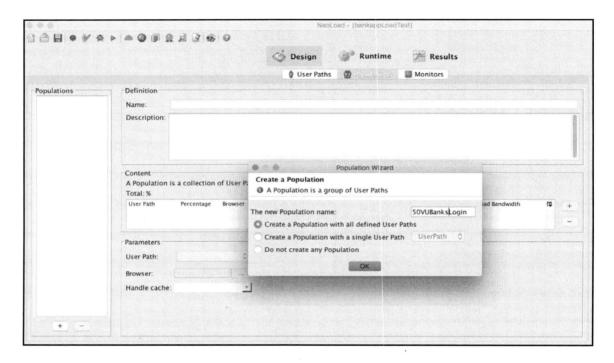

Then, click on the Runtime icon to run the load test with 10 concurrent users for 2 minutes:

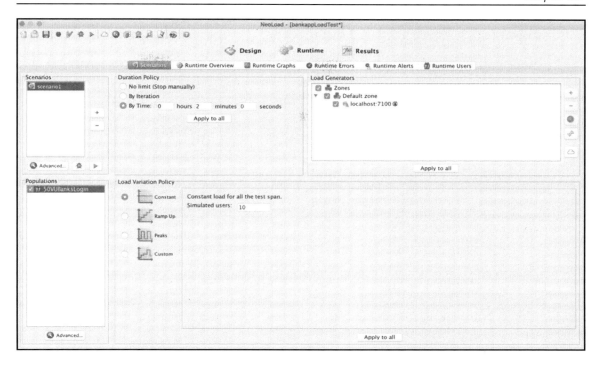

And then, click on the play icon:

Finally, after the test finishes, we can check the results; denoting that we visited 670 pages and made 890 requests during the load test time, using 20 concurrent users:

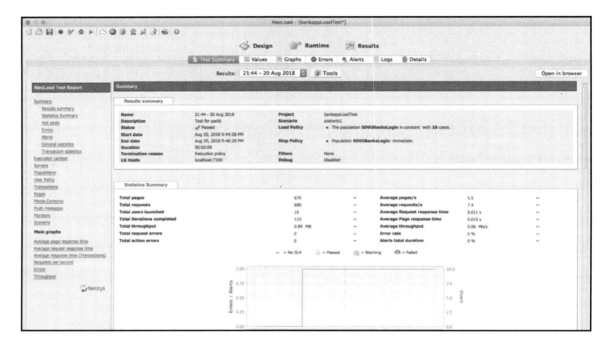

On the other hand, during the load test using VisualVM, we can check the performance of our application and see how it performs at checking the threads, as demonstrated in the following screenshot:

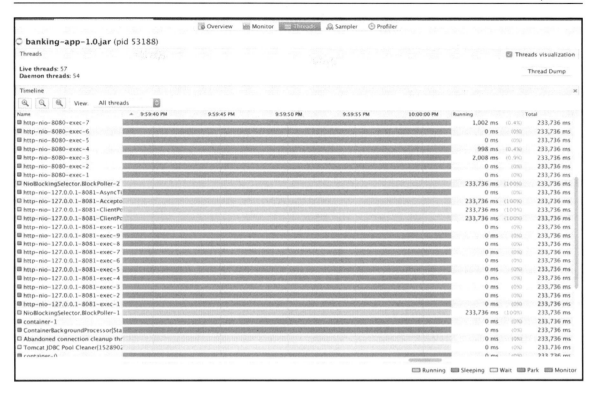

We are going to find that the JVM, memory, and threads, with a simulation of virtual users, look different than just navigating on the application.

It's worth monitoring all the resources of an application when you run load tests to identify where an issue can rise.

Finally, we have learned that using a profiler tool or an APM, in addition to a load test tool, can guarantee that our applications and system work on performance improvements before we launch our code to production environments.

After adding code to improve the performance of an application, it is always a good idea to run performance tests in order to check how well the changes have been implemented.

Summary

Throughout this chapter, we explained the meaning of scalability, availability, and performance. We also learned how to apply some techniques and tools to avoid dealing with performance issues in production and, consequently, how we can improve the performance of our applications to achieve a better response times.

Other Books You May Enjoy

If you enjoyed this book, you may be interested in these other books by Packt:

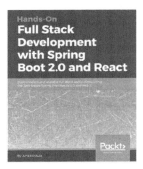

Hands-On Full Stack Development with Spring Boot 2.0 and React
Juha Hinkula

ISBN: 9781789138085

- Create a RESTful web service with Spring Boot
- Understand how to use React for frontend programming
- Gain knowledge of how to create unit tests using JUnit
- Discover the techniques that go into securing the backend using Spring Security
- Learn how to use Material UI in the user interface to make it more user-friendly
- Create a React app by using the Create React App starter kit made by Facebook

Spring Boot 2.0 Projects
Mohamed Shazin Sadakath

ISBN: 9781789136159

- Learn the fundamental features of Spring Boot 2.0
- Customize Spring Boot 2.0 applications
- Build a basic web application
- Use Redis to build a taxi-hailing API
- Create a simple blog management system and a Twitter clone
- Develop a reactive RESTful web service with Kotlin using Spring Boot

Leave a review - let other readers know what you think

Please share your thoughts on this book with others by leaving a review on the site that you bought it from. If you purchased the book from Amazon, please leave us an honest review on this book's Amazon page. This is vital so that other potential readers can see and use your unbiased opinion to make purchasing decisions, we can understand what our customers think about our products, and our authors can see your feedback on the title that they have worked with Packt to create. It will only take a few minutes of your time, but is valuable to other potential customers, our authors, and Packt. Thank you!

Index

A

advantages, microservices
  continuous releases 184
  independent scalability 184
  single responsibility principle alignment 184
  technologies, adopting 185
agile manifesto
  URL 41
Amazon Web services (AWS) 213
AMQP 80
Android client 94
App Dynamics
  URL 308
Application Performance Management (APM) tools
  about 77, 308, 330
  New Relic 309, 311
application performance
  about 329, 330
  high availability 329
  scalability 328
  significance 327
application programming interfaces (API) 183
applications
  containerizing 256, 257, 258
  Docker Gradle plugin 259, 260
architects 11
architecture 11
authentication and authorization as a service 322, 324, 325
authentication and authorization mechanism
  authentication 317
  JSON Web Tokens (JWT) 318
AWS Lambda adapter 231, 233, 236
AWS Lambda
  URL 231
Azure adapter

  about 240, 242, 243, 245
  URL 237

B

Backend as a service (BaaS) 214, 217
Bean Validation
  URL 153
Beans 53
Behavior Driven Development (BDD) 82
bottlenecks
  identifying 331
business dimension
  about 30
  business metrics, identifying 32
  business metrics, tracking 32
  data dimension 33, 34
  user requirements, managing 31

C

C4 model
  about 41
  class diagram 43
  context diagram 42
CAP theorem
  consistency 208
  high availability 208
  partition tolerance 208
Certificate Authority (CA) 122
CI server
  key concepts 296
circuit breaker pattern
  about 209
  Hystrix 210
client-server architectures
  about 72
  account balance endpoint client 92
  AMQP 80, 83

Android client 94
applying 76
authentication endpoint client 91
banking-api 84
banking-client 90
banking-domain 83
boundaries 85
client 75
clients, building 92
CORBA 80
domain 86
implementing, with Spring 78
JavaFX client 93
network 76
persistence 86
request 75
RESTful web services 79
scaling 73
server 72, 78
server, implementing 83
server, monitoring 86, 88
service 86
SOAP web services 79
sockets 80
testing 88, 90
thin client 96
CMD command 255
code-writing process 190
command-line interface (CLI)
  URL 235
Command-Query Responsibility Segregation
  (CQRS)
  about 150
  complex domain models 151
  persistent information 152
  scaling 154
  URL 61, 203
conformist relationship 75
container orchestration
  with Kubernetes 269
containers
  about 248, 249
  CMD command 255
  commands 250
  concepts 249

ENV command 255
executing 250
EXPOSE command 255
FROM command 254
images 249
images, building 254
images, working with 253
MAINTAINER command 254
RUN command 254
working with 252
continuous delivery (CD) 281
continuous integration (CI) 280
Conway's law 23, 25
CORBA 80
Create, Read, Update, Delete (CRUD) 52
cryptography 320

D

data input validation 320
DataDog
  URL 308
Denial-of-Service (DoS) 317
dependency inversion (DI) principle 23
development process
  accelerating 189
DevOps culture
  about 279
  DevOps adoption 281
  motivations 280
dimensions
  about 30
  business dimension 30
  operations dimension 37
  technical dimension 35
Docker Compose
  about 265
  containers, linking 266
  depends_on option 267, 269
  links option 267
  URL 189
Docker Gradle plugin
  about 259, 260
  URL 259
don't repeat yourself (DRY) principle 181
Dynatrace

URL 308

E

edge services
  about 202, 203
  Zuul 204, 206, 207
embracing automation 282
end-to-end (e2e) 190
Enterprise Integration Patterns (EIP)
  supporting, with Spring Integration 54
Enterprise Service Bus (ESB) 76, 160
ENV command 255
Eureka 197
event-carried state transfer pattern
  about 136
  application performance, enhancing 137
  source application load, reducing 137
  system availability, increasing 138
event-driven architectures (EDA)
  about 127
  command 128
  Command-Query Responsibility Segregation
    (CQRS) 150
  concepts 127
  event 128, 129
  event notification pattern 130, 132, 134, 136
  event sourcing 140, 143, 145, 148, 150
  event-carried state transfer pattern 136
  patterns 130
EXPOSE command 255

F

FIG 265
FROM command 254
full request signature 319
Function as a service (FaaS) 218
function as a service (FaaS)
  about 214, 319
  implementing, with Spring Cloud Functions 224

H

high availability 329
high cohesion 17
horizontal scalability 328
HSQL

URL 165
Hystrix 210

I

Infrastructure as code
  about 283
  DevOps practices 285
  environments, supporting 286
  profiles, selecting 287
  Spring application 285
  Vagrant 288
interface segregation principle (ISP) 21

J

JaCoCo
  URL 112
Java Development Kit (JDK) 46
Java Virtual Machine (JVM) 35
JavaFX client 93
Jenkins 296
JSON Web Tokens RFC
  URL 81

K

Kali Linux
  URL 321
KISS principle
  URL 18
Kubernetes
  container orchestration 269
  labels 271
  pod 269
  replication controllers 272, 273
  services 274

L

labels 271
Liskov substitution principle (LSP) 21
load tests
  example 337, 340, 342, 344, 345
low coupling 14, 17

M

MAINTAINER command 254
Maven wrapper
  URL 49
microservices
  advantages 183
  autonomous 182
  CAP theorem 208
  circuit breaker pattern 209
  configuration client, implementing 194
  configuration server, implementing 194
  disadvantages 186, 187
  dynamic configuration 192, 193
  edge services 202
  Eureka 197
  implementing 191
  modeling 187, 188
  Netflix Eureka service registry, implementing 198
  Netflix Ribbon 201
  principles 182
  registration 196
  service discovery 196
  service registry client, implementing 199
  size 182
Microsoft Azure Functions
  URL 237
Minimum Viable Product (MVP) 31
mobile backend as a service (MBaaS) 214
Model-View-Controller (MVC) architecture
  about 99, 100
  application, securing 120
  authentication 121, 122, 123
  authentication, implementing 123, 126
  benefits 103
  Controller (C) 101, 103
  Model (M) 100
  pitfalls 104, 106
  Spring MVC 106, 109
  test coverage 112, 114
  testing 109, 111
  Thymeleaf 116, 119
  UI frameworks 115
  used, for implementing applications 106
  View (V) 101

monitoring
  about 304
  application monitoring 304
  business monitoring 304
  Spring application 308
  Spring applications 304, 306
multiple-container environments
  Docker Compose 265
  provisioning 264

N

Nanobox
  URL 189
Netflix Eureka service registry
  implementing 198
Netflix Ribbon 201
New Relic
  about 309, 311
  URL 77, 308, 309
Newman
  URL 89

O

OAuth (Open Authorization) 319
OAuth 2 319
Object Relational Mapping (ORM) 337
object-oriented programming (OOP) 18, 249
Open Web Application Security Project (OWASP) 321
Open–Closed Principle (OCP) 19
operations dimension
  about 37
  application, deploying 37, 40
  cloud, versus on-premise 39
  components, interactions 37
  infrastructure 38
  infrastructure, dealing 37
  testing 39
  versioning 38
oracle-java8
  URL 255

P

penetration test (pen test) 321
performance issues, avoiding

about 330
applications, profiling 332
bottlenecks, identifying 331
load tests 337, 340, 342, 344, 345
SQL query, optimizing 336
Pipe-and-Filter architecture
about 157
boarding 159
filters 158
pipes 159
use cases 160
plain old Java objects (POJOs) 192, 233
pod 269
production environment 191
project reactor
about 63
back pressure 66
flux 65
mono 64

R

Ration Unified Process (RUP) 31
Reactive Manifesto
URL 62
reactive REST services 68
Reactive Spring Data 67
registries
about 260
images, publishing 261, 263
release management
about 291
Continuous delivery 293
continuous deployment 293
Continuous integration (CI) 292
Jenkins 296
pipelines 291
pipelines, automating 293
replication controllers 272, 273
reporting databases
URL 154
request 75
RESTful web services 79
Retrofit
URL 91
RUN command 254

S

scalability
about 328
horizontal scalability 328
vertical scalability 328
Secure Sockets Layer (SSL) protocol 320
security
advantages 315
authentication and authorization 317
cryptography 320
data input validation 320
key security recommendations 317
OWASP Top 10 321
sensitive data 320
social engineering 320
sensitive data 320
serverless architecture
about 214
adopting, for SPA 222
Backend as a service 217
benefits 216
concerns 219
file storage 215
framework support 220
Function as a service 218
infrastructure 215
pitfalls 216
security 220
troubleshooting 221
use cases 221
vendor lock-in 219
Service Level Agreement (SLA) 329
service registry client
implementing 199
services 274
Silos
about 278
breaking 279
Single Responsibility Principle (SRP) 18
Single-page applications (SPAs)
about 217
serverless architectures, adopting 222
SOAP web services 79
social engineering 320

sockets 80
software architecture
  components 13
  defining 8
  future, predicting 10
  high cohesion 17
  low coupling 14, 17
  principles 13
  scenarios 9
Software Development Life Cycle (SDLC) 7, 278,
  316
SOLID principles
  about 18
  dependency inversion (DI) principle 23
  interface segregation principle (ISP) 21
  Liskov substitution principle 20
  Open–Closed Principle (OCP) 19
  Single Responsibility Principle (SRP) 18
Spock
  URL 83
Spring Batch
  about 55, 161, 162, 165, 167
  pipes, implementing 168, 170, 171, 173, 175,
    179
  process step 56
  read step 55
  references 161
  URL 168
  write step 56
Spring Cloud Functions
  adapters 231
  AWS Lambda adapter 231, 236
  Azure adapter 237, 242, 243, 245
  example, coding 226, 230
  FaaS, implementing 223
  URL 223, 225
Spring Cloud
  about 59
  API gateway 61
  circuit breaker 61
  configuration server 60
  edge service 60
  microproxy 61
  service registry 60
Spring Data

about 52
URL 52
Spring Initializr
  about 47
  URL 169, 226
Spring MVC 106, 109
Spring projects
  about 46
  application.properties file 51
  applications, securing with Spring Security 56
  autoconfiguration 48
  DemoApplication.java 50
  DemoApplicationTests.java 51
  dependency management 48
  EIPs, supporting with Spring Integration 53
  HATEOAS, embracing 58
  in Nutshell 48
  microservices 59
  mvnw 49
  mvnw.cmd 49
  pom.xml 49
  processor interface 63
  project reactor 63
  publisher 62
  reactive programming 62
  Reactive REST services 68
  Reactive Spring Data 67
  redeployment, avoiding with developer tools 51
  servlet container integration 48
  Spring Batch 55
  Spring Cloud 59
  Spring Data 52
  Spring Initializr 47
  subscriber 62
  subscription 63
Spring Security
  applications, securing 56
Spring
  about 46
  client-server architectures, implementing 78
SQL query
  optimizing 336
Symposium on Principles of Distributed Computing
  (SPDC) 208

T

technical dimension 35
technology
  selecting 25, 27
test coverage 112
thin clients 96
Thymeleaf 116, 119
tools, for profiling java application
  Visual VM 332, 334, 335
Transport Layer Security (TLS) protocol 320
twelve-fact app
  URL 192

U

Uniform Resource Identifiers (URIs) 58
user stories 31

V

Vagrant
  about 288
  URL 189
  working with 288
Version Control System (VCS) 38
vertical scalability 328
Virtual Machines (VMs) 248
Visual VM 332, 334, 335

W

Web Services Description Language (WSDL) 79

Y

YAML
  URL 51

Z

Zuul 204, 206, 207

Printed in Poland
by Amazon Fulfillment
Poland Sp. z o.o., Wrocław